Lawrence Bruner

Report of the Entomologist

Lawrence Bruner

Report of the Entomologist

ISBN/EAN: 9783741130571

Manufactured in Europe, USA, Canada, Australia, Japa

Cover: Foto ©Thomas Meinert / pixelio.de

Manufactured and distributed by brebook publishing software
(www.brebook.com)

Lawrence Bruner

Report of the Entomologist

REPORT OF THE ENTOMOLOGIST.

INTRODUCTION.

Sir: I have the honor to present herewith my annual report for the year 1886. It is confined to the consideration of a few prominent and important insects that have not before been fully treated of in Department publications, and I have omitted from it, because of the limitation as to number of pages allotted to the Entomologist, many briefer notes and articles that have been prepared as the result of the year's work. These omitted portions will at once be prepared for special bulletins.

The fruit interests of the Pacific coast have of late years been more and more threatened by injurious insects, and in the present report the leading place is given to the consideration of the Cottony Cushion-scale (*Icerya purchasi*), which is perhaps the greatest pest that the fruit-growers in that section have to contend with. I was urged last spring by many prominent horticulturists and by Hon. W. W. Morrow, M. C. from the fourth district of California, to personally visit the infested region, but as this was impossible then on account of impaired health and important duties in the East, Messrs. D. W. Coquillett and Albert Koebele were sent to Los Angeles early in the year, with instructions to carry on through the summer an extensive series of experiments and observations upon the species. It will be seen from the context that this is one of those insects which have, naturally, extremely limited powers of spreading, and that its introduction from one continent to another and its subsequent spread might easily have been prevented had vigilance and intelligent appreciation of the dangers of such an introduction prevailed in years gone by as they are beginning to prevail now. The article is supplemented by detailed reports on experiments by Messrs. Coquillett and Koebele, which indicate the difficulties of controlling the pest, but at the same time show that these difficulties may be overcome.

The kerosene emulsions, in different proportions, which have proved so entirely satisfactory against the scale-insects of the Orange in Florida, have in general failed to win the good opinion of orange-growers in California. Mr. Matthew Cooke and other writers in the latter State have pronounced the kerosene emulsions inferior to caustic soda and caustic potash, and even to strong solutions of whale-oil soap.

Until this year I have been unable to offset the decision of these gentlemen with the result of careful experiment. though I have always believed their want of success was due to imperfect preparation of the emulsions or imperfect application of them. I was also inclined to give some credence to the theory advanced by Prof. E. W. Hilgard, that the dryness of the atmosphere in California induced a more rapid evaporation of the kerosene in the emulsion, which accounted for its inferior results. Moreover, the Cottony Cushion-scale is much less susceptible to the action of insecticides than any Floridian species on account of the protection afforded by the large waxy mass which it secretes, as well as on account of its great vitality.

The detailed reports on remedies just referred to show that kerosene emulsions must still be placed at the head of the list, not only for ordinary scale-insects, but for this *Icerya*, so far as efficacy is concerned, though other remedies have the advantage of being cheaper. In the proportion of 1 part of the soap emulsion to 15 parts of water it proves a perfect remedy for their Red Scale (*Aspidiotus aurantii*), a species which has done incalculable damage in Australia and has created much alarm in California. After a thorough application of the mixture in March Mr. Coquillett found that every scale-insect was killed, and at the expiration of two months all had dropped from the leaves. Used in the same proportion on the Cottony Cushion-scale, however, it does not kill the old females with the egg-masses, nor all of the eggs. Used at twice this strength it kills all of the eggs, as well as the old females, and even when properly used at the rate of 1 part of the emulsion to 5 parts of water it leaves the tree uninjured.

Mr. Coquillett reports, with reference to the much-praised caustic soda, that it has no effect on the eggs of the *Icerya*, even when applied so strong as to burn the bark brown and kill all the leaves. Similarly, whale-oil soap, one pound to two gallons of water, does not kill the eggs directly, nor does hard soap and water in the same proportions, although the effect of the latter seems greater than that of the former. They both, however, harden the egg-masses so that a large proportion of the young larvæ are unable to escape. The experiments add greatly to the value of ordinary tobacco, for one of the most effectual washes used is made by boiling one pound of tobacco leaves in one gallon of water until the strength has been extracted from the leaves, and then adding enough water to make two gallons. This wash, however, costs about 5 cents per gallon, and is too expensive for ordinary use. Mr. Koebele, experimenting through August, September, and October, found that kerosene emulsified with soft-soap penetrates the egg-sacs well, kills the old scales, and leaves the tree uninjured. Emulsions of crude petroleum, although much cheaper, he found very apt to injure the trees. He devoted his chief attention, on account of their great cheapness, to the preparation of soaps and resin compounds. He succeeded in making a number of these mixtures, which, when properly diluted, need not cost more than from one-third to one-half of a cent per gallon, and which, if thoroughly applied, will bring about very satisfactory results, killing the insects and either penetrating or hardening the egg-masses so as to prevent the hatching of the young. I am strongly of the opinion that the value of the soap washes depends somewhat on the season of their application, and that the greater success of Mr. Koebele with them as compared with that of Mr. Coquillett was probably due to the fact that his experiments were made during the dry or rainless season.

In connection with the subject of kerosene emulsions, I may put on record here an important discovery made last spring in carrying on further experiments at the office in emulsifying this oil. It is that the white of eggs with a little sugar may be used as a satisfactory substitute for milk where this is not accessible.

If the white of 2 eggs, about 3 tablespoonfuls of sugar, ¾ quart of water, and 1¼ quarts of kerosene are worked through a force-pump and cyclone-nozzle for from 5 to 10 minutes a cream-like emulsion is produced, which can be diluted with water to any desired amount without any separation of the oil; provided that the emulsion is not allowed to stand for any length of time.

Another investigation that has occupied considerable of my time lately is that in reference to the Southern Buffalo Gnats. The loss occasioned by the attacks of these upon domestic animals has been of late years very great, and the Division has been strongly appealed to by influential stock-raisers in the lower Mississippi Valley for information. Messrs. F. M. Webster, Otto Lugger, and Francis Fillion have each been directed to make special investigations and experiments during the year in different parts of the South, and Dr. Warren King, of Vicksburg, has aided in various ways. At the time when these investigations began the particular species concerned had not been determined; nor was anything known of their habits in the early stages. These habits were surmised from what was known of other species of the genus both in this country and Europe, which, as a rule, breed in clear, rapid, and rocky streams; but it was a question how our Southern species could breed so numerously in the lower alluvial Mississippi country.

It results from the investigation that there are more particularly concerned two species, which may be known and distinguished as the Southern Buffalo Gnat (the larger and more common of the species) and the Turkey Gnat, the names by which they are very generally known in the country affected. They are both undescribed species, and I have given them the names of *Simulium pecuarum* and *S. meridionale* respectively. The habits of both species are similar, and both have been found to breed in the more swiftly running currents of bayous and larger streams which are permanent and do not dry up in midsummer. The larvæ are found attached to the masses of drift-wood and leaves which form at points, and which, by impediment, induce a more rapid current on the surface. Very full details will be found in the article, and at its close I have discussed the bearing which seasons of overflow may possibly have on the increase of these insects. Much yet remains to be ascertained, however, especially as to oviposition, the eggs, and the early habits of the larvæ.

Another insect that will be found fully treated of is the common Fall Web-worm (*Hyphantria cunea*), which abounded during the past year in the Eastern States in a phenomenal way, and which was so destructive to the shade trees of the Capital as to attract an unusual share of attention and to call forth many requests for information. Many facts hitherto unpublished, both as to its habits and natural enemies, will be found recorded, while advantage has been taken of the very favorable opportunity afforded by the exceptional increase of the species in Washington City to carefully study its relative preference for different trees. I have already published in my report for the year 1883, and in Bulletin 6 of this Division, in considering the Imported Elm Leaf-beetle, full directions for protecting trees from leaf-devouring insects, and as it is inadvisable to repeat what is already accessible in published form, I have given but a brief summary of the means available for protecting trees from this Fall Web-worm. Moreover, the spraying appliances that are most useful against the scale-insects, and treated of in considering the Cottony Cushion-scale of California, are equally applicable here, and in so far as they differ from those already described and published in previous reports they will be found treated of in connection with said scale. So far as the city of Washington is concerned (and the same will apply to all cities) there can be little doubt that the great increase of this Fall Web-worm of late years has been largely due to two circumstances: First, the prevalence of the English Sparrow and its indisposition or inability to feed upon this worm, while making more room for it by destroying other less injurious and smooth species; secondly, the use of the wooden tree-boxes, which afford such excellent winter shelter for the cocoons.

Some recent experience is recorded with regard to Joint Worms, and the interesting fact is brought out that alternation of generation occurs among them, and that in the genus *Isosoma*, to which they belong, two forms, which have hitherto been considered good species, are in reality seasonal dimorphic forms of one and the same species, as I have always suspected would prove to be the case.

The year 1886 may be said, entomologically, to have been an ordinary one, and notwithstanding the exceptional injury by some, there has been, perhaps, less damage than usual from injurious species.

Among these last must be mentioned the Hop Aphis (*Phorodon humuli*), which was so destructive in the great hop regions of New York State as to have caused an almost total loss. The best evidence I have been able to obtain from correspondents is that in a great many cases no harvest was made, and on an average only about 10 per cent. was harvested. In this connection I have taken steps to carry on a series of practical experiments the coming year, and I may state as a matter of interest that, from investigations made last September in the hop fields I am led to believe that I have discovered the winter egg of this hop-louse upon plum trees, so that its mode of hibernation, which has hitherto been a mystery, has thus been settled. Full verification of this fact, however, cannot be obtained without another season's observation, and for this reason I have been unwilling so far to publish anything in detail.

In my last report I showed that, so far as experiments in silk-culture are concerned, no decisive results could well be hoped for until the Serrell automatic reel could be tested at some point in Washington where the details could be well controlled and observations made by myself and assistants, and where the work could be carried on for at least two years. Congress therefore appropriated $10,000 for this particular purpose, and the reeling stations at San Francisco, New Orleans, and Philadelphia have been abandoned. The brief report of the work in this direction, which will be found in the following pages, must be looked upon as preliminary; for, while the figures given look somewhat discouraging, no fair and proper estimate can be made before another year. The confirmation which our reeling has so far given of the value of the Osage Orange as silk-worm food is interesting, and entirely in keeping with what I expected and what I have previously recorded.

Work has been continued at the apicultural station at Aurora, Ill., as far as the means would permit, and a report on some of the experiments by Nelson W. McLain, in charge of the station, is embodied, while some further reports will be included in a special bulletin. I have endeavored by occasional consultations with Mr. McLain to keep the experiments in lines that have been more or less neglected by bee-keepers and in which there was hope of valuable results. The most important of these are in the direction of controlling fertilization. Most of the improvement in bee-culture in the past has been in the direction of mechanical appliances, while these experiments have in mind the improvement of the bee itself, so as to increase its honey-yielding power, and thus advance the interest in the same way that the dairy interest has been advanced by improving the milk and butter producing qualities of the cow.

A year ago Congress added $5,000 to the appropriation of the Division for the promotion of economic ornithology, and charged the Entomologist with carrying on the work. This appropriation was made at the instance of Professor Baird, myself, and Dr. C. Hart Merriam, and in obedience to a memorial from the American Ornithologists' Union. Work was begun by your appointing Dr. Merriam as a special agent in charge, and Dr. A. K. Fisher and a clerk to assist. The scope of the work planned was indicated in my last annual report, it being arranged that the part relating to food habits should be dealt with by myself and former associates because of its entomological bearing; while to Dr. Merriam was assigned all the other phases of the work, he being particularly interested in the migrations of birds as chairman of the committee on migrations of the Union above mentioned.

Early in July, 1885, a circular was prepared (Circular 20, Division of Entomology) setting forth the objects of the investigation, and asking information concerning the food-habits of certain well-known birds which were supposed to be beneficial or injurious to the farmer. About 2,000 copies of this circular were distributed to farmers and ornithologists throughout the country, and a large number of replies were received. During the winter two additional circulars (Circulars 24 and 27, Division of Entomology), accompanied by three schedules, were prepared, which related to the migration and geographical distribution of North American birds. These were sent to the keepers of light-houses along the coasts and lakes and to the regular observers of the American Ornithologists' Union.

Special attention was given during the year to the English Sparrow question, and a large amount of information has been collected. The ravages of birds in the rice fields of the South was another matter which early received attention, and Dr. Fisher was sent on an extended tour through the rice-growing districts, giving particular attention to those of Georgia and Louisiana. The formation of a collection of the stomachs, crops, and gizzards of birds was early undertaken, and has been continued to the present time.

From the outset I have recognized that while the ornithological work, so far as it related to food-habits, was legitimately placed in the Entomological Division, because of its intimate connection with the subject of entomology, yet there were many other lines of inquiry that have no particular bearing on entomology, and could not well be prosecuted in earnest without detracting from the time which should be devoted to the more legitimate sphere of the Division. As soon, therefore, as it was ascertained that there was some prospect of getting a new Division created I strongly urged such action, and a new Division of Ornithology and Mammalogy was created last June by Senate amendment to the House bill. it having been previously arranged that the Entomologist should take charge of the question of food-habits so far as they relate to insects. Unfortunately, however, the appropriation to the new Division was taken from the Entomological Division, thus reducing the means of this last below what it was two years ago, so that the work has been correspondingly crippled by the stoppage of investigations already begun (especially in California and the South), by the discharge of some of the employés and the reduction in salary of some of the others.

So much of the time devoted to ornithology during the year having been taken up in original investigations and the accumulation of material, Dr. Merriam has submitted no formal report, and the results of the investigations, so far as they have been written up, will be published directly under the new Division.

In this connection, as evidence of the interest abroad in applied entomology, i would refer to the holding of an international exhibition of machinery and contrivances for applied remedies against fungi and insects that are destructive to cultivated plants. This congress was held in October at Florence, and his Excellency, B. Grimaldi, the minister of agriculture, industry, and commerce for Italy, was very anxious to have the Division represented by such discoveries and mechanical appliances as have been developed in its work of late years. He was also very anxious to have a representative from the Department to take part in the discussions of the congress to be held in connection with the exhibition. The Entomologist was in fact made one of the jurors, and it is to be regretted that, by the terms of our appropriation, the Department was unable to have entomological representation at said congress. From reports of the congress that have come to hand, kindly furnished by Prof. Gustav Foëx, in charge of the experimental school of agriculture at Montpellier, and of Henri Grosjean, of Paris, it is evident that they have made good use of the remedies and contrivances published and recorded in our annual reports, and that, with the exception of experience against the Grape-vine Phylloxera, there was not very much that would have interested us in America.

The work of the Division is best represented by its published results, as, after all, its value is proportioned to the manner in which it is placed upon record and made available to the public, though there is of necessity a great amount of work that is not accounted for in print. In the matter of published and contemplated reports and bulletins, the following list represents the activity of the Division fairly well:

The publications of the present year have been as follows:

Bulletin No. 8. The Periodical Cicada. An account of Cicada septendecim and its tredecim race, with a chronology of all broods known. pp. 46.

Bulletin No. 11. Reports of Experiments with Various Insecticide Substances, chiefly upon insects affecting garden crops. pp. 34.

Bulletin No. 8. Second edition.

Insects affecting the Orange. Report by H. G. Hubbard on the insects affecting the culture of the Orange and other plants of the Citrus family, with practical suggestions for their control or extermination. pp. 227; figs., 95; plates, 14.

Fourth Report of the United States Entomological Commission, by C. V. Riley, being a revised edition of Bulletin No. 3, and the final report on the Cotton Worm, together with a chapter on the Boll Worm. pp. 546; figs., 45; plates, 64.

Report of the Entomologist for the year 1885. pp. 154; plates, 9.

Bulletin No. 12. Miscellaneous Notes on the Work of the Division of Entomology for the season of 1885. pp. 45; 1 plate.

Bulletin No. 9. The Mulberry Silk-worm; being a manual of instructions in silk-culture. Sixth revised edition of Special No. 11. pp. 62; figs., 29.

Those in course of preparation are:

Final Report on Insects injurious to Forest Trees (nearly completed).

Bibliography of Economic Entomology. A critical list of the economic writings of American entomologists.

Report on Insects affecting Domestic Animals.

Report on Remedies. A critical and classificatory treatise upon all the remedies which have been recommended against injurious insects.

Report on the Insects affecting Garden Crops of Florida.
Report on the Insects affecting the Grains.
Report on Insects affecting the Hop Crop.
Report on Insects affecting the Cranberry Crop.
Report upon the Grape-vine Phylloxera.
Monograph of the Acrididæ (destructive Grasshoppers).
Monograph of the Noctuidæ (Cut-worms, &c.).
Bulletin on Acronyctas (destructive tree-caterpillars).
Report on the Insectivorous Habits of Birds.
Several bulletins.

Dr. Packard has continued work on the Report on Forest Insects. He spent a portion of March and April in Northern and Central Florida studying and collecting the species injurious to Live and Water Oak, as well as to the Pines and Cypress. His observations go to corroborate those of others who have studied the Florida insect fauna, viz, that while a large proportion of the insects feeding on the oaks in Central Florida differ from those found in the Northern States, yet the pine insects from Maine to Florida belong to nearly one and the same fauna. During the summer months he worked in Maine, on the shores of Casco Bay, and a considerable amount of work was also done near Jackson, in New Hampshire, and around Providence. A report by him on some of the insects observed, and especially on a worm injurious to spruce buds, has been submitted, and will be published in the next bulletin.

Mr. F. M. Webster has continued investigations on the insects affecting our grains and forage plants, and his report, included herewith, contains a number of interesting observations, and also a list of 102 species of insects frequenting Buckwheat, with notes of their relative abundance and their method of attacking the plant.

Mr. Lawrence Bruner has continued work in Nebraska, and a special report from him will be published in bulletin form.

Prof. Herbert Osborn, of Ames, Iowa, has continued to assist me in work upon the insect parasites of domestic animals.

Miss M. E. Murtfeldt and Mr. J. G. Barlow were each engaged during the year for brief periods in various observations in Missouri, and Mr. William H. Ashmead similarly for a brief period in Florida.

Work by Mr. B. P. Mann on the Bibliography of Economic Entomology has been interrupted by the reduction in the appropriation, but otherwise the Divisional force at the Department remains the same, Messrs. E. A. Schwarz and Theo. Pergande assisting in the office work.

The illustrations to this report have been made by Miss Lillie Sullivan and Dr. George Marx, with the supervision of myself or of Mr. Howard.

I take pleasure, in conclusion, in acknowledging my indebtedness to Mr. Otto Lugger for assistance in the preparation of the article on the Buffalo Gnats and for the satisfactory manner in which he carried on his observations at Memphis, and particularly to Mr. L. O. Howard, who has had charge of the Division during my absence, and who has materially assisted me throughout both in the office correspondence and the preparation of reports. December 24, 1886.

Respectfully submitted,

C. V. RILEY,
Entomologist.

Hon. NORMAN J. COLMAN,
Commissioner of Agriculture.

30 AG—'86

MISCELLANEOUS INSECTS.

THE COTTONY CUSHION-SCALE.

(*Icerya purchasi* Maskell.)

Order HEMIPTERA; family COCCIDÆ.

[Plates I, II, III, IV, and V.]

INTRODUCTORY.

We have, during the year, been conducting a special investigation of the habits of and remedies for the so-called Cottony Cushion-scale of California, an insect which for the last eight years has occupied much of the attention of the horticulturists of that State. We have been much interested in this pest since it was originally sent to us while in Missouri by Mr. R. H. Stretch from San Francisco in 1872, and have watched its increase and spread, until it became evident from its alarming prolificacy, from the great diversity of its food-plants, from its supposed immunity from the attacks of natural enemies, and from the protection against the action of insecticides afforded by its abundant waxy excretions, that especial study and experiment were much needed.

The following account of the insect is prepared from published accounts and unpublished correspondence; from our biologic notes made at the office in Washington, chiefly in 1878, 1880, and 1886; but more especially from our recent experience in the field (which the delay in publishing the report has enabled us to partly embody), and the observations of Messrs. Coquillett and Koebele, whose reports on experiments made to destroy it will be found given in full among the reports of agents.

GEOGRAPHICAL DISTRIBUTION.

So far as we have been able to learn, up to the date of present writing, the Cottony Cushion-scale is found only in California, in Australia, in South Africa, and in New Zealand. We shall discuss its introduction into California and its present limitations in that State in subsequent sections of this paper, and what we know of its spread in the other countries mentioned is here considered.

IN AUSTRALIA.—As will appear farther on, the evidence collected goes to prove that this insect is indigenous to Australia and has been exported from this colony to the two other colonies in which it occurs and to the United States. We have very few facts as to its occurrence in Australia and these are taken at second hand. We have addressed communications to a number of naturalists in different portions of that country, but their replies have at this writing not been received. From the "Report of the Commission appointed by his excellency the governor to inquire into and report upon the means of exterminating the insect of the family 'Coccidæ,' commonly known as the 'Australian Bug,'" published at Cape Town, 1877, and from the letter of Mr. Roland Trimen, dated February 5, 1877, and published by the government secretary of Cape Colony as "Government Notice No. 113, 1877," we find that at that time specimens of the insect were sent from Cape Town to different portions of Australia, and that replies were received as follows: The Queensland authorities simply promised inquiry and report. The government of South Australia did not recognize the insect in question as a native of that colony. The inquiry to Victoria was referred to Prof. Frederick McCoy, director of the National Museum at Melbourne, who identified the insect as a new *Dorthesia*, "common in Victoria on different kinds of *Acacia*."

This is the extent of our information. Mr. Maskell, in his second paper on this species (Transactions and Proceedings New Zealand Institute, XIV, p. 226, 1881), writes: "When in Australia a few months ago I observed at Ballarat an insect, certainly an *Icerya*, but I think not *I. purchasi;* but I had no opportunity of bringing away a single specimen." There exists, then, a possibility at least that the insect under consideration is found at Ballarat as well as around Melbourne.

IN CAPE COLONY.—We find in the "Report of the Commission," &c., just cited, the following information on the spread of the insect in this colony:

From the answers received it would seem that the insect, having first appeared and succeeded in establishing itself in Cape Town and the vicinity, gradually spread along the lines of traffic by land and sea to different parts of the colony; and we may mention, in evidence of its irregular dispersal by chance methods of conveyance, that it was observed in the village of Ookiep, Namaqualand, only a few months after its first discovery in the Cape Town Botanical Gardens in 1873, and yet was not seen in the neighboring division of Stellenbosch till the later end of 1876.

The limits to which the insect had extended at the time of the publication of the report of the commission (1877, presumably the latter part of the year) included the following localities: Cape Town and neighborhood, Simon's Town, Stellenbosch (Mulders Vlei), Malmesbury, Paarl, Wellington, Namaqualand (Ookiep), Bredasdorp, George (Brak River), Uitenhage, East London.

We have no information as to the present status of the insect in this colony, as the replies to our letters of inquiry have not yet come to hand.*

IN NEW ZEALAND.—From the paper containing Mr. Maskell's original description of *Icerya purchasi* (Trans. and Proc. N. Z. Inst., XI, 220, 1878), we learn that the insect was first noticed at Auckland. A note by Mr. E. A. MacKechnie (Ibid., XIV, 549, 1881) indicated that it had greatly increased in presumably the same neighborhood in 1881. In Mr. Maskell's second paper (Ibid., p. 226) he mentions in a foot-note that he had just received the insect from Napier. In his third paper (Ibid., XVI, 140, 1883) he writes as follows:

Icerya purchasi has spread greatly in the last two years. It had just reached Napier at the date of my last paper. It has now established itself in that district not only in gardens, but in the native forests. In Auckland it is attacking all sorts of plants. * * * It has reached Nelson, and I have had many communications from that place complaining of its ravages· * * * Whether this pest will spread in our colder southern climate (Christchurch) as it has in the warmer north remains to be seen. Our gardeners here are not in much dread of outdoor insects; they confine their attention to those in greenhouses. They may be right; still the winter even in Canterbury is not severe enough to kill these insects, and I know that in the Christchurch public gardens many trees have had to be burnt simply on account of the ravages of *Coccidæ*.

We have no information on this point from this colony later than 1883, but have taken steps to ascertain the present spread of the pest.

---

*Just as the report is being sent to the printer we learn from Miss Ormerod that she has received specimens from Port Elizabeth, Cape Colony.

IMPORTATION OF THE SPECIES INTO CALIFORNIA.

The first printed record, with which we are acquainted, of the occurrence of the Cottony Cushion-scale in California is Mr. Stretch's article in the Proceedings of the California Academy of Sciences, Vol. IV, read September 16, 1872. In opening this paper he refers to the fact that "at a former meeting certain insects forwarded to this society from Menlo Park, San Mateo County, by Mr. Gordon," were referred to him for examination. A careful search through the previous proceedings fails to show any mention of this previous sending, though at the meeting of July 1, 1872, Mr. John Hewston, jr., "exhibited some limbs of Australian Acacia from San Mateo which were infested by a species of Coccus, and stated that the insect had not only been detected in its depredations upon said tree, but also upon the orange trees." This latter reference may very possibly have been to the Cottony Cushion-scale, and if so it is interesting, as indicating already a spread of some miles from Menlo Park.

All the slight evidence possessed points to the introduction of this scale on Australian Acacia by Mr. George Gordon about 1868 or 1869. Mr. Stretch says:

This being all the information to be derived from the specimens referred to me, I visited Menlo Park in search of further information, and received a very hearty welcome from Mr. Gordon. The supposition is that the insect was imported from Australia some three years ago; at any rate it seemed to originate on the *Acacia latifolia*.

This was evidently Mr. Gordon's supposition, and the plain inference is that about three years previous to this time certain Acacias had been imported by Mr. Gordon from Australia as plants or cuttings contrary to the general custom, although it is not stated in so many words.

Dr. A. W. Saxe, of Santa Clara, Cal., in 1877, wrote:*

"So far as I can ascertain, it was brought to California on some plants imported from Australia by the late George Gordon, of Menlo Park (the sugar refiner)."

In the introduction to our annual report as Entomologist to this Department for 1878 we referred to the serious complaints that came from the Pacific coast of injury by it to orchard and ornamental trees, and from specimens received from Dr. Saxe (Mr. Maskell's papers being unknown here then) referred it to the genus *Dorthesia*, and remarked:

It is an Australian insect, and has of late years been introduced on Australian plants into South Africa, where, as I learn from one of my correspondents, Mr. Roland Trimen, curator of the South African Museum, it has multiplied at a terrible rate, and become such a scourge as to attract the attention of the government. It has evidently been introduced (probably on the Blue Gum or *Eucalyptus*) to California, either direct from Australia or from South Africa, and will doubtless become quite a scourge; because most introduced insects are brought over without the natural enemies which keep them in check in their native country and consequently multiply at a prodigious rate. It will be naturally partial to Australian trees, and shows a preference for Acacia, Eucalyptus, Orange, Rose, Privet, and Spiræa.

Professor Comstock, in the Annual Report of the Department of Agriculture for 1880, p. 348, cited this article of Dr. Saxe's as the earliest article with which he was acquainted, and repeated Dr. Saxe's opinion as to the introduction of the insect.

Beyond this we are able to get no information upon the subject, and these data are in all probability the first connected with the introduction of the Cottony Cushion-scale. There may possibly have been

---

* *California Agriculturist and Artisan*, December, 1877.

subsequent and independent importations, but that this is the one from which the main spread originated there can be little doubt.

ITS SPREAD AND PRESENT LIMITATION IN CALIFORNIA.

We are indebted to Mr. Matthew Cooke, of Sacramento, for communicating a lengthy and careful account of the localities in which the pest at present exists in California. Mr. Cooke has mapped out ten districts, six in the counties of Marin, San Mateo, Santa Clara, Sacramento, Sonoma, and Napa, in the San Francisco region, and four in the counties of Santa Barbara and Los Angeles, in the southern portion of the State.

The first infested district extends from Menlo Park to San Mateo, a distance of 10 miles. It is bounded on the east by the Southern Pacific Railroad, and extends some 3 miles west, including in consequence some 30 square miles. But little effort, according to Mr. Cooke, has been made to eradicate the pest in this district.

The second infested district is contained within the town limits of San Rafael, Marin County, about 14 miles north of San Francisco. In this district it has been held in check, but there are still some to be found, and its increase is only dependent upon a lapse of vigilance.

The third infested district includes the city of San José and the town of Santa Clara, and contains an area of about 16 square miles. In these towns the scale insects infested the ornamental and shade trees and shrubbery, but did not seem to trouble the deciduous fruit trees to any extent. At San José energetic measures have been taken; the trees have been cut back and their trunks scrubbed until the pest has been thoroughly eradicated. At Santa Clara, however, little has been done, and some places are seriously infested.

The fourth infested district occurs at the city of Sacramento, where only about 120 acres are infested, although it is stated to be rapidly spreading. The insect was first discovered in this district by Mr. Cooke in October, 1885, in about eight gardens. The city trustees appropriated $200, and with this sum it was destroyed, except upon certain premises which the authorities could not enter. Mr. Cooke gives in this connection, as an instance of the rapidity of the multiplication and spread of the insect, the following:

In October, 1885, a patch of these insects covered a space of about 3 by 4 inches was noticed upon a limb of an Acacia tree. From these it spread, and in a little more than a year several Orange and Lemon trees and other plants growing closely in an area of about 160 by 80 feet had become seriously infested.

The fifth infested district is found at Healdsburg, Sonoma County, about 65 miles north by west of San Francisco. Here the insect is mainly comprised within the town limits, and infests the shade trees along the streets and the shrubbery in the gardens.

In Mr. Cooke's sixth district the insect cannot be said to exist at present. It comprises a single garden in the town of Saint Helena, Napa County, about 60 miles north by east of San Francisco. It was found upon a rose bush in that place by Mrs. Richard Wood in October, 1882. The bush was destroyed, and the pest has not been found in that section since.

The seventh infested district includes the city of Los Angeles, where the insect is principally confined, according to Mr. Cooke, to the gardens and suburbs on the eastern side of the city. Mr. Coquillett says that as nearly as can be ascertained the insect was first introduced into Los Angeles in 1878 upon some nursery trees purchased from a San Francisco nurseryman. These trees were planted in a certain nursery, and when the insects were first noticed upon them the owner was requested to burn them. He neglected to do this, and soon after failed in business, and the nursery fell into other hands. The new owner also proved indifferent, and from this point the insects spread into the surrounding orchards, going mainly in the direction of the prevailing winds. Some years ago a tree was found infested at Passadena, 7 miles east of Los Angeles, but it was immediately destroyed, and the insect has not been heard of since. At Pomona, 32 miles east of Los Angeles, the same thing happened in 1883. Two trees were found to be infested and were immediately destroyed, and the insect has not appeared since.

The eighth infested district is at Anaheim, Los Angeles County, 27 miles south by east of Los Angeles. Here the insect is purely local and does not seem to be spreading.

The ninth district is at San Gabriel, 9 miles east of Los Angeles. In the vicinity of this place are some of the largest orange groves in California. In 1880 or 1881, according to Mr. Cooke, a Mrs. McGregory bought a pot-plant in Los Angeles, brought it home, and placed it beside a small Orange near her house. In 1882 the neighboring orange trees were found to be infested with the Cottony Cushion-scale. In the fall of 1883 it was found in some of the larger orchards so abundantly as to cause alarm among the growers. By means of a voluntary tax of five cents per tree, some fifteen hundred or two thousand dollars were raised and expended and the pest eradicated. The most radical measures were used. The trees were cut back to the crotches, the branches burned, and the trunks scrubbed. In 1885, however, the insect was again found, but only in a few trees.

The tenth and last district includes the orchards in and around the city of Santa Barbara. According to Mr. Coquillett the scale was introduced into this district in 1878. A number of trees from the same lot which first introduced the pest into Los Angeles was sent to Santa Barbara at about the same time. Mr. Cooke states that he visited this district in July, 1884, and found Mr. Stowe's orchards (10 miles north of the city of Santa Barbara) the most seriously infested spot in the State. Forty acres, principally of lemon trees, were badly damaged, and over many acres the trees had been dug out and burned. Two miles north of Mr. Stowe's, Colonel Hollister's groves also contained the insect in numbers. About 40 acres were partially infested. The latter gentleman made strong endeavors to rid his groves of the insect, and spent a great deal of money, with only partial success. Mr. Cooke states that the course of the insect between Mr. Stowe's and Colonel Hollister's could be plainly traced over a rolling grazing land on the nettles, dock, and other weeds.*

---

* Reports have gained currency that this Icerya was found abundantly around Santa Barbara on wild plants, and especially upon the "Grease-wood," and it has been argued from such reports that the species is indigenous. They have no foundation except in mistaken identity, a large Coccid belonging to the genus *Rhizococcus*, which occurs abundantly on *Artemisia californica*, having undoubtedly given rise to the report. The female of this species, which we shall describe as *Rhizococcus artemisiæ*, secretes a globular mass of white cottony wax, which is more or less distinctly ribbed, and her eggs are of the same color as those of the Icerya; but with these superficial resemblances which have misled, there are profound structural differences.

FOOD-PLANTS.

ORIGINAL FOOD-PLANT OF ICERYA PURCHASI.—There seems good reason to believe that this species is originally an Acacia insect, and that upon one or another of the plants of this genus it was imported from Australia into South Africa, California, and New Zealand. Australia is pre-eminently the home of the Acacias, while none are indigenous to California, nor, so far as we can ascertain, to New Zealand, and, as is well known, the species now found in these two countries have been introduced from Australia.

Professor McCoy, of Melbourne, in his original communication to the government of Cape Colony, in 1876, stated that the insect in question occurred in Victoria on "different kinds of Acacia."

Mr. J. C. Brown* states, on the basis of Mr. Trimen's description, that the "Australian Bug" appears to resemble in several details one of the Coccidae found on the Kangaroo Island Acacia, universally around Adelaide. This statement is so indefinite as to have little weight; yet there is more than a possibility that the Australian insect mentioned is the *Icerya*.

Mr. Trimen, in his report previously mentioned, states that the first specimens seen by him in Cape Colony occurred in 1873, at Clairmont, on Blackwood trees (*Acacia melanoxylon*), obtained from the botanic gardens at Cape Town. He goes on to say:

In the course of a few months the insect increased so prodigiously in number, and the Australian Acacias became laden with them to such an extent, that in the early part of 1874 the large Blackwood trees in the gardens, which were infested to a greater extent than any other plant, had to be cut down.

In New Zealand the first appearance of this insect was also upon an Australian Acacia. Mr. Maskell, in originally describing the insect, in 1878, says: "My specimens of this subdivision were found on a hedge of the Kangaroo Acacia,† in Auckland, in March last. I understood from Mr. Cheeseman and Dr. Purchas, who kindly brought this insect under my notice, that it had only lately appeared in Auckland, and that it was only as yet to be found upon that one hedge."

In California the experience was almost precisely similar. Mr. Stretch, in his paper before the California Academy of Sciences, in 1872, stated that at Menlo Park "it seemed to originate upon *Acacia latifolia*, a species imported from Australia." Miss Anna Rosecrans, writing to the *Pacific Rural Press* of February 17, 1877, says: "It was first noticed at San Rafael on Acacia trees four or five years ago." Dr. Chapin, in the first report of the State Board of Horticultural Commissioners of California, 1882, says: "This scale has been, it is asserted, known to be on the Acacia for seven years in San José, but it is only during the past and present seasons that it has attracted attention" (presumably by its spread to other cultivated plants).

Thus we have much cumulative evidence that the species of the genus Acacia are the preferred food-plants of the Cottony Cushion-scale, and, admitting Australia as its proper home, they are probably its original food.

ITS FOOD-PLANTS IN SOUTH AFRICA.—From Mr. Trimen's 1877 report we gather the following list of plants to which the Australian Bug had spread since 1873:

Acacia melanoxylon.

*On the "Australian Bug" of South Africa. *Journal of Forestry*, May, 1882, VI, p. 44.
†*Acacia armata.*—C. V. R.

Australian Acacias.
"Golden Willow."
Casuarius.
Pittosporum.
"Blue Gum" (rarely).
Australian "Bottle-brush."
Oak.
Orange.
Vine.
Fig.
Laurustinus.
Rose.
Rosemary.
Strawberry.
Verbena.
Plumbago.
Indian Jasmine.
Bougainvillea.
Hawthorn.
Poinsettia.
Hakea.

This list is not added to in the "Report of the Commission," &c., published at Cape Colony in 1877. Mr. Trimen, in the article cited above, gave the preference to the trees and shrubs of Australian origin; but Mr. J. C. Brown (*loc. cit.*) quotes him as writing, under date of March 17 (1882?), that the insect had then mainly attached itself to the orange trees. "Many of the finest plantations have been destroyed and others are on the high road to destruction. You will remember," he says, "how good and cheap oranges used to be here; they have lately been three pence and four pence apiece, and often inferior in quality even at such a price."

ITS FOOD-PLANTS IN NEW ZEALAND.—From the various communications of Mr. Maskell and others in the Transactions and Proceedings of the New Zealand Institute we give the following list of plants which have been especially designated. There has been no attempt, however, on Mr. Maskell's part to give at all a complete list, and in fact, he says,* "In Auckland it is attacking *all sorts* of plants, from Apple and Rose trees to Pines, Cypress, and Gorse":

Common Furze.
Orange.
Lemon.
Acacia decurrens.
Acacia armata.
Apple.
Wattles.
Rose.
Gorse.
Pine.
Cypress.

ITS FOOD-PLANTS IN CALIFORNIA.—Originally starting upon *Acacia latifolia* at Menlo Park, this insect soon spread to numberless other plants. Dr. Saxe, in 1877, mentioned that it already attacked the Acacias, Australian Pea-vine, Rose, Honey-suckle, Ivy-geranium, Laburnum, Pear, and the weeds in the orchard.

---

*Ibid., XVI, p. 140 (1883).

Dr. Chapin, in 1883, mentioned the following:
Pear.
Apple.
Bridal-wreath.
Rose.
Dwarf Box.
Verbena.
Veronica.
Acacia mollissima.
Acacia latifolia.
Acacia limnœris.
Acacia floribunda.
Pittosporum tobria.
Strawberry.
Black Locust.
California Laurel.
Cork Elm.
English Ivy.
Magnolia grandiflora.
White Oak.
Dwarf Flowering Almond.
Wild Grease-wood.

Our recent experience in California, as well as that of Messrs. Coquillett and Koebele last summer, would indicate that, while there are few plants upon which the insect will not temporarily feed if it happen to fall upon them while in the first stage, yet the number of plants upon which it can thrive and multiply is limited. The larva will survive for weeks without food and will wander about in search of suitable food if it should find itself, for one cause or another, on that which is unsuitable. It undoubtedly thrives best on Acacias, and next to these we should place the Citrus fruits, the Quince, and the Pomegranate, and we doubt if it could thrive upon many other trees. The list of its food-plants, or rather of plants upon which it has been found, is longer than is justified, not only because of its power of endurance above noted, but because the young are easily carried by wind or otherwise to plants more or less uncongenial and on which they ultimately perish, while the adults are often dislodged from infested Acacia or Citrus trees onto plants under or near them.

Among the more valuable trees upon which it certainly cannot thrive, and upon which it does not occur when they are grown at some distance from infested Acacia or Citrus trees, are the following: Pines, Cypress, Eucalyptus, Olive, Apricot, Peach, Pear, and Oleander.

The plants upon which Mr. Coquillett found females with egg-masses in limited numbers, and which were growing in situations so remote from any infested Acacia or Citrus trees as to preclude the idea that the adult insects had found their way to these plants from such trees, were as follows:
Pomegranate.
Quince.
Apple.
Peach.
Apricot.
Fig.
Walnut.
Locust.
Willow.

Pepper.
Grape.
Rose.
Castor-bean.
Spearmint.
Rose-geranium.

Mr. Koebele, whose observations have been close and extensive, found that the Quince is always thickly infested, as is also the Pomegranate, while on Pear, Apple, Peach, and Apricot the scales were not numerous in the adult state. Only a few scales, and these nearly always small, were found upon the Castor-oil bean. Some Pecan-trees were noticed on which some of the branches were completely covered with scales. A Willow hedge surrounded by plants which had been infested for over two years did not itself become attacked until the past summer. The Fig he states to be a favorite food-plant. On Eucalyptus he found young scales all summer, and in October he found twigs full of scales of all sizes. A few full-grown individuals were found upon a single Pepper tree (*Schinus molle*) growing in the orchard. The following is a supplementary list of plants upon which Mr. Koebele reported the scales most noticeable:

Portulaca oleracea—Scales often numerous.
Malva rotundifolia.
Grape (*Vitis* spp.)—Scales occurring principally on petiole and leaf.
Medicago denticulata.
Helianthus spp.
Rose (*Rosa* spp.)—Scales growing often to an unusually large size, and very numerous on some varieties.
Epilobium coloratum.
Erigeron canadensis.
Bidens pilosa.
Artemisia ludoviciana.
Ambrosia psilostachya—Hundreds of scales on each plant during July, August, and September.
Sonchus oleraceus.
Plantago spp.
Mentha piperita.
Stachys æquata.
Solanum tuberosum.
Solanum douglasii.
Chenopodium murali.
Chenopodium album.
Amarantus retroflexus.
Polygonum persicaria—Stem often entirely covered by scales.
Rumex crispus.
Urtica holosericea—A favorite plant, on which the scales developed with unusual rapidity and to large size.
Carex spp.
Paspalum spp.
Panicum crus-galli.

CHARACTERS AND LIFE HISTORY.

The genus *Icerya* was first described by Signoret in the Annales de la Société Entomologique de France" for 1875, pp. 351, 352, and was founded on the single species *I. sacchari* (Guérin), which occurs on sugar cane in the Island of Bourbon. He knew only two stages, the full-grown female and the newly hatched larva, but these were described with his customary care.

Mr. Maskell, in describing the species under consideration, places it without much hesitation in this genus, and later, in 1883, still places it in *Icerya*, after examining specimens of *I. sacchari* sent him by M. Signoret. In his original paper (Trans. Proc. N. Z. Inst., 1878, 220). Mr. Maskell describes quite carefully the egg, the young larva, the second stage, and the full-grown female, but had not seen the male larva, cocoon, or adult. Professor Comstock (Ann. Rept. Dept. of Agric., 1880, p. 347) follows Maskell's description quite closely, and introduces no new facts.

There is therefore a necessity for a careful review of the complete life history of the insect, and this we have endeavored to give in the following pages.

THE EGG (Plate II, Fig. 1).—The egg is quite smooth, elongate-ovate in form, and is of a deep orange-yellow color. It measures about 0.7^{mm} in length.

The average number of eggs laid by the female varies according to the vigor of the individual or the condition of the plant upon which she dwells; prolificacy diminishing in proportion as the plant is badly infested—a general law among Coccidæ. Over 800 eggs have been counted in a single egg-mass by Mr. Coquillett, while Mr. Koebele has counted in a single egg-mass, which, by the way, was found upon nettle (*Urtica holosericea*), 940 eggs and 72 young larvæ, while 123 eggs yet remained in the dead body of the female, making a total of 1,135 eggs from the single female.

The time required for the eggs to hatch after leaving the body of the female varies with the temperature. In the winter-time the sacs are usually filled with eggs, while in the hottest part of the summer seldom more than one or two dozen will be found in each sac. Some collected by Mr. Coquillett on the 18th of March did not hatch until the 10th of May; but in mid-summer hatching is only a matter of a few days.

THE FEMALE LARVA—FIRST STAGE (Plate I. Fig. 2, and Plate II, Fig. 2).—The newly hatched female larva (and probably the male is identical with it at this stage of growth, since we have not been able to separate them into males and females) is red in color, inclining somewhat to brown. The body is ovoid in outline, being flattened beneath and convex above. The antennæ are long and 6-jointed. Joint 1 is short and stout, and as broad as long; joints 2, 3, 4, and 5 subcylindrical and subequal, much more slender than joint 1, and twice as long as broad; joint 6 is as long as 4 and 5 together, and forms a long club, at base equaling joint 5 in diameter, but broadening out to twice its width at tip. The basal portion of the club is sometimes distinctly separate from the rest, forming an additional joint. All joints have a few sparse hairs, and the club, in addition to several short ones, bears near its tip four very long ones, each of which is considerably longer than the whole antenna. The legs are thin and brown in color. The coxæ and femora are moderately large, while the tibiæ and tarsi are long and thin, the terminal joints of the latter bearing several long hairs. The upper digitules are represented by simple hairs, but the lower ones are present and are bent near the base. The eyes are prominent and are each mounted on a short tubercle. The mentum is broad and apparently 2-jointed. The rostrum is broad at base and the rostral setæ are not very long. At the tip of the rounded abdomen are 6 small tubercles, 3 each side of tip, each of which carries a long stout hair, which is as long as the whole body.   The body above shows 6 rows of secretory pores, 4 along the middle, and 1 on each side.   More or less regular rows of hairs alternate with these pores.

FEMALE LARVA—SECOND STAGE.—According to Maskell and Comstock, there are but three stages of growth in the female after hatching, and these are readily distinguished by the number of antennal joints; the larva of the first stage having 6, that of the second 9, and the adult 11.   Messrs. Coquillett and Koebele came to the same conclusions, and all have overlooked a form which we have found quite abundantly among the material we have studied, and which seems to constitute an intermediate stage between the so-called first and second, and which is of course produced by an additional molt which we have personally observed in the field.   Hence the so-called "second stage" of these authors becomes third, while the adult female is fourth instead of third, and there are 3 molts instead of 2.

This new intermediate form (Plate II, Fig. 3) differs from the female larva of the first stage in the following respects: It is much more rounded and of a stouter general appearance.   The antennæ have the same number of joints, 6, but their relative proportions are quite different.   The antennæ as a whole are relatively much shorter. Joint 1 is short and stout, its length equalling its breadth; joint 2 equals joint 1 in length, but is not quite so broad; joint 3 is as broad as joint 2, but is twice as long; joints 4 and 5 are equal in length and width, each narrowing somewhat at base and tip, each considerably narrower than joint 3, and each of the same length as joint 2; joint 6 (club) is of an irregular shape; at base it is as narrow as joint 5, but it broadens until it is slightly wider than 2 or 3, and its tip is narrowed again; its shape is that of an irregular rhomboid with rounded angles and sides, the acutest angles at base and tip.   The antennæ carry about the same number of hairs as in the first stage, but those homologous with the four very long hairs of the club in that stage are in this second stage but little longer than the other antennal hairs.   The eyes do not appear on the margin of the body, and are only seen on a ventral view.   The legs are proportionately much shorter, and the femora are stouter; the trochanters are broader distally, and consequently form a broader triangle in shape.   The six tubercles at the anal end of the body are still present, but the hairs which they bear are much shorter.   The secretory pores are no longer arranged in rows, but are scattered sparsely over the back and under the sides.   The back is more hairy, and the short black hairs occur in irregular tufts.

FEMALE LARVA—THIRD STAGE (Plate II, Fig. 4).—That which has heretofore been considered the second stage, and which, as we have just seen, is the third, may be described as follows:

The body is broadly oval in shape and reddish-brown in color, but is soon obscured more or less by the thick, curly, cotton-like excretion. The antennæ are 9-jointed instead of 6, and are subcylindrical, tapering somewhat from base to tip.   Joints 4, 5, 6, 7, and 8 are subequal in length, and each is about as long as broad; joints 2 and 3 are broader and considerably longer; joint 1 is like the corresponding joint in the previous stage; joint 9 (club) is a suboval joint, proportionately much smaller than in the previous stages; it does not exceed joint 8 in width, and it does not quite equal joints 7 and 8 together in length. The long hairs of the club are proportionately quite short.   The insect as a whole is much more hairy than in either of the previous stages.   The hairs are short and black, and show a marked tendency to grow together in tufts; even when their bases are well separated their tips turn toward each other or toward the common center of a group; they are quite thickly scattered over the thorax, but less so over the abdomen; all around the edge of the body they appear in close tufts, and the concentric subdorsal ring of tufts which is so prominent in the next stage is plainly seen in this. The secretory pores are scattered irregularly all over the back, and are more numerous than in the previous stage: they also occur under the lateral edges of the body. They are small and circular, and, seen directly from above, have a double outline, indicating a circular central orifice. Around the edge of the body is a row of much larger pores, brown in color, which protrude from the body, masked by the lateral tufts of hairs, each with a circular crown or lip at tip, from which proceeds a long, fragile, glassy tube. (Plate II, Fig. 6.) The legs and feet are a little stouter than before, the tarsal digitules are shorter, and their enlarged tips quite indistinct. The six anal hairs are still present, though hardly noticeable as they protrude from the mass of shorter hairs.

THE ADULT FEMALE—FOURTH STAGE (Plate II, Fig. 5).—Immediately after the molt by which the insect passes into this stage, it is free from the waxy excretion and presents a broadly oval form, flattened below and quite strongly convex above, with two prominent raised surfaces on the second and third thoracic segments. Its color is still reddish brown, with several darker spots, especially upon the front half and along the sides of the posterior half of the body, and the antennae and legs are black. The antennae are now 11-jointed instead of 9; joint 1 is nearly twice as wide as long: joints 2 and 3 are subequal in length and thickness and are each somewhat longer than broad; joint 4 is a little more than half as long as 3 and is narrower; joints 5, 6, 7, 8, 9, and 10 increase gradually and slightly in length and decrease very slightly in width: joint 11 (club) is irregularly ovoid and is one and one-half times as long as 10; the special hairs are a little shorter than in the previous stage. The whole body is furnished with short, black hairs, more numerous than in the last stage, arranged in tufts, particularly around the edge, where they occur in a double parallel row, the inner row being practically subdorsal and accentuated by a slight ridge. Down the central portion of the dorsum of the abdomen the segments are indicated by the transverse rows of hair tufts. The secretory pores are exceedingly abundant, occurring in enormous numbers just under the lateral edges of the body, and scattered more sparsely over the back. The individual wax filaments which issue from these pores are very delicate and curly, and there is reason to suppose that two or three issue at one time from one pore, as they are frequently seen connected at base; the pore opening, however, seems to have a single simple opening. The inner row of tufts on the back is broken at its anal point by a depression, in which is situated a very large pore, from which the insect occasionally ejects a globule of a semi-liquid honey-dew. This depression is surrounded by an irregular ring of hairs, which are yellowish in color instead of black. The glassy filaments arising from the large tubular pores described in the last stage are now very long and radiate from the body in almost every direction. They break off easily, yet still often reach a length double that of the insect and her egg-sack together. What is probably the opening of the oviduct is situated on the under side of the seventh abdominal segment. It is surrounded by a transversely oval chitinous ring.

THE EGG-SAC (Plate I, Fig. 4).—As the body of the female begins
to swell from the eggs forming inside. the beginning of the egg-sac is
made. The female lies flat on the bark, the edges of the body turned
slightly upwards, and the waxy material of which the sac is composed
begins to issue from countless pores on the under side of the body, but
more especially along the sides below. As the secretion advances the
body is raised, the cephalic end being still attached, until, near the
completion of the sac, the insect is apparently standing on its head,
nearly at right angles to the surface to which it is attached. The egg-
laying commences as soon as a thin layer of the secretion has formed
on the under side of the abdomen, and it continues during the formation of the sac. There soon appears around the edge of the abdomen
a narrow ring of white feltlike wax, which is divided into a number
of flutings (Plate I, Fig. 3). These flutings grow in length and the
mass of eggs and wax under them increases, forcing the female upward until the sac is completed. When completed, it is from two to
two and one-half times the length of the female's body. It is of a
snow-white color, and the outside is covered with 15 of these longitudinal ridges or flutings, of subequal size, except that the middle one
is smaller than the others. The upper part of the sac is firm in texture, but the lower is looser and thinner, and from the middle of the
under side the young make their escape soon after hatching. The
size of the sac and the length of time required in its growth depends,
leaving the weather and the health of the food-plant out of consideration, upon the number of eggs which the female deposits. So long
as oviposition continues, the secretion of wax accompanies it and the
egg-mass grows. Concerning the rate of growth Mr. Coquillet gives
the following instance:

"On the 4th of May of the present season I marked a large number
of females which were located upon the trunk of an orange tree that
was not in a very healthy condition. These females had just begun
to secrete the cottony matter, the latter at this date being in the form
of short but broad tufts around the margin of the abdomen, those at
the hind end of the latter being longest. By the 31st of May the
cottony matter was equal in length to one-third of the female's body,
and by the middle of July it about equaled in length the entire body
of the female. As the egg-masses of some of the females upon the
same tree were longer by one-half than the bodies of the females which
produced them, it is very probable that at least another month must
elapse before the egg-masses of the females which I observed would
be completed. It is altogether likely, however, that these egg-masses
would have been completed in a shorter time had the females been
located upon a healthy tree. The egg-masses found upon healthy
trees attain larger size than those found upon sickly trees, owing
doubtless to the fact that the females living upon trees of the former
kind are more vigorous than those upon unhealthy trees."

THE MALE LARVA—PROBABLE SECOND STAGE.—Neither Mr. Coquillett nor Mr. Koebele were able to distinguish the male larvæ until
these had reached the stage in which they form their cocoons. Among
the specimens studied at the Department, and which were sent alive
from Los Angeles by Mr. Koebele, we have found a larval form
which has not yet been described, and which we strongly suspect
may be the male in the second stage. This form is illustrated at Fig.
7, Plate II. It differs from our supposed second stage of the female
in its more slender form, longer and stouter legs, and longer and
stouter antennæ. The legs and antennæ are not only relatively

longer and stouter, but are absolutely so. The body above is much more thickly clothed with the short stout hairs than the corresponding female stage, and the mentum is longer and darker colored. The antennæ are 6-jointed, and the joints have precisely the same strange relative proportions as in the female. The secretory pores are present, but are not quite so numerous as in the female.

MALE LARVA—THIRD STAGE.—In this, the third or last larval stage, the male is readily distinguished with the naked eye from the female in any stage by the narrower, more elongate, more flattened, and evenly convex form of his body, as well as by his greater activity in crawling about the trunk or branches of a tree. More careful examination shows that the beak is entirely wanting, the tubercle from which it arises in the earlier stages being replaced by a shallow triangular depression. The body is almost naked, being very sparsely covered with a short, white, cottony matter, and is destitute of the short but stout black hairs which are found upon the body of the female during the third and fourth stages of her life. In the absence of black spots and in the 9-jointed antennæ he agrees with the similar or third stage of the female, and the average length when full grown is about 3^{mm} and diameter about 1^{mm}.

THE MALE PUPA AND COCOON.—When the male larva has reached full growth and is ready to transform it wanders about in search of a place of concealment, finally secreting itself under a bit of projecting bark, under some leaves in the crotch of the tree, or even wedging itself down under a mass of females. Very frequently, probably in the majority of cases, it descends to the ground, and hides under a clod of earth or works its way into some crack in the ground. Having concealed itself, it becomes quiescent, and the delicate, flossy substance of which the cocoon is formed begins to exude abundantly from the body. This material is waxy in its character, but is lighter and more flossy and less adhesive than that of which the egg-sac of the female is composed. After a certain amount has been exuded the larva moves backwards very slowly, the exudation continuing until the mass is from 7^{mm} to 10^{mm} in length. From this method of retrogression it happens that the body of the larva is frequently seen protruding posteriorly from the mass, which naturally leads to the erroneous conclusion that the material is secreted more abundantly from the fore part of the body, whereas the reverse is the case. When the mass has reached the proper length the larva casts its skin, which remains in the hind end of the cocoon, and pushes itself forward into the middle of the cocoon.

The pupa (Plate II, Fig. 8) has the same general color as the larva, the antennæ, legs, and wing-pads being paler and the eyes dark. It has also the same general form and size. All the members are free and slightly movable, so that they vary in position, though ordinarily the antennæ are pressed close to the side, reaching to basal part of metathorax(ventrally); the wing-pads also against the side, elongate-ovate in form and reaching to second abdominal joint. The legs are rather shorter than the diameter of body, and the front pair thrust forward. The anal end is deeply excavated, the abdominal joints well separated, the mesonotum well developed, and the pronotum tuberculous or with some 8 prominences; but there are no other structural peculiarities. The surface is, however, more or less thickly covered with waxy filaments, which are sometimes exuded in sufficient quantities to give quite a mealy appearance.

Whenever the pupæ are taken from the cocoon and placed naked in a tin box they exude a certain amount of wax, often enough to partially hide them from view. If disturbed, they twist and bend their bodies quite vigorously.

The cocoon (Plate I, Fig. 5) is of an irregular elongate shape, appearing a little denser in the center, where the pupa has placed itself, and at the edges delicate and translucent. The material of which the cocoon is composed is very delicate, and appears like the finest cotton, but on submission to a gentle heat it melts as readily as the coarser secretion of the female, and leaves the larva or pupa, as the case may be, clean and exposed.

THE ADULT MALE (Plate I, Fig. 1).—A careful description of the male of this species has never been published. It was unknown to Mr. Maskell at the date of his first paper and has not been mentioned in any of his subsequent papers. Mr. Trimen attempted to breed it, but was unsuccessful. He says: "So little is certainly known of the males of the Coccidæ that I have kept from time to time a large number of this Dorthesia under glass in the hope of obtaining the males, but hitherto without success. I once, however, found on my window a male of some Coccus which I thought was very probably that of the introduced species, as it agreed in most of its important characters with Westwood's figure of the male *Dorthesia characias*. It was dark-red, with the wings gray, and very slender and fragile in its structure. It measured $\frac{15}{48}$ inch across the expanded wings."

The male was unknown to Professor Comstock, but was very briefly mentioned by Dr. Chapin in the first report of the Board of State Horticultural Commissioners, Sacramento, 1882, p. 68. He found the male in numbers during a period of two weeks from September 25, 1881, but did not observe it in 1882. It is also mentioned by Matthew Cooke in his "Injurious Insects," &c., 1883, p. 166, and a rough and uncharacteristic figure is given at Fig. 146, Plate 3. His few words of description are: "Male insect, winged; color, thorax and body dark brown; abdomen, red; antennæ, dark colored, with light hairs extending from each joint; wings, brown, iridescent." The following detailed description is drawn up from numerous specimens, both mounted and living:

The adult male is a trifle over 3^{mm} in length, and has an average wing expanse of 7.5^{mm}. The general color is orange-red. The head above is triangular in shape, with the apex blunt and projecting forward between the bases of the antennæ. The eyes are placed at the other apices of the triangle, and are large, prominent, and furnished with well-marked facets. There are no mouth-parts, but on the under side of the head is a stellate black spot with five prongs, one projecting forward on the conical lengthening of the head, one on each side to a point just anterior to the eyes and just posterior to the bases of the antennæ, and the remaining two extending laterally backwards behind the eyes. The antennæ are light brown in color and are composed of ten joints. Joint 1 is stout, almost globular, and nearly as broad as long; joint 2 is half as broad as 1 and is somewhat longer; joint 3 is nearly twice as long as 1 and slightly narrower than 2; joints 4, 5, 6, 7, 8, 9, and 10 are all of about the same length as joint 3, and grow successively a little more slender; each joint, except joint 1, is furnished with two whorls of long light-brown hairs, one near base and the other near tip; each joint is somewhat constricted between its two whorls, joint 2 less so than the others. There are no visible ocelli. The pronotum has two wavy subdorsal longitudinal black lines, and the mesonotum is nearly all black, except an oval patch on the scutum. The metanotal spiracles are black, and there is a transverse crescent-shaped black mark, with a short median backward prolongation. The mesosternum is black. The legs are also nearly black and quite thickly furnished with short hairs. The wings are smoky black, and are covered with rounded wavy elevations, making a reticulate surface, a cross-section of which would appear crenulate. The costa is thick and brown above the subcostal vein, which reaches costa at a trifle more than four-fifths the length of the wing. The only other vein (the median) is given off at about one-sixth the length of the wing, and extends out into the disk a little more than one-half the wing length. There are, in addition, two white lines, one extending out from the fork of the subcostal and the median nearly straight to the tip of the wing, and one from the base in a gradual curve to a point some distance below the tip. Near the base of the wing below is a small ear-shaped prolongation, folded slightly on itself, making a sort of pocket. The halteres are foliate, and furnished at tip with two hooks, which fit into the folded projection at base of wings. The abdomen is slightly hairy, with the joints well marked, and is furnished at tip with two strong projections, each of which bears at tip four long hairs and a few shorter ones. When the insect is at rest the wings lie flat upon the back.

RATE OF GROWTH OF THE DIFFERENT STAGES.

The rate of growth of the insect necessarily depends so much upon surrounding conditions, and especially on the mean temperature, that it is difficult to make any definite statements as to time elapsing between molts or that required for other periods of the insect's growth. No facts have hitherto been published which bear upon this point. Mr. Coquillett's observations show that individuals hatched from eggs on the 4th of March cast the first skin on the 23d of April, and underwent the last molt on the 23d of May. Mr. Koebele also reports a case which bears upon this point, and which is interesting as occurring later in the season. He placed four newly hatched larvæ on a healthy young orange tree, out of doors, August 5. On September 26 two of them passed through the first molt. October 10 one more molted, and on October 23 the fourth cast its first skin. All left the leaves after molting and settled on young twigs. None of them had gone through the last molt when he left Los Angeles, November 6. He was afterwards informed by Mr. Alexander Craw, of Los Angeles, that nearly all of the insects were full-grown in February, and he therefore concluded that the individuals observed by him would not attain full growth before that time.

The mature male larva requires on an average about ten days from the time it begins to form the cocoon before assuming the pupa state, and the pupa state lasts from two to three weeks. The more reliable information we have been able to obtain, would show that at Los Angeles the average number of generations each year is three.

HABITS.

The newly hatched larvæ settle upon the leaves and tender twigs, insert their beaks, and imbibe the sap. On passing into the third stage they seem to prefer to settle upon the smaller twigs, although a few are found upon the leaves and still fewer upon the larger branches and trunk. The adults, however, almost invariably prefer the trunk and largest branches.

The insect is rarely found in any of its stages upon the fruit.

The species differs markedly from most Coccidæ in being active during the greater part of its life, though most of the traveling is done by the female immediately after the third molt and by the male just before settling to make his cocoon. At these periods they wander up and down the trunk and larger limbs until they find some suitable place, when they settle down, the male to pupate and the female to insert her beak and develop her eggs and their characteristic waxy covering. She is capable of slow motion even after oviposition has commenced, but rarely does move unless from some exceptional cause. In thus settling after their last wanderings both sexes are fond of shelter and will get under any projecting piece of

31 AG—'86

bark or under bandages placed around the tree, the male often creeping under clods of earth. Both the female and the male, in adolescence, are most active during the hotter parts of the day and remain stationary at night; but the perfect or winged male is rather sluggish during the day, usually remaining motionless on the under side of the leaves of low plants or high trees, in crevices of the bark, or wedged in between females on the tree. There seems, in fact, to be a well-marked attempt at concealment. The recently developed individuals are found abundantly on or under clods of earth near their pupal cocoons, and they issue most numerously during the latter part of the afternoon. They are at first weak, awkward, and ungainly, and instinctively seek some projection on the tree or elevation on the ground from which to launch on the wing.

At the approach of night they become imbued with a very high degree of activity and dart rapidly about on the wing. At such times they swarm around the infested trees, and many of the females, even some with large egg-masses, hold their bodies raised obliquely from the bark, as though aware of the presence of the males. In September and October Mr. Koebele noticed that the males began their flight about 5 o'clock, and as soon as it was fairly dark they again settled down to rest. None have been observed flying at night and none have been attracted to the electric lights.

EXUDATION OF THE HONEY-DEW.

It required but a few hours upon our first visit to Los Angeles, the latter part of March, to become familiar with the insect in all its habits and conditions, as at that season the species is to be found in all conditions from the egg through all the stages of both sexes. But the characteristic of this remarkable insect which most obviously attracted our attention and distinguished it from all other species of the family, even where there were no gravid females with the fluted cushion, was the saccharine exudation. As with most Aphids and Coccids, this sweet liquid is exuded at all stages of growth, but is most copious from the adult female just before oviposition begins. It is expelled with considerable force from the large pore already described, and in hot weather with sufficient rapidity to produce all the effects of honey-dew. Usually it is limpid enough to soak and discolor the trunk and to drop as it accumulates from the leaves, sometimes being so copious as to remind one of a shower; but at other times, and especially during dry weather, the sugar condenses and forms large drops or masses of white, semi-opaque, sirupy liquid, which adheres to and often completely covers the insect, so that the trunk of the tree looks much as if it had been bespattered with caustic potash or melted stearine. At other times the liquid parts evaporate entirely and leave masses of pure white powdery sugar.

Honey-loving insects seek this sugary secretion in numbers, and it is always followed by the black mold or smut (*Capnodium citri*), which is so universal an accompaniment of all honey-secreting Homoptera, living as it does on the saccharine deposit. The secretion being so very copious from Icerya, the smut is equally thick and copious in her wake. Indeed, the great prevalence of this smut in the Icerya-infested groves of California (rendering it necessary to wash or cleanse the gathered fruit) is as characteristic of the Pacific coast as the rusty effect of the Rust-mite (which is unknown there) is of the orange groves of Florida.

MODE OF SPREAD AND DISTRIBUTION.

The spread of this species will be aided by very much the same agencies that affect the spread and dissemination of other species of scale-insects. We have already, in 1868, in treating of the Oyster-shell Bark-louse of the Apple,* and again four years later,† discussed the principal methods by which such spread is promoted, viz., by the agency of wind and running water; by the young being carried upon birds and other animals, particularly flying insects frequenting the same trees; but primarily by transport upon scions and nursery stock.

In insects like the Coccidæ, where the locomotive power is confined for the most part to a few days in early larval life, the species would be very much restricted in range, and would never pass from one country to another, except by some of the agencies above indicated. Our observations since we first wrote upon this subject, as well as the extended observations of Mr. Hubbard in Florida, and given in the special report on Insects affecting the Orange, as also Mr. Coquillett's observations on the distribution of the particular species in question, all go to confirm the potency of these means of distribution. Thus Mr. Hubbard found that lady-birds (Coccinellidæ), and more particularly gossamer spiders, are active agencies in such distribution. The agency of the wind, as indicated by the more rapid spreading in the direction of prevailing winds, has often been verified. Mr. Coquillett reports: "In the infested part of this city (Los Angeles) is a large vineyard, and on both the north and south sides of it is an orange orchard infested by these insects; but, while the recently hatched insects occur on the vines as far out as the tenth row of grape-vines on the south side of the vineyard, they are not found upon the vines beyond the third row on the north side, the wind, as stated above, blowing from the southwest. No adult females are to be found on any part of this vineyard, and the young insects must have been carried by the wind from the infested orange trees on either side of the vineyard." Our own experience in California showed that similar evidence of the influence of the prevailing wind in promoting the spread of the species is general.

While Mr. Hubbard's observations show that the action of the wind is indirect rather than direct, by influencing the flight of winged insects and the floating of spiders which transport the scale-insects, yet we have every reason to believe that winds have a much more direct influence than is generally supposed, especially in the case of severe storms passing over infested districts at the right season. We laid emphasis on this in our earlier writings, and Mr. Coquillett, while admitting the influence of birds, insects, and water in the transportation of our *Icerya*, lays greatest stress upon the direct agency of the wind. Young scale-insects are not easily dislodged, but where a tree is badly infested there is every reason to believe that they instinctively drop from the terminal twigs, and their specific gravity is so slight, that they may be carried long distances in strong wind currents.

In regard to the influence of birds upon the spread of the Cottony Cushion-scale, Mr. Coquillett observed that whenever the nest of a bird is found upon a tree recently infested with this insect, the latter will be found to be most numerous in the immediate vicinity of the

---

* First Report Insects of Missouri, p. 15.
† Fifth Report Insects of Missouri, pp. 85, 86.

nest, thus indicating that the young had been accidentally brought there and in considerable numbers by the old birds.   There is no doubt also that the irrigating ditches have a very marked influence on the spread of the species, as many of the ditches pass under infested trees, and the waxy secretion serves both to protect the insect from the water and to facilitate floating.

While, therefore, the gradual spread from orchard to orchard is in the main through the agency of other flying insects and gossamer spiders, yet the transportation of the pests to long distances must necessarily be effected through the agency of high winds, birds, and man in commercial intercourse, the latter being probably the only means by which the species have been introduced from one country to another separated by wide ocean areas.

NATURAL ENEMIES.

BIRDS.—The natural enemies of the Cottony Cushion-scale seem to be very few in number, not only in California but also in South Africa and New Zealand.   In South Africa the only bird which is recorded as feeding upon this scale is the common "White Eye" (*Zosterops capensis*), and this is given by Mr. Trimen upon hearsay evidence only: "I have not noticed any of our small birds attacking the *Dorthesia*, but Mr. C. B. Elliott tells me that his boys have observed the little 'White Eye' * * * pecking at them."   From what we have been able to learn of the habits of this bird, however, we are inclined to think that it is attracted rather by the abundant secretion of honey-dew and the minute insects caught in it than by the scale-insects themselves.

Neither Mr. Coquillett nor Mr. Koebele observed any bird feeding upon it.   The reason for this exemption is probably the copious secretion of wax, which is doubtless distasteful.   Several reliable persons report that ducks and chickens feed greedily upon those scale-insects which are dislodged from the trees.   On one occasion a brood of six young ducks gorged themselves upon scales which had been washed from the trees with pure water, and on the same day two ducks died.   On the day following three more died, while the sixth recovered after an illness of several days.   This disastrous effect was probably due to the greed with which the scales were eaten, as they were said to produce no such result with chickens which ate them at the same time.

PREDACEOUS INSECTS.—The only predaceous insect observed by Mr. Coquillett to feed upon the Cottony Cushion-scale was the larva of a species of Lace-wing fly (*Chrysopa* sp.), which was not bred and cannot be named more exactly.

The Ambiguous Lady-bird (*Hippodamia ambigua*) has been noticed feeding upon the eggs when they were exposed to view by the egg-sac being broken open; but neither this nor any other species of Lady-bird was seen to feed upon the adult insect, although commonly attracted by the honey-dew secreted.

Among the predaceous insects found by Mr. Koebele and sent to us for study we may mention first the larva of a small moth (*Blastobasis iceryæella* n. sp.. Plate III. Fig. 3), although as yet we are not certain that it ordinarily preys upon the living and uninjured scale-insects or their eggs.   Like certain other so-called predaceous Lepidoptera, it may be attracted primarily by the waxy secretions of the bark-lice, and only incidentally destroy the insects and their eggs.

These larvæ were often found feeding in the egg-masses of females
which had been destroyed by soap washes, and also in sacs the eggs
of which had hatched some time previously, but never upon fresh
eggs. One of the larvæ, kept in a glass tube with living scales and
fresh eggs, fed slightly on the waxy mass, but did not thrive until
after the scales died. It then fed upon the dead scales and molted,
but died before transforming. Two nearly full-grown larvæ fed readily on dead scales which were still soft, and passed through their transformations successfully. The same insect fed readily upon the Black
Scale (*Lecanium oleœ*), in this case eating the living insects and their
eggs, forming a silken tube along the twig, and passing from one scale
to another, just as does the Coccid-eating Dakruma (*Dakruma coccidivora*)* in feeding upon the Cottony Maple Scale at the East.

This is probably the same insect as that mentioned by Professor
Comstock, Annual Report Department of Agriculture, 1880, p. 336, as
follows : " Upon one occasion (August 25, 1880), I found within the
body of a full-grown female [of *L. oleœ*] a lepidopterous larva. * * *
The specimen, however, was lost, and no more have been found since."
From the fact that this larva destroys living Black Scales, we have
every reason to believe that it will also feed upon living Cottony
Cushion-scales, and will not confine itself, as heretofore observed, to
the dead females and their empty egg-sacs.

Blastobasis aphidiella, Riley MS., we have reared from the larvæ
feeding on the contents of Phylloxera hickory galls.

The genus *Blastobasis* Zeller is distinguished by the first antennal joint being compressed and much broader than the flagellum ; its
lower side concave, the anterior edge above its base furnished with
erect hairs ; its apex above provided in the male with a scaly tooth ;
the flagellum in the male is filiform, faintly serrate, and furnished
with short ciliæ, its base curved and anteriorly excised ; in the female
it is simple. The palpi are as long as thorax and rather stout in
the male, faintly compressed and covered with coarse scales, the last
joint slightly over half the length of the middle one and its apex
pointed. The ocelli are present. The front wings are narrow, their
apical portion quite slender and pointed ; eleven-veined, vein 1 *b* distinct. The hind wings have seven well-separated veins. This is not
the place to discuss the variation which the species of the genus are
subject to: but they are small in size, quite uniform in general color
and markings, but varying so in the intensity and the details of orna-
mentation that the species are not easily separated, and we shall not
be at all surprised if future experience should justify the combining
of several which are now separated.

BLASTOBASIS ICERYÆELLA n. sp.—Expanse 13ᵐᵐ to 15ᵐᵐ. General color pale
cinereous. *Head* gray; eyes dull black, fringed posteriorly by rather long yellowish hairs, which curve over them like eyelashes; palpi above pale yellowish-gray; in
some specimens the inferior surface is almost black, whilst in others there is only a
slight sprinkling of blackish scales; antennæ uniformly gray, with a slight yellowish tinge and faintly darker annulation, the tuft of the basal joint almost white.
Primaries cinereous, sprinkled quite densely with blackish scales; a linear, blackish,
transverse band more or less distinct (in one male only indicated by a small dusky
spot at costa), starting from basal third of costa and obliquing posteriorly, it termi-
nates at about the middle of inner margin; its inner edge is bordered by a more or
less distinct paler gray line; the black discal spot, which in other species is usually

---

* We have bred a species of *Dakruma* the past season, indistinguishable from *D.
coccidivora*, from the Cochineal insect (*Coccus cacti*) received from Dr. A. F. Car-
rothers, of San Antonio, Tex., who collected the specimens at his ranch (Iuka ranch)
near Cotulla, La Salle County, Texas.

external of the band, in this species forms part of the band; the two black spots on a transverse line with anal angle are always present, though the posterior one is sometimes more or less obliterated; these spots are generally relieved posteriorly by a patch of paler scales, while posteriorly and exteriorly of this pale patch the black scales are sometimes increased so as to resemble a transverse posterior band with a pale interruption. Under surface uniformly gray, with slight brassy reflection. Secondaries pale gray above, glossy below, with brassy reflection. Fringes of all wings still paler, with a yellowish, silky luster. Legs pale gray, the anterior or external surface of the front and middle legs, including coxæ, being in some specimens dark gray or almost black, while in others there is only a slight sprinkling of darker scales. In one specimen there is noticed a quite dark band near the apex of the middle tibiæ; hind legs whitish, sometimes with a faintly dusky, longitudinal streak externally on the tibiæ; abdomen of a lighter or darker silvery gray, generally somewhat darker towards the end, the anal tuft of the male more or less yellowish.

Described from four ♂ s and one ♀ reared from Icerya-feeding larvæ.

We have not seen good specimens of this larva, and may therefore quote Mr. Koebele's brief description, drawn up from fresh specimens:

The larva while young is of a reddish-white color, with a narrow, deeper red dorsal line. The piliferous warts are prominent, whitish, with rather stiff white hairs. The head and prothoracic shield are light yellow (testaceous), and bear also a few hairs. The full-grown larva is from 5^{min} to 6^{mm} long and brownish in color. The narrow, whitish dorsal line is bordered with a mottled liver-brown, and the whitish line beneath this again with a heavier brown subdorsal line. The under side and the feet are still reddish-white, while the head and prothoracic shield are pitch black.

This species is closely related to *Blastobasis chalcofrontella*, and also somewhat to *Blastobasis quisquiliella*, from both of which, however, it may at once be distinguished by the blackish band of the front wings, which in them is wanting or only indicated by a small dusky shade at the costa. The head of *B. chalcofrontella* is also broader and of a yellowish-white color, and the palpi and legs more concolorous with the body, and the general tint of the wings more yellowish.

In *B. quisquiliella* the head, palpi, and legs are more rufous and the general aspect more like *B. chalcofrontella*.

With *B. nubiliella* and *glandulella* it cannot be confounded, as both are generally larger and darker, though some specimens of *nubiliella* are larger than the smaller specimens of *iceryaella*. The band on primaries of *nubiliella* instead of being linear broadens towards the costa so as to form a transversely elongate, triangular spot, which in some particularly well-marked specimens is quite conspicuous.

In *B. glandulella* the band is not indicated or but faintly indicated, and it is at once distinguished by the much larger size and uniformly darker coloration.

A common Tenebrionid beetle (*Blapstinus brevicollis* Lec., Plate III, Fig.2) was found by Mr. Koebele to occur abundantly among the rubbish at the foot of the trees infested by Icerya. Egg-sacs which had been completely eaten out and the eggs devoured were found in close conjunction with several of these beetles, and in consequence a few beetles were placed in a pill-box with female scales and large egg-masses. In a few days the eggs were all eaten, but the insects themselves were not disturbed. It is probable that this is not the normal habit of this beetle, yet it may without much question be put down as an occasional destroyer of Icerya eggs. The habits of the allied *Epitragus tomentosus*, as described by Mr. Hubbard in his report on Insects Affecting the Orange, p. 75 (Fig. 36), render this all the more probable. The *Epitragus* was observed to feed upon scale-insects of all kinds in Florida, tearing the scale from the bark and devouring its contents, and sometimes also the substance of the scale itself.

The larva of a Dermestid beetle (*Perimegatoma cylindricum* Kirby, var. *angulare*) was also found among the Cottony Cushion-scales, but as it would only feed on dead scales in confinement, it is not likely that it is truly predaceous.

Prominent among the true bugs found upon the infested trees is the large brown *Largus succinctus* (Plate III, Fig. 4). This is said to destroy the scale-insects, although Mr. Koebele could never see it do so. He noticed it feeding upon the honey-dew, and on one occasion noticed two immature specimens with their beaks inserted in a male larva of Icerya. They ran away on his approach, and the larva was found to be dead; but, as there were numbers of other dead larvæ about, he did not consider that there was any evidence of the predaceous habits of the *Largus*. On the contrary, he observed this insect often with its beak inserted into young shoots of Orange. The other Heteroptera found by him among the scales were the well-known *Piesma cinerea* Say, *Corizus hyalinus* Fabr (Plate III, Fig. 5), *Peritrechus luniger* Say, *Beosus* sp., *Lyctocoris* sp., and *Piezostethus* sp. These last five species have been kindly examined by Mr. Uhler, our best authority in the suborder, and he reports the undetermined species as probably new.

The most efficient destroyer of the Cottony Cushion-scale at Los Angeles is perhaps a species of earwig, family Forficulidæ (Plate III, Fig. 6), neither the genus nor species of which we are able to determine, from the fact that we have only seen immature specimens. According to Mr. Koebele this insect is often met with among the scales, and, from observations which he made, feeds greedily upon the Icerya in all stages, tearing open the egg-masses and eating the eggs, and also tearing and eating the mature insects as well as the larvæ. The breeding habits of the mother earwig and her care of her flock of young have been observed by Mr. Koebele, but have been so well studied by European authors as to need no detail here.

Mr. Koebele also reports the occurrence in the scale masses, in large numbers, of a minute whitish mite, which becomes of a reddish color when full fed, and which he thinks destroys the female scales. We have not seen specimens of this mite, and are therefore unable to determine it.

In a recent communication from Miss Ormerod, already mentioned on p. 467, she writes as follows of a predaceous insect discovered by her correspondent, Mr. Bairstow, of Port Elizabeth, Cape Colony:

It will perhaps be of some interest to mention that Mr. Bairstow has found a species of Coccinella which has proved (as far as our coleopterists are aware) to be previously undescribed, to be so exceedingly serviceable in destroying the "Australian bug," as they call it, that he has been supplying it to applicants. Dr. Baly examined the specimens sent over for me, and I propose to notice it, with full technical description and a figure, as *Rodolia iceryæ*.

PARASITES.—It is a somewhat remarkable fact that no true parasites were ever bred from the Cottony Cushion-scale until the past summer, and still more remarkable that in the course of their careful investigations, extending over a space of six months, neither Mr. Coquillett nor Mr. Koebele succeeded in finding a single parasite upon this insect. From a number of scales, however, sent to Washington by Mr. Koebele November 10, we bred, on December 8, two specimens of a small Chalcid, which is, without question, a true parasite of

Icerya, as the female scales from which they escaped were found each with a small round hole in its back.

This little parasite (Plate III, Fig. 1) is prettily marked with black and yellow.   It is new to our fauna and may have been imported with its host.   We turned it over to Mr. Howard for study, and as he finds it necessary to erect a new genus for it, we append his generic and specific characterizations :

ISODROMUS n. g., Howard.

Female.—The antennæ arise near the border of the mouth; the scape is not widened; *the pedicel is much longer than the first funicle joint:* the funicle joints increase slightly in length from 1 to 6 and considerably in width, so that joint 6 is more than twice as wide as joint 1; the club is half as long as the funicle and is obliquely truncate from base to tip.   The head is thin antero-posteriorly; the facial impression is slight; *the inner borders of the eyes are nearly parallel*; the ocelli are placed at the corners of a right-angled triangle.   The scapulæ meet on a long line at middle.   The hind femora have a very delicate longitudinal furrow below.   The marginal vein of the fore wings is entirely wanting; the stigmal is moderately long and *bends abruptly downward, forming at first a right angle with the submarginal,* afterwards curving slightly outwards; *the postmarginal is absent.   The large mesopleura are covered with a number of longitudinal ridges.*
Male unknown.

This genus belongs to the *Encyrtinæ,* and is more closely related to *Homalotylus* than to any other described genus.   Its structural affinity to this genus is quite marked, but it is well separated by the characters italicized above.   It differs in habit also, as *Homalotylus* is parasitic upon coleopterous larvæ of the families Coccinellidæ and Chrysomelidæ.

ISODROMUS ICERYÆ, n. sp., Howard.

Female.—Length 2.2ᵐᵐ; expanse 4.2ᵐᵐ; greatest width of fore wing 0.7ᵐᵐ.   Head and thorax nearly smooth; head very delicately punctured and furnished with a very few larger impressions.   Pronotum and mesonotum very delicately shagreened; mesoscutum and hind border of pronotum with a number of closely applied white hairs.   The general color is shining black; all of the head except eyes and an occipital black blotch, the hind border of both pronotum and mesoscutum, all of the tegulæ except tip, a blotch each side of the mesoscutellum and one at tip, the under side of thorax and base of the abdomen, the upper side of the first abdominal joint, and a small spot at the abdominal spiracles, yellow.   The yellow of the head is nearly orange, while the rest is more of a lemon.   The antennæ are honey-yellow throughout, becoming dusky towards tip.   All the legs, including coxæ, are yellow; hind femora dark above, black at knees; hind tibiæ with two black bands.   Wings clear.   Described from 2 specimens.

REMEDIES AND PREVENTIVE MEASURES.

We have indicated in the introduction to this report the more important results of the experiments carried on at Los Angeles by Messrs. Coquillett and Koebele, and as their reports are later given in full we shall refrain from entering into detail here, and state only a few of the more important convictions that impressed us after the first week's experience in the orange groves of California.

IMPORTATION OF PARASITES.—The general importance of the introduction of parasites which affect a species in its native land, and which have not accompanied it into the land of its introduction, has been insisted on in our earlier writings and in those of others, and the ease with which this may be done in the case of the more minute parasites of scale insects adds to its importance in their connection.   Considering the fearful losses already occasioned to California orange-growers by two species (the *Icerya* in question and the California Red Scale), introduced from Australia, we know of no way in which the Department could more advantageously expend a thousand dollars than by sending an expert to Australia to study the parasites of the species there and secure the safe transport of the same to the Pacific coast; and the fact that the Commissioner of Agriculture is prevented from doing so by restrictions imposed on the Division of Entomology is a sad commentary on the narrow Congressional policy which seeks to limit and control administrative action in details which can neither be properly understood nor anticipated by committees.

PREVENTIVE ACTION.—The value of clean culture and fertilizing where necesary to induce vigorous growth, but more particularly of wise pruning, so as to let in the sun and rain to the heart of the tree, has been set forth in the special report of the Division on the Insects affecting the Orange, by Mr. Hubbard, and apply equally to California as to Florida. We have also been particularly impressed with the value of wind-breaks of coniferous trees not affected by the Coccidæ that infest the Orange, both as shelter to the trees and as screens to prevent the spread of the *Icerya* from infested trees outside the grove.

SPRAYING WITH INSECTICIDES.—The orange-growers of the Pacific have suffered greatly from the advice and recommendations of biased or interested persons, who were prejudiced in favor of their own particular remedies, and were for a long time unwilling to profit by the results of thorough and careful experiments which we have for some years conducted in the East, and which are in the main embodied in Mr. Hubbard's report. A pretty thorough personal survey of the field has convinced us that while the resin soaps experimented with by Mr. Koebele are a valuable addition to our insecticides for the orange Coccidæ, yet in the main our experience in Florida is repeated in California, and all the more satisfactory washes have kerosene as their effective base. There has been, and is, however, a very great waste in applying it, and where from 10 to 50 or more gallons have been used on a single tree, from 2 to 4 would suffice.

We cannot urge too strongly the fact that in the case of this *Icerya*, as most other orange-feeding Coccidæ, it is practically impossible, with the most careful and thorough spraying, to reach every one of the myriad individuals on a good-sized tree. Some few, protected by leaf-curl, bark-scale, or other shelter, will escape, and with their fecund progeny soon spread over the tree again if left unmolested. Hence two or three sprayings at intervals of not more than a month are far preferable to any single treatment, however thorough; and this is particularly true of the *Icerya*, which occurs on so many other plants, and which in badly infested groves is crawling over the ground between trees. It is now the custom to use the time of a team and 2 men for fifteen to twenty minutes or more, and 10 gallons and upward of liquid on a single medium-sized tree. In this way the tree is soaked until the fluid rains to the ground and is lost in great quantities, some growers using sheet-iron drip-plates around the base of the tree to save and re-use the otherwise wasted material. This is all wrong so far as the oil emulsion is concerned, as the oil, rising to the surface, falls from the leaves and wastes more proportionally than the water.

The essence of successful spraying of the kerosene emulsion consists in forcing it as a mist from the heart of the tree first and then from the periphery, allowing as little as possible to fall to the ground and permitting each spray particle to adhere. It is best done in the cool of the day, and, where possible, in calm and cloudy weather. With one-fifth of the time and material now expended in California the spraying should be successfully done, so that three sprayings at proper intervals will be cheaper and far more satisfactory than only one as ordinarily conducted. In this particular neither Mr. Coquillett's nor Mr. Koebele's experiments are entirely satisfactory, as we were so far from the field while they were being carried on as to render any special direction of them impossible. Both strove for the practically impossible, viz, the destruction of all insects by a single application. Mr. Koebele's estimate of the cost of the kerosene wash is also too high, as he used it much stronger than necessary. The resin compounds may doubtless be used to advantage in connection with the kerosene emulsions; but anything which will give permanence and preventive character to the wash will add greatly to its value. Without going into details as to reasons, we would therefore recommend the addition to every 50 gallons of the kerosene-soap wash, made after the usual formula, 3 ounces of arsenious acid. Though the arsenical preparations are mainly effective against mandibulate insects, by poisoning through the stomach, they have also more or less effect by contact, and we are strongly of the opinion (which we hope soon to verify) that this combination, for the first time recommended, will give the spray more lasting effect, and that the few insects which escape the direct spray will be destroyed as they subsequently leave their protecting retreats or hatch from eggs and crawl about the tree. As a means of arresting the growth of the black-mold (which is, however, only the indirect consequence of the Coccid), so troublesome an accompaniment of the *Icerya*, a small proportion of sulphate of copper might also be added.

Just as there is now a great wastage of time and material in drenching a tree, so the spraying nozzle most in vogue in California is also wasteful. That most commonly used is the San José nozzle, in which the water is simply forced through a slightly flaring terminal slit in a more or less direct and copious jet. The force and directness of the spray give this nozzle its popularity under the mistaken spraying notions which prevail, and to this we must add the fact that, being a patented contrivance, it is well advertised and on the market.

The cyclone nozzle has not yet had proper trial to impress its advantages, having scarcely been known prior to the experiments of Messrs. Coquillett and Koebele. That made and sold by G. N. Milco is patterned in size and aperture after that which we designed to spray from near the surface of the ground. What is wanted for an orange grove or for trees is a bunch of nozzles of twice the ordinary size and capacity, the size of the outlet to be regulated by the force of the pump. There is no form of nozzle so simple and so easily adjustable to all purposes. We strongly recommend a bunch of four nozzles of twice the ordinary size and thickness, one arranged so as to have the outlet distally or at one end of the piping (which may be ordinary gas-pipe) and the other three on branches, so that the outlet is at right angles, each about an inch below the other, and so placed that they are separated by one-third the circumference of the main pipe. Such a bunch, with apertures properly adjusted to the occasion, worked from the center of the tree, will envelop it in a perfect ball of floating mist, which in a very short time will imbue all accessible parts. For tall trees a more forcible direct spray might be sent from the end by substituting an ordinary jet and the wire extension, which is simply an extension tube screwed over the nipple, the end of the tube being covered with wire netting, which breaks up the liquid forced through it, and which for force and fine division of the particles has some advantages over the San José nozzle. Finally, if a series of blind caps and several sets of caps of varying aperture are kept on hand, the spray may be adjusted at will, and to suit the conditions of wind, pump force, &c., that have to be dealt with.

FUMIGATING.—Fumigating the trees will always have the disadvantage, as compared with spraying, that the mechanism is more cumbersome, the time required greater, and the first cost in making preparation heavier; and these factors will always give spraying the advantage with small proprietors or those who have to deal with young trees. As an offset to these drawbacks fumigation has the merit of more effectually reaching all the insects upon a tree, and this alone would under some circumstances justify the greater first cost and trouble in preparing movable tents for the purpose, providing always that a gas, vapor, or fume be discovered that will rapidly kill all the insects without injuring the tree; virtues not easily combined in such subtile media.

In Florida proper spraying has been found to be so effectual and satisfactory that no elaborate experiments in fumigating have been undertaken, and we are fully satisfied that proper spraying will also prove sufficient in California. But so much poor work has been done and so many defective washes used that many growers have become discouraged, and quite a disposition has been shown to either cut down the trees or resort to fumigation as a last resource. In connection with Mr. Alexander Craw, Mr. Coquillett has conducted some experiments in the Wolfskill orchard at Los Angeles, which lead them to believe that they have discovered a gas which possesses the requisite qualities, and trees that had been treated and which we examined pretty carefully would seem to justify their hopes. Several ingenious movable-tent contrivances are also being developed in Los Angeles County that give promise of practical utility and feasibility, and which we may have more to say about on some future occasion.

BANDAGES AROUND THE TRUNK.—There is always danger that a tree once sprayed will get reinfested from the insects that have not been reached upon adjacent plants or upon the ground, and which in time crawl up the trunk. Any of the sticky bandages used for the canker-worm will check this ascent, but when placed directly on the trunk may do more harm than good. They should be placed upon strips of tar or other stout paper or felting, tied by a cord around the middle, the upper end flared slightly outward, and the space between it and the trunk filled with soil, to prevent the insects from creeping beneath. Cotton should not be used for this purpose, as birds for nesting purposes carry away particles of it containing the young insects, and thus help to disseminate them.

CONCLUSION.—All possible care should be taken in cultivating and harvesting the crop to prevent dissemination of the young upon clothing, packing-boxes, &c., and too much care cannot be exercised in endeavors to prevent the introduction of the species from infested to non-infested regions. Next to destructive locusts no insect has been more fully legislated against than this *Icerya* in California. Yet while some good has resulted, the laws have too often proved inoperative, either through the negligence or ignorance of the officers appointed to execute them, or, more often, the indifference of the courts and their unwillingness to enforce them with vigor.

The pest has come to stay. No human endeavor can exterminate it. But it may be controlled, and while the greatest possible co-operation should be urged and, if possible, enforced, yet each orange-grower must in the end depend upon his own exertion; and we say to them, individually and collectively, that there is no occasion for discouragement. This insect has made profitable orange-growing on the Pacific coast more difficult and more of a science; but, by making it impossible at the same time for the shiftless to succeed in their business, it will come to be looked upon as a not unmixed evil.

BUFFALO GNATS.

Order DIPTERA; family SIMULIDÆ.

[Plates VI, VII, VIII, and IX.]

For many years past one of the greatest insect foes the stock-raisers of the lower Mississippi Valley have had to contend with has been the so-called Southern Buffalo Gnat. This insect is a small fly, closely related to the well-known "Black Fly" of the North, to the famous "Columbacz Gnat" of Hungary, and to other less known but as noxious species of the genus *Simulium*, found abundantly in Lapland, Brazil, and Australia. These flies swarm at certain seasons in immense numbers, and by their bite, multiplied a thousand fold, cause great destruction amongst mules, horses, cattle, hogs, sheep, and poultry.

Although we possess in the United States a great number of species of the genus *Simulium*, only a few of them are so very troublesome and noxious as to have attracted special attention. The great majority of the species are quite local, and occur only in such limited numbers as not to form swarms of sufficient strength to occasion any serious damage, although they are very troublesome at times in some regions. The popular name "Southern Buffalo Gnat" includes at least two distinct species, and others will doubtless be found to contribute to the injury when the regions are better studied entomologically. In any general account of the distribution of the Southern Buffalo Gnats it must be borne in mind that these two species are frequently called by the same name, and that even other flies not at all related to them are called Buffalo Gnats by the inhabitants of the infested regions.

Although two or more species of *Simulium* are thus confounded, the following general statements will describe the actions of all species. They resemble each other in their life-history so closely, that one description of it will apply to that of all.

The popular name Buffalo Gnat has not been chosen because these gnats ever attack the animal of that name, but because of a fancied resemblance to the shape of the same. Looking at the insect from the side, it reveals a very large, hump-backed thorax, with the head—furnished with two short antennæ, like minature horns—in the act of butting an enemy. The name "Turkey Gnat," however, has been given to one of the species concerned, because at appears at a time when turkeys are setting and suffer so much by them. "Goose Gnat" is another name used for the same insect for a similar reason.

Believing that it is always best in popular nomenclature to adopt names already known and given by the people, we shall throughout this article designate the chief depredator as the "Southern Buffalo Gnat" and the second one as the "Turkey Gnat." We shall treat first of the "Southern Buffalo Gnat," but as both species occur to a great extent through the same region, most of what is said of the one species will apply also to the other, their habits being essentially the same. We shall call particular attention to the "Turkey Gnat" only when it is necessary to show any differences, whether as to distribution, habit, or character.

THE SOUTHERN BUFFALO GNAT.

(*Simulium pecuarum* n. sp.)

GEOGRAPHICAL DISTRIBUTION.

The region infested by the Southern Buffalo Gnat is much more extensive than formerly known. In some years at least it comprises the whole of the Mississippi Valley from the mouth of the Red River, in Louisiana, to Saint Louis, Mo. All the land adjacent to the many rivers and creeks that empty from the east and the west into the Mississippi River is invaded by swarms. They are driven about by the wind, and reach points far away from their breeding-places. The exact localities reached by such swarms can as yet not be given, but may be mapped out after further investigations.

In *Louisiana* all the land inclosed by the Mississippi and Red Rivers, with perhaps the exception of the extreme western counties, is usually invaded by the Buffalo Gnats during a gnat year. South of the Red River they become scarce, less aggressive, and appear only at very irregular intervals.

In *Mississippi* all the counties bordering on the river that gives the name to the State are more or less invaded during gnat years.

All *Arkansas*, excepting perhaps the western counties, shares the same fate. In the numerous creeks and rivers of this State and of Louisiana the Buffalo Gnat breeds most abundantly.

In *Tennessee* the same conditions prevail as in Mississippi, but the swarms do not reach so far east as in the latter State.

In *Missouri* the Buffalo Gnats infest only the southeastern counties.

Kentucky does not fare as well as Missouri, since swarms of them frequently ascend the Ohio River for some distance.

Illinois and *Indiana* are also more or less invaded; in the former, it is the region bordering upon the Mississippi and Wabash Rivers; in the latter, that on the Ohio and Wabash Rivers. In 1886 Buffalo Gnats appeared in large swarms at De Soto, in Jackson County, Illinois, and along the White River, in Davies County, Indiana.

In Eastern *Kansas* swarms have repeatedly done great damage.

EARLY HISTORY.

From the very fact that the Buffalo Gnats have been constantly denominated by the same term, inevitable confusion must necessarily exist in their early history. Such is indicated by the appended reports of the special agents, who of course could not tell to which of the species the information received applied.

It seems that no authentic record exists in Louisiana about the occurrence of the Southern Buffalo Gnat prior to the year 1850. It has been reported, however, that they had previously appeared in 1846.

In 1861 and 1862 they were very troublesome in portions of Mississippi and Louisiana; in 1863 and 1864 they abounded about Shreveport, La., and in Chicot County, Arkansas.   None are reported to occur in 1865, but in 1866 they invaded the alluvial country between the Arkansas and Red Rivers east of the Washita.   In 1873 and 1874 serious injury was occasioned by them in several regions in Louisiana. But in 1882 and 1884 they were more destructive than ever before, doing immense damage to live stock of all kinds.   Although not generally very numerous in 1885, they appeared in sufficient numbers in several counties of Louisiana to kill quite a number of mules.   In 1886 they appeared generally throughout the whole extent of the region infested by them, and they appeared rather unexpectedly, because it was so unprecedentedly late in the season.

In Indiana this insect was well known as far back as 1843, when the settlers used to watch for it every year, as swarms would appear in certain regions with more or less regularity, often occasioning considerable damage.

It was ascertained from a number of gentlemen in Tennessee and Mississippi that the Buffalo Gnats were well known to their ancestors who first settled in that region at a time when Indians were their neighbors.

But every one questioned in the States of Louisiana, Mississippi, Tennessee, and Arkansas would voice this universal opinion, viz, that Buffalo Gnats come only with high water and are contemporary with an overflow.   The connection between an overflow and the appearance of the Buffalo Gnats will be considered farther on.

TIME OF APPEARANCE.

The time of the appearance of the Southern Buffalo Gnat is regulated by the earliness or lateness of spring, and it consequently appears much earlier in the southern parts of the Mississippi Valley. As a rule, it can be expected soon after the first continuous warm spell in early spring.   The first swarms were observed last year in Louisiana on March 11; in Mississippi and Tennessee, May 1; and in Indiana and Illinois, May 12.   Small and local swarms may appear somewhat earlier or later in the neighborhood of their breeding-places. The Turkey Gnat appears usually later, although in 1886 it appeared near Memphis, Tenn., as early as April 5; the swarms were quite local, however, and strictly confined to the vicinity of creeks that produced them.   In Louisiana they appeared, as usual, much later than the true Buffalo Gnat, and some were found as late as June 6, and the bayous disclosed others still in their pupal state.

The great majority of the species of this genus are northern insects, and appear there in the winged form all through the summer.   The larvæ require cold water for development.   As we go farther south this *cold water* can only be found in the more elevated regions or in winter or the early months of spring.   Earliness of season or high altitude are there the substitutes for the lower temperature of more northern latitude.

DURATION OF AN INVASION.

Swarms of Buffalo Gnats usually appear with the first continuous warm weather of early spring.   They lead a roving kind of life, being drifted about with the wind, which frequently carries them long distances beyond their usual haunts. At first the members composing a swarm are very active and blood-thirsty; but they soon die, and the swarm decreases gradually and soon disappears entirely. New swarms appear continually and replace the former ones. The duration of an invasion throughout the regions infested varies from a few days to five or six weeks. If cold weather follow their appearance, the gnats become semi-dormant; they are not killed by it nor by rain, but revive and become aggressive again with the first warm rays of the sun. Hot weather, however, soon kills them and puts an end to any further injury. The duration of life of a single individual is short; at least specimens confined even in large and well-lit boxes soon die. Buffalo Gnats that have once imbibed blood of any animal also soon die, as seen by the large numbers found dried up in stables in which they have been carried attached to mules or horses. In the fields gnats filled to repletion with blood drop to the ground and crawl away, soon to die. They suffer, therefore, from their blood-thirsty habits, and this seems to be quite a general rule with all those blood-sucking species which are known to annoy man and other warm-blooded animals; for the love of blood generally proves ruinous to those individuals which are anxious to indulge in it, as we have shown to be the case with the Harvest Mite or Jigger.*

CHARACTER OF A SWARM.

The number of individuals comprising a swarm cannot be computed, as swarms vary greatly in size. Their presence is at once indicated by the actions of the various animals in the field. Horses and mules snort, switch their tails, stamp the ground, and show great restlessness and symptoms of fear. If not harnessed to plow and wagon they will try to escape by running away. Cattle rush wildly about in search of relief. Formerly, when deer were still numerous, they would be so tormented by these insects as to leave their hiding-places and run away, seeking protection even in the presence of their greatest enemy, man. Approaching animals in the field, we notice at once small black bodies, exceedingly swift in their flight, darting about their victims in search of a suitable spot to draw blood. But even during a very general invasion by these gnats these insects are not uniformly distributed throughout the region infested, but they select certain places. Only low and moist ground is frequented by them; exposed or sunny spots are never visited. There may be no indications of gnats in a whole neighborhood, and the unprepared farmer, dreaming of no danger to his mules or horses in passing dense thickets of bushes, &c., near the roadside, is suddenly attacked by a swarm of these pests, and is frequently unable to reach a place of safety in time to save his cattle. As suddenly as such swarms appear, just as suddenly do they disappear. During a gnat season cautious farmers never travel with their horses or mules without providing themselves with some kind of protective grease.

When Buffalo Gnats are very numerous the whole air in the vicinity of our domestic animals is filled with them at times, and looking towards the suffering brute, one sees it surrounded by a kind of haze formed by these flying insects. Sweeping rapidly with the hand through the air one can collect hundreds of gnats by a single stroke. They crawl into everything, and the plowman has constantly to brush

*See *Amer. Naturalist*, vol. vii, 1873, p. 19.

them away from his face, which does not always prevent them from entering and filling his mouth, nose, and ears; he is so tormented by them, and frequently by their bite as well, that he has to cease working for the time being. Thousands try to enter the houses in villages and cities, and the windows are frequently completely covered with them.

MODE OF ATTACK.

The flight of all species of *Simulium* is very swift and powerful. They possess, in comparison with most other flies, an enormously large thorax, consisting of a very tough, chitinous integument, that furnishes ample attachment for the strong muscles which propel them during their long and continuous flights.

The Southern Buffalo Gnat is exceedingly active in all its motions, and is at its bloody work as soon as it has gained a foothold upon an animal. The individual flight is inconspicuous and rarely more than a few feet from the ground. It is also usually noiseless, but when one passes rapidly close to the ear of a person the sound produced is faintly like that of a passing bullet, and no one who has listened to it will ever forget it, but will always connect it with their presence. If the insects are not very hungry, or if influenced by too warm or too dry an atmosphere, they circle around a mule or a horse very much like so many small bees; if hungry, however, they lose no time whatever, but with a few nervous jerks settle upon the selected spots and immediately go to work. They are never quiet, but are most active during early morning and towards evening. They also fly during moonlight nights. During the hottest portions of the day, from 11 a. m. to 4 p. m., they are more or less inactive. Their favorite time of attack is a cloudy, dark day, or when rain is threatening. If the gnats try to enter houses or stables by means of the windows, they constantly butt their heads against the panes of glass, until they become so exhausted that they drop to the ground and die. Specimens kept in confinement in large vessels, with the bottoms covered with moss and soil and containing a wet sponge and a saucer filled with water, die within forty hours. During all this time they never cease trying to escape. The sense of smell (and sight) of these insects must be well developed, because they unerringly find animals a long distance away from their breeding-places. If very numerous, they cover the whole animal, without making any selection of position.

The smaller Turkey Gnats are not so blood-thirsty, nor do they form such large swarms. The snorting, biting, switching of tails, and the general restlessness of the stock in the fields soon reveal the presence of their foes. The gnats will, upon arrival, rapidly circle around the animal, select a point of attack, fasten themselves upon the chosen spot, and immediately commence to bite. The genital and anal regions, the ears and portions of body between the forelegs—in short, those parts where the skin is most easily punctured—are selected by these insects. The attack is so rapid, that in course of one minute the body of the tormentor is seen to expand with blood, which shows plainly through the epidermis of the abdomen. The bitten part of the animal shows a nipplelike projection, and if the insect is removed by force a drop of blood as large as a good-sized pin's head will ooze out. Other gnats will almost at once pounce upon the same spot and continue the biting. All those veins which project under the skin of the animal are also favorable points of attack, and their course is made visible by the hordes of gnats fastened upon them.

The great danger of an attack by these insects lies in the unexpectedness of their appearance. As already mentioned there may be no indication of their presence in any neighborhood and the roads are free of them. But with the change of the prevailing wind they may appear, and when one is passing certain localities, such as low, wet, and shady ground, or dense thickets of underbrush, they will start forth like a cloud, and cover the animals at once. Open fields may be entirely free from gnats, but if animals pass certain places in them out dart the tormentors, and the animals attacked can only save themselves by running to high places exposed to the full rays of the sun. The gnats, following the animals for some distance, leave as suddenly as they appeared, and hide themselves again in the thickets. In the cities they appear suddenly with certain winds, chiefly with those blowing from the south, southeast, and west, and usually disappear again with winds blowing from the opposite direction.

ANIMALS INJURED.

Domestic animals are attacked in the following order, varying somewhat in different localities, viz, mules, horses, cattle, sheep, setting turkeys and hens, hogs, dogs, and cats. The death-rate of mules is highest, both because they seem to be more susceptible to the bite, and because they are almost exclusively used in the Southern States for farm work. Horses also suffer greatly. Cattle, when weakened by winter exposure and by scarcity of food, succumb easily to the continued attacks of their winged foes. Hogs show at first the effects of the bite but very little; yet large numbers die soon after the attack, while others die about six weeks after the disappearance of the Buffalo Gnats; they usually perish from large ulcerating sores, which cause blood-poisoning. Many persons claim that the so-called *charbon* is produced by the bites of these gnats, a statement which is, of course, not borne out by facts. Sheep, although well protected by their wool, suffer greatly by bites upon the unprotected portions of their skins, and injure themselves still more by crowding too close to fires, which are built to produce protecting smoke. Many sheep crowd so close to the fire as to be burned to death. Setting turkeys and hens are frequently forced by the gnats to leave their nests. Young fowls are killed outright. The gnats, in attacking fowls of all kinds, force their way under the wings of their victims, where they cannot be dislodged. Dogs and cats are also greatly tormented, and will not remain outdoors during a Buffalo Gnat invasion if they can help it. Deer, forgetful of any other threatening danger, are tormented to such a degree as to lose all fear, and approach the smoldering fires; in their agony they sometimes allow people to rub the gnats from their bodies, and will, in their frantic endeavors for relief, even lie down in the glowing embers or hot ashes.

EFFECT OF THE BITES.

Animals bitten by many Buffalo Gnats show all the symptoms of colic, and many people believe that these bites bring on that disease. Mules especially are thus affected, yet large numbers of *post mortem* examinations made by Dr. Warren King, of Vicksburg, and others, failed to show any relationship between this disease and the bites, nor were any facts obtained which would justify the correctness of such a popular conclusion. Dr. King opines that the effects of these bites on animals are much the same as that of the rattlesnake on the human system.   This seems to be the generally accepted opinion among the more intelligent planters.   The animal attacked becomes at first frantic, but within a very short time it ceases to show symptoms of pain, submits passively to the infliction, rolls over, and dies; sometimes all within the space of three or four hours.   Even if bitten by a very great number of gnats death does not necessarily follow, and then it is not always suddenly fatal.   Mules which at night do not appear to be seriously injured will often be found dead next morning.

Animals of various kinds become gradually accustomed to these bites, and during a long-continued invasion but few are killed towards the end of it.   It is a prevailing notion that the bite of the gnats appearing first is the most poisonous.   It would seem to be more probable, however, that the poison introduced into the systems of animals—unless sufficient to prove fatal—may to some extent serve as an antidote against that introduced later, and if this poison should remain in the system with any stability, such a fact would also account for native or acclimated stock being less susceptible to the poison from bites than that recently imported.   There is no doubt that stock freshly imported from Kentucky to Tennessee and Mississippi is more apt to be killed than that raised in the infested portions of these States, and that, having withstood one invasion, a second one proves fatal but seldom.   One reason why Buffalo Gnats appearing very early in the season are more dangerous may be found in the fact that the stock, weakened by exposure during the winter, have had as yet no chance to gain in strength by feeding upon the early vegetation, which it obtains previous to and during a later invasion.   Consequently, the resisting power of animals is greater later in the season. Experience has also taught owners of stock how to protect the same, and in comparison with former gnat seasons fewer animals are killed of late.   Prof. J. A. Schoenbauer, who wrote nearly one hundred years ago about the Kolumbacz Gnats of Hungary, witnessed the *post mortem* examination of a horse killed by these gnats.   Upon dissection it was found that not only was the anus entirely filled with the flies, but also the genital orifices, the nasal passages, and the bronchial tube and its ramifications.   A case of this kind must be very exceptional.   No doubt gnats will sometimes enter these passages, but as a rule death is not occasioned in this manner.   The loss of blood and the terrible irritation of the skin by so many poisonous bites are reasons sufficient to account for the reflex irritation of the nerves and blood poisoning.

HOW ANIMALS PROTECT THEMSELVES.

The different kinds of animals, knowing their tormenters by instinct or experience, have various methods of protecting themselves against their attacks.   To run away is the first impulse of all; but it is of no avail, since their enemies are too swift to be outrun.

Horses and mules, if not harnessed or tied, become perfectly frantic, and rush away hither and thither, roll themselves upon the ground, dash off again wildly, and repeat these actions until they become entirely exhausted.   If they succeed in reaching an elevated spot free from trees and accessible to the full rays of the sun, they escape further severe molestation.

Cattle act in a very similar way, but instead of searching for higher, sunny spots, they prefer to rush through dense thickets, such as are formed by canes, and thus rid themselves of many tormentors, but all in vain. If creeks are near by, some find partial protection by immersing themselves in the water.

Hogs also run madly about. If mud is accessible, they do not fail to make good use of that material and wallow in it.

Sheep run about blindly, crying piteously all the time.

Dogs and cats are sensible enough to search for dark shelters in stables or remain in the house.

Poultry of various kinds seek relief by flying in high trees. They assist each other in picking off their tormentors, thus partly freeing themselves.

Deer try to find relief by running away from the gnats.

But all such methods avail but little without the assistance of man. Fires are started everywhere to produce a dense smoke. As soon as the tormented animals notice such smoke they all show their good sense by rushing to it, invariably selecting that side of the fire where the smoke is densest. Here they crowd together, and many are injured by too close proximity to the glowing embers. Nor can they be driven away by hunger; and only during a dark night, or in the brightest light of the midday sun, do some of them venture out in search of food.

PREVENTIVES.

Smudges have thus far proved the best method of protecting animals in the field against Buffalo Gnats. Thoughtful planters are in the habit of collecting and storing during the year all kinds of material that will produce a dense and stifling smoke; such materials are old leather, cast-off clothing, dried dung, &c. As soon as large swarms of gnats appear, and the stock is threatened by them, fires are started in different parts of the plantation, and are kept burning as long as the danger lasts. Anything that will produce smoke is thrown upon the smoldering logs, and the most offensive is considered the most useful. If the time for plowing has arrived, smudges are located in the fields in such a manner that the smoke is drifted by the wind over the teams at work. Such smoke-producing fires are also kept burning in the cities, and they are found in front of every livery and street-car stable, as well as of such stores as employ draft horses or mules. If these animals have to be upon the roads, they may usually be somewhat protected by tin pails in which some smudge is kept, and which are suspended from their necks and from the wagons.

Animals may also be protected with a layer of mud or a coat of sirup. It has been found that animals which have shed their rough winter coat of hair and have become smooth are not as much troubled as others still covered with long hairs. The gnats find it much more difficult to obtain a foothold upon a smooth skin, and the clipping of the hair in early spring is therefore advisable.

Buffalo Gnats have a great aversion to entering dark places, and stables thoroughly darkened are safe places for stock of all kinds in a gnat season. The odor of ammonia prevailing in such stables may also to some extent prevent the insects from entering. Planters with a small acreage, therefore, prefer to keep their horses and mules in the stable instead of working them in the field. For the same reason the owners of livery stables will not allow their animals to be taken outside the city limits if gnats are numerous enough to be dangerous.

But the great majority of planters cannot wait for the disappearance of the pest, and have to resort to other defensive means. Various external applications have been used to this effect: Decoctions of Alder leaves, Tobacco, Pennyroyal, and other herbs, have been tried with a view of preventing gnats from biting mules while at work; but all of them have proven ineffective. At a time when small swarms of Turkey Gnats were tormenting mules plowing in the field one side of the animal was moistened by Mr. Lugger with various insecticides, while the other side was not protected at all. By following the animal and watching the gnats it was soon observed that any offensive-smelling substance would drive the gnats from the protected side to the unprotected one. Kerosene emulsion, pyrethrum powder suspended in water, diluted carbon-bisulphide, and dissolved tobacco-soap were all used in turn, and all seemed to produce the same effect. Several times the whole animal was carefully sponged with the one or the other of the above substances. For a time the gnats would not settle upon the animal; but in the course of two hours the beneficial effect of these insecticides was gone, and the insects were no longer kept away.

Experience shows that the best preventive is grease of various kinds. The following kinds are the most important: Cotton-seed oil alone, or mixed with tar, fish oil, gnat oil; a combination of stinking oils alone, or mixed with tar or kerosene oil, crude coal oil, kerosene oil, kerosene oil mixed with axle-grease, and others. To be effective, the grease must be used at least twice during the day, because as soon as its offensive odor disappears it becomes inoperative. All such applications are of no advantage, however, on stock running at large. Gnat oil is very extensively used, but it is like the rest of the remedies—very apt to remove the hair.* In fact, all these different kinds of oil and grease are more or less injurious to the animals, because a continued coating with them weakens the system.

The employés of the Hudson's Bay Company protect themselves and their stock against the bites of the "Black Fly" by the use of oil of tar, and as long experience has shown it to be a simple and easily applied wash, we strongly recommend its use. A quantity of coal tar is placed in the bottom of a large shallow receptacle of some sort, and a small quantity of oil of tar, or oil of turpentine, or any similar material, is stirred in. The receptacle is then filled with water, which is left standing for several days until well impregnated with the odor. The animals to be protected are then washed with this water as often as seems to be necessary.

As long as stock in the infested region is suffered to run at large, and is neither provided with shelter nor food during the winter months, it will suffer severely from the gnats. Animals well cared for can stand the attacks of the gnats far better, and do not perish as readily. Ill-treated and unhealthy mules and those bruised and cut are the first to die, and the prevailing opinion of intelligent planters is to the effect that well-cared-for mules, if greased twice a day when working in the field, seldom die even when attacked.

---

*According to Messrs. Fahlen & Kleinschmidt, chemists, of Memphis, Tenn., "Gnat oil is any kind of stinking oil; it should not contain drying oils, such as Oleum lini and O. gossypii." They use fish oil, and to increase its perfume add Ol. animale fœtidum, 4 ounces to 10 gallons. But since fish oil costs 50 to 75 cents per gallon, some mix it with crude petroleum; this addition, however, has the tendency to kill the hair roots. Ol. hedeomæ (pennyroyal) is too costly, and therefore not frequently used. Fish oil and Ol. animale fœtidum have given the best satisfaction.

REMEDIES FOR THE BITES.

A number of remedies to counteract the poison of the Buffalo Gnats have been tried, but none of them have been sufficiently tested or have proved uniformly effective.

Dr. Warren King, of Vicksburg, Miss., recommends rubbing the affected animals thoroughly with water of ammonia, and administering internally a mixture of 40 to 50 grains of carbonate of ammonia to 1 pint of whisky, repeating the dose every three or four hours until relieved. He claims to have never lost an animal under this treatment, although they were sometimes apparently beyond recovery. This remedy is not generally known, but certainly contains sufficient merit to warrant a thorough and careful trial.

Some planters claim to have cured their stock simply by continued doses of whisky alone and by keeping the sick animal in cool and darkened stables.

Blood-letting is also recommended, both as a preventive and as a cure, but may be considered as of very doubtful utility, except in cases where heroic treatment is required. Mules badly injured and in a dying condition are bled until the blood, which at first is nearly black, appears of a natural color again.

Dying animals have frequently been saved by immersion in the cold water of running streams. Evidently all these remedies have a tendency to allay the fever produced by incipient blood-poisoning.

ATTACKING MAN.

A number of cases have from time to time been reported by various newspapers in the infested region of human beings being killed by these insects. Inquiry has sometimes failed to prove the truth of such reports; yet sufficient facts are on record to show that if the gnats attack a person suddenly in large swarms and find him unprepared or far away from any shelter they may cause death.

Dr. Bromby, in Madison Parish, La., had a case of death caused, he believes, by the gnats. A Mrs. Breeme, having lost, in the spring of 1883, 17 mules of her stock, was suddenly taken sick. She told the doctor that she had been bitten by mosquitoes. She died in great agony from blood-poisoning.

In 1884 several persons were killed by Buffalo Gnats. Mr. H. A. Winter, from near Helena, Ark., while on a hunting trip, was attacked by them one and a half miles from home, while passing some low ground. Running towards a house, he was seen to fall dead. All exposed parts of his body had turned black. Another man was killed near Wynne Station, Arkansas, on the Iron Mountain Railroad.

DAMAGE DONE IN VARIOUS YEARS.

The damage occasioned by Buffalo Gnats throughout the infested region cannot be estimated, owing to the fact that no statistics have ever been collected in a systematic manner. But the loss in certain localities has been immense, and greatest when the insects appeared in the very early spring. Of late years the losses have increased because the country has become more densely settled and not because the bite of the gnats has become more dangerous. The following statements are based on reports from reliable individuals and from records in local papers examined by Mr. Lugger:

As far as can be learned the damage in Louisiana was but slight prior to 1850; but many animals were killed in 1861, 1862, 1863, 1864, and 1866. In this latter year the parish of Tallulah, Louisiana, lost over 200 head of mules, and upwards of 400 mules and horses were killed within a few days in the parishes of Madison, Tensas, and Concordia, all in the same State. In other States they also did great damage. In 1868 many mules were killed in the low lands of Daviess County, Kentucky. Although frequently causing more or less trouble and loss, they did not appear again in such overwhelming numbers until 1872, 1873, 1874, 1881, 1882, 1884, 1885, and 1886. In 1872 it was reported that the loss of mules and horses in Crittenden County, Arkansas, exceeded the loss from all diseases. In 1873 they caused serious injury in many parishes of Louisiana. In 1874 the loss occasioned in one county in Southwest Tennessee was estimated at $500,000. The gnats have been especially injurious since the Mississippi floods of 1881 and 1882; in the latter year they were more destructive to stock than ever before, appearing in immense numbers in Eastern Kansas, Western Tennessee, and Western Mississippi, and the great destruction of cattle, horses, and mules caused by them added greatly to the distress of the inhabitants of those sections of the country caused by unprecedented floods. Many localities along the Mississippi River in Arkansas also suffered severely. In 1884 Buffalo Gnats appeared again in great numbers and were fully as destructive as in 1882. In Franklin Parish, Louisiana, within a week from their first appearance, they had caused the death of 300 head of stock. They were equally numerous throughout the whole region infested, and for the first time in the history of the pest they attacked horses and mules on the streets of the cities of Vicksburg and Memphis. No general outbreak took place in 1885; yet gnats appeared in sufficient numbers to kill quite a number of mules in various parishes of Louisiana, especially in Tensas and Franklin. Buffalo Gnats appeared again in immense numbers in 1886, and extended throughout the entire lower Mississippi Valley, and swarms were even observed and doing damage far away from the region usually invaded. They came very late in the season, and consequently animals were in better condition to withstand their attacks. The damage was great, however, in many localities where planters had not taken steps to protect their stock.

Besides the actual loss by death of their stock, planters lose much valuable time in preparing their fields for the crops. It so happens that the gnats appear at a time in which the ground becomes fit to be prepared for cotton, and as it is very important to give that plant as much time as possible to mature, every day is very valuable in early spring. Planters owning large estates have to use their mules for plowing, notwithstanding the gnats, while farmers on a small scale can keep their animals in the stable, thus protecting them.

POPULAR OPINIONS ABOUT THE EARLY STATES OF THE BUFFALO GNATS.

The early states of both Buffalo and Turkey Gnats were as a rule perfectly unknown to the inhabitants of the infested regions when our investigations began. Yet the great, and in some seasons absorbing, interest taken in them gave rise to many speculations as to their origin. Many theories had been advanced from time to time and were discussed in the newspapers, and no facts had been observed to throw light upon the many mooted points yet obscure in the popular mind.

From the very fact that the region infested by these insects contains many swamps, it was claimed by many that the gnats originated in them and nowhere else. Others were convinced that low and moist soil would produce them, since it had been observed that such localities would harbor gnats in abundance, and that their swarms would rise from the grass if animals approached.

Even such absurd theories as that the Mississippi water coming in contact with decayed leaves and similar material would spontaneously create them were stoutly maintained by some, while others claimed that the gnats were produced out of mud without undergoing any transformation whatever. There exists also a prevalent opinion among the more intelligent that the eggs are deposited upon grass, weeds, &c., where they remain until the water of an overflow reaches and submerges them, when incubation takes place. In this manner eggs were supposed to remain sometimes for years, or until the necessary conditions for incubation arrived with the cold water of the Mississippi River.

Many larvæ, which are found in large numbers about decayed logs and under rotten leaves in the woods, have given rise to the belief that such were the young of their dreaded foe. The larvæ of a family of flies, the *Chironomidæ*, which occur in vast numbers in all the water of the infested region as well as elsewhere, look somewhat like those of the *Simulium*. Their general appearance and their actions are very similar, and consequently they have frequently been mistaken for the young of the real culprit, and, in fact, were at first mistaken by our agents. But the flies resulting from these larvæ are very different, looking very much like mosquitoes with feathered antennæ: they also swarm in very early spring, but are innocent of any harm to animals.

We reproduce at Plate IX, Fig. 1, a figure of a *Chironomus* larva which was found in the pods of *Utricularia* at Vineland. N. J., by Mrs. Mary Treat. The figure was made by us at Mrs. Treat's request, and was published as Fig. 9, of her article entitled "Is the Valve of *Utricularia* Sensitive?" in Harper's *New Monthly Magazine*, February, 1876, Vol. LII, pp. 382–387. We have also figured on the same plate, at Fig. 2, *a* and *b*, the pupa of the same species and the adult of *Chironomus plumosus*, a species common to both Europe and America, and which was collected in great numbers by Mr. W. H. Seaman at Chautauqua Lake, New York, August, 1886.

HABITS AND NATURAL HISTORY.

THE EGG.—The eggs of the different species of the genus *Simulium* occurring in the lower Mississippi Valley have not as yet been discovered,* but sufficient is known. from analogy with closely allied species in this country as well as in Europe, to indicate the localities in which to search for the eggs of one of the species, the smaller Turkey Gnat, which is so common in the vicinity of small and rapid streams. These creeks descend from an elevated region not inundated by the Mississippi River. They are, however, greatly affected by an over-

---

* While this report is going through the press, word reaches us at Los Angeles, Cal., from Mr. Webster, who was sent to Louisiana especially to look for them, that the eggs have been discovered by him.—C. V. R.

flow, since the back water arrests the downward current and eventually forces the water back, thus completely filling the creek-beds
with turbid river water. In such creek-beds trees of various kinds
abound, as well as great masses of dead and fallen timber, too heavy
to be floated away. All such projecting points offer sufficient space
for the fly to deposit eggs upon, and such places we intend to have
closely investigated the coming spring at a time in which the water
is highest and in a neighborhood where flies are known to breed.

As mentioned in our report for 1884. Dr. W. S. Barnard has described and figured in the *American Entomologist* (Vol. III, pp. 191–
193, August, 1880) the eggs and early states of a species of *Simulium*
common in the mountain streams in the vicinity of Ithaca, N. Y.
These eggs (Plate VIII, Fig. 7) were found on the rocks on the banks
a few inches above the surface of the water, and we give herewith a
description of them as a means of facilitating the finding of those of
the southern species here treated of. The eggs are deposited in a com-
pact layer ; their shape is long ovoid, but on account of their softness
and close proximity to each other they become distorted and poly-
hedral ; one end is frequently flattened or concave. Each egg measures 0.40^{mm} by 0.18^{mm}. In Hungary the eggs of the Columbacz
Midge (*S. columbaczensis* Schönbauer) have also been studied by
Edward Tomosvary, and the observations have been published since
his death by Dr. Géza Horváth.* It seems that this species is, as
far as its habits are concerned, more intimately related to our smaller
species than the larger and more dangerous Buffalo Gnat. Its eggs,
which are enveloped in a yellowish-white slime and deposited towards
the end of May or beginning of June, are also deposited upon stones
or grass over which the water flows and in the brooks of the more
elevated regions. The female of that species is said to deposit on an
average from 5,000 to 10,000 eggs, but no detailed description is given,
while we have found only about 500 in the ovaries of our species.

But when and where does the larger and true Buffalo Gnat deposit
its eggs? At present nothing is known about it. Messrs. Lugger
and Webster left too soon to discover the eggs, because no gnats were
expected so unprecedently late in the season ; while Mr. Fillion did not
reach the affected region until too late. At the time in which the
Buffalo Gnat swarms all the low land is flooded and the water in the
bayous has reached a depth of 20 and more feet above the usual summer depth of 2 to 5 feet. The water at such a time has spread over
thousands of square miles, and only the taller trees are above it.
Over such an extent of surface it would naturally be almost impossible to find these small eggs; but it is now known that the members
composing the swarms of Buffalo Gnats are all females, which, led by
a mad desire for blood, leave their breeding-places not to return
again, but to perish in consequence of this appetite. To perpetuate
the species, therefore, copulation of the sexes must take place almost
immediately after acquiring wings, that is, at or near the places of
their birth, which latter the males do not seem to leave at all. Eggs,
no doubt, will be found at such places. If deposited anywhere else
their chances of hatching, or rather the chances of the newly-born
larvæ remaining in the water after the subsidence of the same, would
be slight indeed.

It admits of but little doubt that the eggs will hatch very soon
after being deposited, for it is not likely, as has been claimed by

* A. Kolumbácsi légy, Dr. Horváth Géza, in *Rovartani Lapok*, I. Kotet, 10.
fuzet, Budapest, 1884.

some, that the eggs will remain dormant for a whole year, or even two and more years, in the place where deposited, only to hatch when reached by another overflow. Such theories are not borne out by any observed facts, and they are, moreover, contrary to the usual habits of similar insects.

Since some of the breeding places of the two species of insects are now well known, the finding of the eggs will only be a question of time.

THE LARVA.—The peculiar aquatic larvæ of both the Buffalo and Turkey Gnats resemble those of the other known species, and their distinctive features will be shown in the closing descriptive portions of the paper. Generally speaking, they are less than half an inch in length, subcylindrical, attenuated in the middle, and enlarged toward both ends; the posterior third of the body is much stouter than the anterior third, and almost club-shaped. The color of the larva varies greatly, and is usually more or less like that of the substance upon which it is fastened; it is marked by two dirty, greenish-gray, irregular spots upon each joint, on a whitish and translucent ground. The head, which is almost square, is yellowish, marked with a few darker spots and lines, and with a pair of small, black, approximate spots on each side that look like eyes, but are not. Besides the usual mouth organs the head possesses two additional brown and fan-shaped bodies, which are usually spread out and kept in constant motion when catching food; they open and close like a fan, and if folded can be partially withdrawn into the mouth. The smooth body of the larva is composed of twelve joints or segments, five of which form the club-shaped anal portion of the body. On the under side of the thoracic portion there is a subconical, retractile process, crowned with a circular row of short and sharp bristles. The anal extremity consists also of a subcylindrical, truncated protuberance, which is crowned with rows of bristles similar to those of the thoracic proleg. The larva possesses no stigmata, but immediately below the anal protuberance, on the under side of the body, there are three short, cylindrical, soft, curved, and retractile tentacles, to which the large tracheæ lead, and which are probably the organs of respiration.

In some of the most mature larvæ two kidney-shaped black spots are visible just above the thoracic proleg, one on each side. · If closely investigated with a good lens it is seen that the tufts of filaments serving the future pupa for respiration are already formed under the larval skin. All these filaments arise from the same spot and are branches of a single internal tube.

Habits of the Larvæ.—The larvæ of the different species of *Simulium* are so very uniform in their modes of life that the description of the habits of one will suffice for all.

The most essential condition for the well-being of these aquatic creatures is rapid motion of the water in which they live. Wherever water of such a description is found in the region infested by Buffalo and Turkey Gnats the one or the other species can be found.

The next important condition of a suitable breeding-place is the presence of some stationary material in the water upon which to fasten themselves.

Water in rapid motion is only found in certain well-defined places, either in streams coming from an elevated plateau or in streams meandering through a level country. In the former any sudden bend and any obstruction, no matter how small, will produce accelerated motion of the water; in the latter, sudden bends are the chief cause. In the former. there are numerous places where larvæ can securely fasten themselves, because large numbers of sticks partly embedded in mud are not disturbed by the rising water. Against such immersed sticks, as well as against fence-rails, &c.. which cross such streams, numerous dead leaves are lodged and anchored by the mud. All such obstructions, forming small whirlpools just below them, are places in which the larvæ of the Turkey Gnats are found. Larger submerged logs, wholly or partly submerged stumps, brush, bushes, or any other material of like nature in the larger creeks and bayous give the larvæ of the Buffalo Gnat suitable places to anchor to.

Upon such material they cluster together, and, fastened by the posterior protuberance to the leaf, they assume an erect position, or make their way upward or downward with a looping gait. Frequently attached by a minute thread, they sway with the ripples at or near the surface of the water, often as many as half a dozen being attached by a single thread. While these larvæ make their way up and down these submerged objects with perfect freedom they do not venture above the water, and when about to pupate select a situation well down toward the bottom of the stream.

The larvæ of the Turkey Gnat are more often found fastened to submerged dead leaves in the smaller and more shallow creeks or branches. These larvæ are evidently somewhat social in their habits, as they crowd together upon one leaf in numbers varying from ten to thirty, and, judging from their uniform size, they must be the offspring of the same parent. As the current away from obstructions caused by twigs and leaves, decreases in swiftness, so do the larvæ decrease in numbers, until only a few feet away but one or two can be found. When first found, in early March, they are quite small, but they grow rapidly during the latter part of March and early April. They are quite stationary when not disturbed. Besides being fastened to the leaf by the last posterior segment, they are also securely anchored by a very fine silken thread. When disturbed they loosen their hold at once and float downstream, suspended and retarded by this thread, which very rapidly increases in length while the larvæ are drifting with the current. While thus drifting they jerk about in a lively manner, searching for a new resting-place, and sink to the bottom quite gradually. Owing to their small size, and to the fact already stated, that their color is in harmony with their surroundings or with the leaf upon which they are fastened, these larvæ are difficult to detect in a depth of 3 to 4 inches. When removed and put in a glass vessel they soon settle against the sides of their prison, and can then be studied with a lens.

The larva can move about very rapidly in the manner of a spanworm, but with this difference, that it always remains anchored by means of a thread, which lengthens as the animal proceeds. Being very restless and active in such confinement, it will keep on looping for hours, at a rate of twenty to twenty-five loops per minute. It can move both forward and backward; the forward motion being produced by fastening the single thoracic leg to the side or bottom of the vessel, loosening the anal proleg, bringing it close to the former, and letting the latter go at almost the same moment; the backward motion being simply a reversal. In the course of six to eight hours the larva becomes weak and sickly; it will drop to the bottom of the vessel if disturbed, but will no longer try to escape. All the larvæ thus imprisoned, in repeated trials, died in the course of twenty-four hours. A colony of nearly full-grown larvæ, in a small creek, shared the same fate when the overflow of the Mississippi River created a back flow and made the water in this creek stationary for some time.

All the creeks and branches in which such larvæ were found by Mr. Lugger descend in beds composed of clay. The Rocky Bottom Branch, a tributary to the Horn Lake Creek, Mississippi, has worn out a bed in a solid deposit of stratified ferruginous sandstone, intermixed with conglomerations of the same substance. The water, 6 to 8 inches deep in normal seasons, even during the summer months, runs over this stony bed in very rapid currents, forming everywhere little cascades, and no better breeding-places for the larvæ of any *Simulium* could be imagined. Yet none could be found, plainly indicating that the species under consideration must be able to fasten to submerged material to find a suitable home.

Food of the Larvæ.—The larvæ of the Southern Buffalo Gnat are carnivorous in their habits, although they do not, perhaps, reject floating particles of a vegetable origin. Their mouth is not adapted for biting off any pieces from a large or solid substance, but is constructed to catch and ingulf small objects. To obtain these the fanlike organs peculiar to these larvæ create currents of water directed towards the mouth. Any small and floating matter drifted by the current of water into the vicinity of these fans is attracted by the ciliary motions of the component rays of the same, and thus reaches the space embraced by them, and they, bending over the mouth, direct the further motions of the particles. If of the proper kind they are eaten, otherwise they are expelled by a sudden opening or parting of the fans. They do not feed, as has been claimed, upon plants which they are unable to bite off or chew, and which do not exist in the water at the time when the larvæ grow most rapidly. A searching investigation of the water in their breeding-places revealed the fact that it was swarming with animal life, and was filled with the larval forms of small crustaceans belonging to various families, but chiefly to those of Coptopods and Isopods. An abundant supply of food must also be found in the presence of immense numbers of freshwater sponges, polyps, and animalcula. Larvæ of the Southern Buffalo Gnat kept in glass vessels were observed to swallow these minute crustaceans, and none of this food was seen to be expelled again. A number of square diatoms, jointed together in a chain, have also been observed in the intestines of these larvæ by the aid of the microscope. The presence of such quantities of animal food will also account for the observed fact that the larvæ grow so very rapidly during the early spring, since this is the time of the year in which most of the small fresh-water crustaceans spawn and produce living young, and food is, therefore, much more abundant at this season than at any other.

There may be, and very likely is, a connection between an overflow by the Mississippi River and the amount and kind of food produced by it. During the long-continued heat of summer nearly all the swamp-land, as well as the majority of the bayous, dry up, either partially or entirely, and water remains only in small pools, in springs, and in perennial creeks. The animal life in all these places becomes more and more concentrated, while they fairly swarm with small creatures of all kinds, and if the larvæ of the gnats could lead a roving kind of existence, or could thrive in warm water, there would be no lack of food for them at this season. As great numbers of small creatures found in the evaporating and fast-disappearing water possess the faculty of coming to life again even after having been dried up for a long time, an inundation resurrects vast numbers of them, and brings them furthermore within reach of the larvæ. These, however, are not active during the heat of summer, and an inundation at that time will not affect them at all; but if it should take place early in spring, this additional source of food would soon mature vast numbers otherwise doomed to die.

PUPA AND COCOON.—As soon as the larvæ are fully grown they descend towards the bottom of the water to make their peculiar pouches, and many pupæ are found at a depth of 8 to 10 feet below the surface; others much higher up. But in shallow water they may be found clustered one above the other, just above the bottom of the stream, their instinct having evidently taught them to provide for a sudden fall in the water. Notwithstanding this, with the water falling in the bayous and larger creeks at the rate of 1 foot per day, many pupæ are left high and dry. Those of the Turkey Gnats, which are always found just above the bottom of the smaller perennial creeks, are not thus endangered by a low stage of the water, which rises and falls suddenly with every heavy rain, but remains of uniform depth at other times.

In one of the breeding-places of the Southern Buffalo Gnats, at the junction of Crop and Mill Bayous, in Tensas Parish, Louisiana, Mr. Fillion found immense numbers of the dry and empty pouches as late as June 10, 1886; they were attached to vines, trunks of living trees, and leaves retained by the vines. All these pouches were found near the highest point reached by the overflow, forming a zone or belt from 3 to 4 feet in width. On July 15, the current, very swift in June, had almost ceased to be noticeable, and the stream had decreased from a width of 45 feet to that of 20 feet; the Crop Bayou was partly dry, and no obstructions or vines of any kind reached the water, which flowed in clear dry banks. The belt of dry pouches was at the latter date high above the water, the lowest being found some 13 feet above it, while the highest reached to the mark left by the overflow.

The cocoon or pouch spun by these larvæ is conical, grayish or brownish, semi-transparent, and has its upper half squarely cut off; it is fastened to sticks, leaves, or logs. The larva in spinning does not leave its foothold, but running in the center of its work, uses its mouth to spin this snug little house. In it it changes to a pupa, which has its anterior end protruding above the upper rim. These pupæ are at first of a light brown color, afterwards changing to a pinkish cast, and, just previous to the hatching of the fly, to black. During the first of the coloration epochs they are attached to the vegetable substances upon which the pouch has been fastened by the thoracic filaments, by threads about the body, and by the anal extremity; but during the last two the pupæ hang by the short anal attachment alone to the threads at the bottom of the pouch, and rise more and more out of the pouch, until at last they swing about freely in the current, attached only by the drawn-out threads.

The pupa itself is distinguished from most other Dipterous pupæ by the presence of a tuft of respiratory filaments starting from each side of the thorax. These tufts, as already stated, foreshadowed by two dark spots upon the sides of the thoracic segments in the larva, are composed of a greater or less number of very slender filaments, varying in number in the different species of *Simulium*. Along the posterior margins of each of the third and fourth dorsal segments there are eight minute spines; the tip of the abdomen is also armed with two larger and bent spines or hooks, by which the pupa is secured to the inside of the open pouch. Remaining but a very short time in the pupal state, prolonged or shortened by atmospheric influences, they give forth the winged insects. The length of the pupal state in the case of the Turkey Gnat averages five days. Both larval and pupal skins remain for some time in the empty pouch.

The perfect insects issue from their pupæ under water, and surrounded, according to some writers, by a bubble of air. The silky hairs of the fly, however, are protection enough to prevent it from drowning. The winged insect pops to the surface like a cork, runs a few inches over the water, and darts away with great swiftness.

THE IMAGO.—The perfect fly varies in length from 3^{mm} to 4.5^{mm}, the females being usually the larger; the Turkey Gnat is somewhat smaller. Both insects are, like all other species of *Simulium*, characterized by their peculiar short and thick shape. The head is bent under, and is nearly as wide as the very large and humped thorax. The thick antennæ are composed of twelve stout joints; the four-jointed palpi terminate in long and fine joints; the posterior shanks and the first joint of the hind tarsi are somewhat dilated. The free labrum is as sharp as a dagger, and the very prominent proboscis is well adapted for drawing blood. The insects possess no ocelli, but their eyes are large; in the male they join at the forehead, but in the female they are farther apart. The mouth organs of the male are also not so well developed as in the female, being soft and unable to draw blood. The bodies of these gnats are quite hard and can resist considerable pressure. The color of the Southern Buffalo Gnat is black, but covered with grayish-brown, short, and silken hairs, which are arranged upon the thorax in such a manner as to show three parallel longitudinal black stripes; the abdomen is more densely covered with similar hairs, and shows, furthermore, a dorsal broad, whitish stripe, which widens towards the posterior end. The legs are more reddish, but also covered with hairs of the same color as elsewhere; the balancers are yellowish-white and the wings ample. The general appearance of the Turkey Gnat is very similar, but it is lighter in color.

The gnats are exceedingly active, and endowed with very acute, senses, which enable them to find unerringly animals a long distance away. Only females seem to form these aggressive swarms, since not a single male has been found in the large numbers captured and investigated. The male stays near the place of its birth, and since females once gorged with blood do not and cannot return, copulation and the depositing of eggs must take place very soon after emerging from the water. These points have as yet to be investigated.

NUMBER OF BROODS.

All species of the genus *Simulium*, the life-histories of which have been studied, are single-brooded, and no doubt Buffalo and Turkey Gnats form no exception to that rule. Extending as they do over such a vast area, we should expect their swarms in some seasons to form and appear continuously for five or six weeks before the whole brood had matured and disappeared. No Buffalo Gnats have ever been found in the infested region during the summer, fall, or winter, even when inundations have occurred in these seasons, and there are no indications of a second or third brood in the same year.

ENEMIES OF THE BUFFALO GNAT.

The Buffalo Gnats in their winged form have but few enemies among birds, because they usually appear at a time in the early spring when but few of our insectivorous birds have returned from their southward migrations. Besides the Mocking-bird and the Winter Wren, birds which remain in the more southern portions of the infested regions, no other birds have been observed to catch and feed upon them. Hens and chickens eat large numbers of such gnats as have become helpless by being gorged with blood. A single premature Dragon-fly, or Mosquito Hawk, and a brightly colored Hawk-fly (*Asilidæ*) were observed by Mr. Lugger to catch them in the fields. But the larvæ of the gnats do not fare so well. Although somewhat protected by their color and position in the water, many are discovered by small fishes belonging to the family *Cyprinidæ*, which frequent even the smallest creeks, and greedily eat them; other fishes in the larger creeks will probably act in the same way. The carnivorous larvæ of Water-beetles, as well as other aquatic insects, no doubt find them as well suited to their taste. The pupæ escape detection much better, because they do not move, and are, as a rule, hidden by the fine floating mud of the water which partially covers them and their pouches.

No insect enemies of any of the *Simulium* larvæ have been heretofore observed either in this country or in Europe. It is therefore interesting to note that the larva of a species of the neuropterous genus *Hydropsyche*, has been found by Mr. Howard near Washington feeding upon the larvæ of a local species of *Simulium*. The facts were communicated by him to the Entomological Society of Washington at its September (1886) meeting, and we quote his account of his observations:

In the month of August, on the larger stones in parts of Rock Creek, District of Columbia, where the current was swiftest, and particularly on such rocks as were tilted so as to bring a portion of the surface close to the surface of the water, were observed hundreds of peculiar funnel-shaped larval cases or webs (Plate IX, Fig 5) of a species of this interesting Trichopterous genus. The cases varied greatly in size. The mouth of the funnel in some instances was not more than 3^{mm} in diameter and in others reached fully 10^{mm}. The tube of the funnel was in every case bent nearly at right angles with the mouth, and the larva ensconced within it waited for its prey to be caught in the broadened mouth. It was noticed that the cases were preferably placed at the edge of slight depressions in the rocky surface, so that the tubular portion was protected from the full force of the current. The broad funnel-shaped expansion was woven in wide meshes with exceedingly strong silk, and was supported at the sides and top by bits of twigs and small portions of the stems of water plants. The central portion was so open as to allow the water to pass through readily. The tube was strong and tight and was covered with bits of leaves and twigs. It was open at either end. On the surface of a rock about 18 inches in diameter 166 of these nets were counted. At this portion of the stream the larvæ of a *Simulium* (probably *S. venustum*, Say) were very abundant. They occurred chiefly on the small water plants which grow in these rapid places, and were found in considerable numbers on the surface of the rocks on which the cases of *Hydropsyche* occurred. They must have been washed into the mouths of these nets in great numbers, and probably furnished the principal food of the carnivorous larvæ. The *Hydropsyche* larvæ (Plate IX, Fig. 3, and enlarged head, Fig. 4) were very active and difficult to capture, unless the stones were removed entire from the water. Placed in standing water they fought vigorously with each other, and after a lapse of twenty-four hours did not seem appreciably affected by the want of fresh water.

Miss Cora H. Clarke has described the nets of a similar species of *Hydropsyche* (Proc. Bost. Soc. Nat. Hist., vol. 22, May 24, 1882), but does not mention the insects which formed the food of the larvæ observed by her.

DESCRIPTIVE.

There are some characters which these two species possess in common with all other species of the genus, though scarcely any of the described species are known in both sexes. It may be well to state, therefore, that the male differs markedly from the female in his much smaller abdomen and relatively larger thorax, by the mouth parts being soft and subobsolete, and more particularly by the eyes being confluent and having two well-marked and distinct sets of facets. As we have already stated, the male is not found flying with the female, and we should not have obtained this sex in the two species here treated of had they not been bred from the larvæ. It is desirable to describe both sexes from fresh and living specimens, as they become sordid in alcohol, and shrink and lose much of their character and color when mounted dry. The females are also somewhat altered in appearance after having been gorged with blood. The prothoracic is the only spiracle traceable in the insects of this genus.

The larvæ of all the species known have very much the same general form and structure, and they differ chiefly in some of the details of the flabelliform fan and of the mouth parts.

The pupa in form foreshadows that of the future fly, and the species differ in this state chiefly in the number of filaments or ramifications thereof that compose the breathing organs. These are invariably situated, one on each side, upon the anterior dorsal margin of the thorax, each originating in a single trunk, which soon branches into rays which are fine hollow tubes, apparently composed of rings, and closed at their extremities. Each tube consists, further, of one or two chitinous layers covered by a finely granulated material. In both the species under consideration there are two of these chitinous layers, of which the inner is very thin and smooth, the outer thicker and furnished with pores. The base of the trunk connects by a stigma-like ring with a true spiral tracheal tube visible beneath the epidermis, and which, bending suddenly inwards, contracts and connects with the internal tracheal system of the corresponding side.[*] At the tip of the last abdominal segment, upon the dorsal surface, are two hooks, which engage in the meshes of the cocoon, to hold the pupa in position. Some few threads of loose silk and the old larval skin are also found in this situation. Minute black hooks, arranged in regular and definite order upon the dorsal and ventral surface of the abdomen, assist the pupa to keep its position inside the open cocoon. These hooks are usually bent upwards.

The cocoons of the various species differ from each other both by their structure and by the method by which they are fastened to plants, stones, &c. Generally speaking, the cocoon is a brownish, obconical, semi-transparent pouch, open above, more or less covered with mud, and directed against the current of the water. The pupa is more or less tightly surrounded by it, and has the anterior portion protruding above the rim of the pouch. The cocoons are formed of irregular threads, which harden rapidly in the water, and in the deeper parts of the cocoons there are also some long loose and disconnected threads.

---

[*] Dr. Vogel, in his description of the tracheal tubes of the pupae of *Simulium*, gives a similar description, stating that, contrary to the published opinion of Siebold, there are no tracheæ inside the tubes.—Mittheilungen der Schweizerischen Ent. Ges., Vol. VII, Heft 7.

SIMULIUM PECUARUM, n. sp.— ♀. (Plate VIII, Fig. 3, and dorsal view, Fig. 5). Length, 2.5 ᵐᵐ to 4 ᵐᵐ. *Head* (Plate VIII, Fig. 2), uniform grayish-slate, clothed with short yellowish hair, which becomes longer behind the eyes; eyes black, with coppery or brassy reflections; *antennæ* black, with whitish pubescence, and with a few bristles on two basal joints, which are tinged with red; joints 1 to 11 gradually diminishing in thickness towards the last, joint 1 shortest, joints 2 and 3 twice as long as joint 1, joints 4, 5, and 6 as long as joint 1, joints 7, 8, 9, and 10 gradually increasing in length, last joint fusiform, twice as long as joint 10; maxillary palpi a little longer than antennæ, blackish, with long grayish bristles. *Thorax* grayish-slate, more or less densely covered with short yellow hairs, and with usually very distinct markings, consisting of two mediodorsal and two subdorsal, broad, longitudinal, sooty-black bands, of which the latter curve to posterior edge of patagium, which is reddish at tip; lateral edges of prothorax with fine black sutures; under side of thorax uniform grayish-slate, with sparse yellow hairs; space around the one large stigma lighter; halteres opaque, reddish-white; legs uniform reddish-brown, densely covered with yellowish hairs; tips of tarsi blackish; wings subhyaline, larger veins and base reddish-brown. *Abdomen* nine-jointed; joints subequal in length, except the last 2, which decrease in length; a longitudinal, broad bluish-gray dorsal band extends from near base of segment 2, where it is broadest, to the tip, curving downward to the anterior lateral edge of segment 7, below this band laterally the color is blackish-brown, with the exception of a broad bluish-gray transverse band on the posterior edge of each of segments 1 to 6; under side of abdomen uniform brownish-gray, without markings; abdomen densely covered with yellowish hair, which is very long upon the posterior edge of segment 1, forming an overlapping fringe.

♂.—Length varying from 1.5ᵐᵐ to 2.2ᵐᵐ. Differs considerably from female. *Head* (Plate VIII, Fig. 1,) not visible from above, being occupied by the very large confluent eyes ; the remaining parts below the eyes are black, with black hairs and bristles ; eyes composed of two different kinds of facets, those above being very large, as large again as those of the female, and those in front and surrounding the dwarfed trophi very minute, the dividing line between the two sizes being abrupt [the figure is not accurate] ; antennæ similar to those of female, more pronounced in color, both the black and reddish being more vivid ; maxillary palpi black, and shorter than the antennæ. *Thorax* black above, with sparse yellow hairs; legs somewhat lighter in color, tips of tarsi not black ; hairs upon legs longer than in those of female. *Wings* hyaline, veins and base yellowish-brown. *Abdomen* black, with grayish-white posterior margins to segments, dorsally and laterally, and covered with longer yellowish hairs.

Described from two bred specimens.

Larva (Plate VI, Fig. 1 and Fig. 2, showing head in three positions).—Average length when full grown, 7ᵐᵐ to 8ᵐᵐ. Subcylindrical, the club-shaped posterior third of body being twice as stout as the thoracic joints, and joint 4 the most constricted. Translucent when living, dirty white in alcohol; immaculate in a very few specimens ; distinctly marked in the great majority with brownish dorsal cross-bands in middle of joints, leaving free a white mediodorsal longitudinal line ; thoracic joints with three irregular rings of the same color ; under side more or less irregularly spotted with brown. *Head* subquadrate, horny, yellowish-brown, with a number of brown spots and lines in regular order (as in figure) and two roundish approximate ocellate black dots on each side under the skin, and seemingly rudimentary organs of sight, from which the future compound eyes originate: *antennæ* (Plate VI, Fig. 5 *a*) uniformly pale, three-jointed, about one-third as long as greatest width of head; joint 1 very stout, fully four times as thick as 2, which is a little longer than 1, straight, slightly tapering towards tip, joint 3 extremely small, a mere triangular tip: *mentum* (Plate VI, Fig. 3 *a*) subtriangular, with apex cut away and replaced by three groups of very small teeth, of which the central group consists of three teeth, the middle one largest, and the groups on side, of four teeth, of which the second from center is largest; sides of mentum, near apex, with two small teeth each; all the teeth are chitinous and black; a long erect bristle, pointing upward and inward, near each side of mentum: *labrum* (Plate VI, Fig. 3 *b*) horny densely covered with hair: *mandibles* (Plate VI, Fig. 5 *b* and *c*) resembling in shape the profile of the inverted last joint of the human thumb, with a series of teeth in place of the nail; teeth difficult to see, owing to the presence of five distinct brushes of hair; upon extreme lower tip of mandibles three large teeth, below them a series of eleven slender and very pointed teeth, of which the first two are the smallest, teeth 3 to 9 increasing and teeth 10 and 11 gradually decreasing in length; a second series of teeth below them consists of two triangular teeth, of which the first is largest: *maxilla* (Plate VI, Fig. 6) stout, fleshy, with an internal thumb-shaped lobe; *maxillary palpus* two-jointed, first joint cylindrical, second very short, crowned with a regular circular

REPORT OF THE ENTOMOLOGIST. 513

row of short spines or warts: *labium* (Plate VI, Fig. 3 c) horny, with two brushes of hair above, between which is a very small *ligula* covered with a small brush of hairs; *fans* (Plate VII, Fig. 1) composed of a stout stem, bearing about forty-six scythe-shaped rays, lined on the inside by very minute, equidistant, erect hairs of equal length. *Thoracic proleg* (Plate VI, Fig. 4) faintly four-jointed, subconical, retractile (introversible), very thin and transparent, crowned with about twenty rows of short, sharp hooks, apparently arranged in a circular manner; the hooks, of which ten are in each row, seem to be movable to a certain extent, and are fastened or hinged to small chitinous rods in the epidermis. *Tip of abdomen* (Plate VI, Fig. 7) formed by a subcylindrical body, crowned with rows of hooks. *Breathing organs* below these hooks and on the upper side of abdomen; they consist of three short, cylindrical, soft and retractile tentacles, which connect with the large internal tracheæ (Plate VI, Fig. 7).

In full-grown larvæ a spot more or less dark (as in our figure) is seen on each side of thoracic joint; it is produced by the formation of the coiled breathing tubes of the future pupa.

Pupa.—Average length, 5^{mm}. General color, when fresh, honey yellow; prothoracic filaments brown, and the abdomen dorsally also tinged with brown, except a mediodorsal space; all the members have also a fine brown marginal line. Prothoracic filaments consisting of six main rays issuing from the basal prominence and subdivided two or three times, so that in most cases as many as forty-eight terminal filaments can be counted. Abdominal joints 3, 4, and 5, each with eight well-separated dark-brown and anteriorly-recurved hooks (Plate VI, Fig. 8), the four on each side separated by a mediodorsal space; those on joint 3 less conspicuous than those on joints 4 and 5; joint 6 without armature; joints 7, 8, 9, and also subjoint less distinctly armed near anterior margin with a continuous dorsal row of very minute posteriorly recurved points; ventrally joints 6, 7, and 8 have each four very minute anteriorly recurved hooks.

Cocoon.—Average length, 3.5^{mm}. Not completely made and not entirely covering the pupa, but tightly surrounding its larger portion. Shape very irregular, with no distinct rim at the upper edge, which is more or less ragged. The threads composing it are very coarse, and the meshes rather open and ordinarily filled with mud. Not always fastened separately to objects, but frequently crowded together, without forming, however, such coral-like aggregations as in some of the Northern species.

SIMULIUM MERIDIONALE, n. sp.— ♀. Length, 2.5^{mm} to 3^{mm}. (Plate VIII, Fig. 6.) *Head* uniform slate-blue, verging to greenish or cerulean blue in some lights, clothed with silvery pubescence, which becomes longer behind the eyes; parts below antennæ and trophi more densely pubescent, producing the effect of a white face; eyes with a metallic, coppery luster; antennæ black, with very dense white pubescence; no bristles on basal two joints, which are but very slightly tinged with red; joint 1 shortest; joints 2, 3, and 11 subequal in length; joint 3 widest; joints 4 to 9 subequal in length; joint 10 but slightly shorter than joint 11, which is fusiform; joints 3 to 11 gradually decreasing in width; maxillary palpi as long as antennæ, blackish, with long whitish bristles. *Thorax* slate-blue, with less dense silvery-white pubescence; markings quite distinct, producing the effect of a sculpture, and consisting of three black longitudinal lines, the median narrow, widening a little at apex, and the outer ones curving inwards at base and outwards near apex, sometimes reaching to base of patagium, which appears whitish on account of dense pubescence; on the lateral edges of prothorax are fine black sutures; under side uniform slate-blue, with sparse pubescence; space around the large stigma almost white; halteres white, very faintly tinged with red. *Abdomen* nine-jointed, joints subequal in length, except the last two, which decrease; markings entirely different from those of *S. pecuarum*, formed by velvety black, dark blue and bluish-white, almost silvery, colors; the dark blue appears upon dorsal surface of the last five segments, spreading from a roundish median spot on 5 to the immaculate blue of the last two segments; segments 2, 3, and 4 have each a black cross-bar, and 5, 6, and 7 two narrow black submedian stripes, which disappear almost entirely upon 7; the bluish-white forms an outer edge to all the black and extends over the whole lower surface of abdomen, with the exception of more or less well-marked black cross-lines in middle of each segment; a bluish-white or silvery pubescence covers the entire abdomen, but is very sparse upon the dorsal parts. *Legs* brownish-black; tarsi almost black, and more or less densely covered with whitish hairs. *Wings* subhyaline, veins bluish-white, base ferruginous.

Described from many bred and captured specimens.

♂.—(Plate VIII, Fig. 4.) Length 1.5^{mm} to 2^{mm}. Very different in appearance from female. *Eyes* confluent, very large, brilliant coppery; a very marked difference in the size of the facets, those on upper surface being very large and metallic-coppery, those below and surrounding trophi becoming suddenly small, black, with bronze

33 AG—'86

reflections; *trophi* reddish-black, dwarfed; *antennæ* black, with light yellowish-brown pubescence in front. *Thorax* above intense black, velvety, with a bluish luster; under side grayish. *Legs* reddish, with black tarsi; *wings* hyaline, veins and base bluish-white. *Abdomen* above black, with posterior margins of segments edged with gray; under side of segments 2 and 3 light reddish-gray, the others blackish with gray posterior margins. Sexual organs black. Thorax and abdomen very sparsely clothed with white pubescence. •

Described from three bred specimens.

Larva.—(Plate VII, Fig. 2.) Length when full-grown 5.5^{mm} to 7^{mm}. Normal shape and general appearance. Differs from *S. pecuarum* by the much more irregular markings of segments and head. A majority of the larvæ possess one or two lateral spots on club-shaped posterior third of body. *Head* lacks the regular arrangement of spots and lines, which become confused; the two black spots on each side present. *Antennæ* (Plate VII, Fig. 3a) uniformly pale, much longer than in *pecuarum*, slender and 3-jointed; first joint almost twice as long as joints 2 and 3 together, and a little bent; at base three times and at tip twice as thick as second joint, which is nearly uniform in width, tapering but very slightly towards tip; joint 3 small and pointed, about one-fifth as long as joint 2. *Mentum* (Plate VII, Fig. 4) similar to that of *S. pecuarum*, but distinguished by a flatter apex, by the possession of three erect bristles on each side, starting from round pores, which decrease in size towards base; a fourth very small bristle close to base and in line with the bristles above; the sides of mentum have on each side four sharp teeth. *Labrum* and *labium* not different from those of *pecuarum*. *Mandibles* (Plate VII, Fig. 3b and 3c) possess but seven teeth in first row; the three first nearly uniform in length; teeth 4 to 7 gradually decrease in length; tooth 4 much the longest of all; the two teeth in second row similar to those of *pecuarum*. *Maxillæ* and *maxillary palpus* also similar. *Fans* similar, but the hairs lining the inside of the scythe-shaped rays are thicker and nearer together. *Proleg* more slender; last joint bearing a crown of hooks, usually bent suddenly toward head. Tip of abdomen similar to that of *pecuarum*. *Breathing organs* (Plate VII, Fig. 5) quite different; the three main trunks branch each six times, and the branches enter the trunk from both sides. Full-grown larvæ show also the newly formed coiled breathing tubes of the pupæ through their skin.

Described from many specimens.

Pupa.—(Plate VII, Fig. 6.) Average length, 3.5^{mm}. Shape and coloration as in *S. pecuarum*. The thoracic filaments consist only of the six original rays, which do not branch. Upon dorsal surface of the posterior margins of abdominal joints 4 and 5 is a row of eight anteriorly curved hooks similar to those of *pecuarum*, but none on joint 3; anterior margins of joint 9 and of subjoint with a continuous row of smaller anteriorly curved hooks; joints 7 and 8 unarmed dorsally; ventrally joints 6, 7, and 8 have each four minor hooks.

Cocoon.—(Plate VII, Fig. 6.) Length, 3.5^{mm}. Neater than that of any other species known to me, being formed of fine threads, lined with gelatinous ones. The web is quite dense, uniform, with well-defined, sometimes thickened rims. The cocoon is always securely fastened singly to leaf or stick, and even if many are fastened upon the same leaf they do not crowd each other. It fits snugly about the pupa, which is so securely anchored inside as to be with difficulty extricated.

REMEDIES TRIED AND PROPOSED AGAINST THE LARVÆ.

The results of a number of different experiments with insecticides upon the larvæ of the Buffalo Gnats made by Mr. Lugger during the early spring indicates that it is nearly if not quite impossible to reduce their numbers by killing them in the streams. To attempt to do so when all these streams are swollen, and frequently from 10 to 20 yards wide and half as deep, would be sheer waste of time. When the water is very low and much more sluggish in its motion, thus bringing the chemicals in contact with the larvæ, an application of them might be more effective. Great caution must be used in any efforts in this direction, however, as both man and beast are in many localities entirely dependent upon these streams for their water supply and the introduction of poisonous substances might cause much trouble.

Some of the experiments were made by confining the larvæ in glass tubes and submitting them to a current of water to which the following decoctions and solutions had been added, viz: China berries, salt, lime, sulphur, tar water, kerosene emulsion, and carbon-bisul-

phide. Strong tar water killed them; diluted it proved harmless.
Kerosene emulsion diluted to contain 5 per cent. kerosene was effective; three ounces of carbon-bisulphide in 7 quarts of water proved
fatal within ten minutes; the other insecticides were ineffective. It
would be very costly to put enough of these materials in the water
to produce the desired effect.

Other experiments in smaller creeks, in which numerous larvæ of
the Turkey Gnat were observed, were carried out in a different way.
The materials tried were freshly burned lime, emulsion of kerosene,
powdered pyrethrum, carbon-bisulphide, powdered cocculus indicus,
and tobacco soap. With the exception of the lime, which was thrown
into the water in pieces of the size of an Irish potato, all the others
were in a watery solution or suspension. Repeated trials with all the
chemicals produced the same effect. As soon as the larvæ came in
contact with any of the insecticides they would immediately loosen
their hold upon the leaf and drop down-stream. When the insecticides became so much diluted as not to incommode the larvæ any
longer, these would again fasten to leaves. By using a larger amount
of the various substances many larvæ were killed, as well as most of
the small fish and aquatic insects.

But if the breeding-places in the creeks have to be searched out to
apply the insecticides, it would be much more simple to remove all
the logs, sticks, and leaves. All the fences across the branches should
be removed, or rather should be replaced by wire fences, which would
neither impede the current nor catch as many sticks and leaves. Logs
and larger twigs, if not embedded too deep in the mud of the creek
bed or banks, will always be removed by any high water; a very common occurrence in the Buffalo Gnat region. Old leaves, made heavy
by the adhering mud, would also be carried away by any high water
if the obstructions in these creeks were removed, and with these sticks
and leaves many if not most of the larvæ would be carried away
either into the main rivers or the lower level of the creeks or lakes,
where there is no current and where they would soon perish.

If the general opinion that broken levees are to blame for the destructive swarms of Buffalo Gnats prove to be the correct one, the
restoration of such levees would, within a few years at most, restore
the former immunity from these insects. This time would be materially hastened by the removal of obstructions in all such parts of the
bayous where they would come in contact with the swiftest current.

OVERFLOWS AND BUFFALO GNATS.

It is very generally claimed by the inhabitants of the infested region that as long as the States bordering upon the Mississippi River
had a perfect levee system, which prevented the water from escaping
into the inland bayous, no damage was occasioned by Buffalo Gnats,
not even in districts now badly infested. It is further claimed that
the Buffalo Gnats appear with every overflow, and only with an overflow if such overflow occur at the proper season and with the proper
temperature, viz, during the first continuous warm days of March,
April, or May.

The chronological data already given seem to prove such assertions
correct. Too much weight should not, however, be attached to these
data. The region is as yet rather thinly settled, and no systematic
records of the appearance of Buffalo Gnats in injurious numbers have
ever been kept. A general and widespread appearance of these

insects seems to take place, however, only during an inundation, and, granting the connection between the two phenomena, the causes for it are yet obscure. It was by the elucidation of this problem that we hoped to discover some means of preventing the injury of the flies by preventing the multiplication of the larvæ.

Inundations in the lower Mississippi Valley are not occasioned by local rains, but by the immense volume of water brought down by the river and its more northern tributaries, and such overflows first take place in the northern regions infested by the Buffalo Gnats, and not in the southern. The earlier appearance of these insects in the South would seem to invalidate the prevailing belief that an overflow brings them. Similar conditions prevail in Hungary, where a closely allied insect does so much injury to all kinds of live stock. There the gnats appear every spring in varying numbers, forming local swarms which move about with the wind: but no general invasion takes place until the river Danube inundates the region infested.

Is it not probable that swarms of these gnats are forced by the conditions consequent upon an inundation to extend their flight beyond their usual haunts to the more elevated and drier regions, and that in this fact we have at least one of the causes of the connection? Small swarms, otherwise local and unobserved, would thus, during a period of high water, be forced to band together in such immense armies. There must be other reasons, not yet clearly demonstrated, why these insects appear in such vast swarms with an overflow, and this problem can only be solved by a critical study of many breeding-places during several seasons over the whole region involved.

Some peculiarities of the swarms of Buffalo Gnats have been observed, and these may, by closer study in future, throw some light upon the problem. It is to be noted that all the specimens composing these swarms are females, and that not one male has been found among them either here or in Europe. There is every reason to believe that none of the females composing the blood-thirsty swarms return to the localities where they were born and developed. Experience indicates that once gorged with blood they die. The swarms dwindle in proportion as they are carried away or move from their breeding-places.

Close investigation with the microscope has failed to reveal any eggs in the ovaries of the females composing these swarms, and if they deposit eggs at all it is before congregating to attack animals.

These singular facts invite speculation and theory, but it were unwise to indulge in these before we have learned more about the eggs, when and where deposited, and whether the females depositing them are in any way different from those comprising the swarms. Dr. Fritz Müller has published in the *Archivos do Museu Nacional do Rio de Janeiro*, Vol. IV, p. 47, pl. IV–VII, * some very interesting observations on another fly (*Paltosoma torrentium*), the larva of which is only found in the torrents and cascades of certain streams descending the mountains of Brazil. There the pupæ fastened by the flat venter to the rocks under water, and change into the perfect flies. He found by opening the mature pupæ that there are always two forms of females associated with one form of male. The one form of female possesses a rudimentary mouth, only fit to sip

---

* Reviews of his paper appeared in *Kosmos*, Vol. VIII, pp. 37–42; *Nature*, July 7, 1881, p. 214; *Entomologist's Monthly Magazine*, February, 1881, p. 206 and pp. 180–182, and March, 1881, pp. 225, 226.

honey while the other has a mouth well adapted to penetrate, the skin of warm-blooded animals and to suck blood.

The male *Simulium*, so far as known, is only found near where it developed. The structure of its mouth prevents it from biting, and it shows no inclination to join the roving swarms of females. Hence pairing of the sexes must take place in the vicinity of birth, and the eggs are probably deposited soon afterwards. It is also possible, as in the case of other Diptera, that the eggs are already well developed in the pupa.

The condition of the inundated region forbids an indiscriminate selection of places to deposit in, since the young larvæ must in time find suitable swift currents of water after the subsidence to the normal level. Such breeding-places we hope to be able to map out in future.

It has also been claimed that a number of successive broods of the Buffalo Gnat appear in early spring. If such were the case the relationship between the presence of the gnats and an overflow could be very readily imagined; but we have already shown that there is absolutely no proof thus far of more than one annual brood.

Mr. Webster, while studying in the neighborhood of Vicksburg last spring, was impressed with the idea that the connection between the *Simulium* increase and overflows was dependent upon the condition of the levees, in that the river water in swelling the waters of the bayous not only creates a stronger current in the main bayou, but brings the current in contact with many trees and shrubs, as well as stumps and vines, along the bayous, thereby offering much greater chance for the larvæ to attach themselves.

While we were at first inclined to give some weight to this view, and it seemed to afford an additional important argument in favor of keeping the levees in good condition, a survey of the whole field leads us to abandon this as the most important cause in the increase of the gnats during the period of the overflow, and to adopt the theory already advanced, viz, that the connection is at least partly due to the gnats being driven by the advancing waters from the lower to the higher lands.

Another theory, not supplanting this last but supplementing it, we would advance here: There is no doubt but that the advance of the waters from the main river and their commingling with the clearer streams and tributaries carry a suddenly increased food-supply, in the way of minute crustacea and other aquatic creatures, to the *Simulium* larvæ just at the season when these are about to transform. It is quite probable that development in these larvæ remains more or less latent or stationary during the cold winter months or when the water in which they occur is depleted of minute animal life, and that a sudden access of food would accelerate the final transformations.

A possible third connection between the overflow and this increase may arise from the fact that the larvæ, when the water rises, leave their attachments, or that the débris upon which they are fastened becomes itself started by the flood current, and that in consequence the larvæ from hundreds of smaller streams and tributaries are carried away by the rising water and impelled into the current of the large streams, by which they may be carried for many miles, spreading out at last in the overflowed region at just the time when they are ready for their final transformations. On this theory the larvæ from regions far distant become massed in the overflowed region and vastly augment the numbers which have naturally bred there.

THE FALL WEB-WORM.

(*Hyphantria cunea*, Drury.)*

Order LEPIDOPTERA; family BOMBYCIDÆ.

[Plates X and XI.]

This insect has from time to time attracted general attention by its great injuries to both fruit and shade trees. Many authors have written about it, and consequently it has received quite a number of different names. The popular name "Fall Web-worm," first given to it by Harris, in his "Insects injurious to Vegetation," is sufficiently appropriate as indicating the season when the webs are most numerous. The term is, however, most expressive for the New England and other Northern States, where the insect is single-brooded, appearing there during August and September, while in more southern regions it is double-brooded. In our third Missouri report we first called attention to its double-broodedness at Saint Louis, and we find that it is invariably two-brooded at Baltimore and Washington. Except in seasons of extreme increase, however, the first brood does no widespread damage, while the Fall brood nearly always attracts attention.

We have decided to call attention to this insect somewhat in detail in this report because of its exceptional prevalence and injury in the Atlantic States during the year 1886, and because it became a public nuisance in the city of Washington, and the District Commissioners have formally requested information from us on the subject.

NATURAL HISTORY.

LIMITATION OF BROODS.—At Washington we may say in general that the first brood appears soon after the leaves have fully developed, and numerous webs can be found about the first of June, while the second brood appears from the middle of July on through August and September. In Massachusetts and other Northern States the first moths issue in June and July; the caterpillars hatch from the last of June until the middle of August, reach full growth and wander about seeking places for transformation from the end of August to the end of September.

The species invariably hibernates in the chrysalis state within its cocoon, and the issuing of the first brood of moths is, as a consequence, tolerably regular as to time, *i. e.*, they will be found issuing and flying slowly about during the evening, and more particularly

---

* We have adopted the name *Hyphantria cunea*, following Clemens's reasons for separating *Hyphantria* from *Spilosoma*. He shows (Proc. Ac. Nat. Sci. Phil., 1860, p. 530) that, while agreeing in the wings, *Hyphantria* differs in the labial palpi, the second joint of which is very short and the terminal joint nearly rudimentary, and in the hind tibiæ, which have but one pair of small apical spurs.
The following is the synonymy of the species:
Phalæna (Bombyx) cunea Drury, 1782.
Phalæna punctatissima Abbott and Smith, 1797.
Cycnia cunea Huebner, 1821.
Spilosoma cunea (Drury), Westwood's Ed. Drury, 1837.
Hyphantria textor Harris, 1841.
Euproctis textor (Harris); Walker, 1855.
Hyphantria punctata Fitch, 1856.
Hyphantria textor Harris, Clemens, 1861.
Spilosoma cunea Drury, Brooklyn Soc. Check-list of Macro-Lep., 1882.
Hyphantria cunea (Drury), Grote's Check-list, 1882.

at night, during the whole month of May, the bulk of them early or late in the month, according as the season may be early or late. They couple and oviposit very soon after issuing, and in ordinary seasons we may safely count on the bulk of the eggs being laid by the end of May.   During the month of June the moths become scarcer, and the bulk of them have perished by the middle of that month, while the webs of the caterpillars become more and more conspicuous.   The second brood of moths begins to appear in July, and its occurrence extends over a longer period than is the case with the first or spring brood.   The second brood of caterpillars may be found from the end of July to the end of September, hatching most extensively, however, about the first of August.

In Massachusetts and other Northern States the first moths issue in June and July; the caterpillars hatch from the last of June until the middle of August, reach full growth, and wander about seeking places for transformation from the end of August to the end of September.

The following general remarks upon the different stages refer to Washington and localities where the same conditions hold.

THE EGGS (Plate X, Fig. 3a).—The female moth deposits her eggs in a cluster on a leaf, sometimes upon the upper and sometimes on the lower side, usually near the end of a branch.   Each cluster consists of a great many eggs, which are deposited close together and sparsely interspersed with hair-like scales.   In three instances those deposited by a single female were counted.   The result was 394, 427, and 502, or an average of 441 eggs.   But in addition to such large clusters each female will deposit eggs in smaller and less regular patches, so that at least 500 eggs may be considered as the real number produced by a single individual.   The egg, measuring 0.4^{mm}, is of a bright golden-yellow color, quite globular, and ornamented by numerous regular pits, which give it under a magnifying lens the appearance of a beautiful golden thimble.   As the eggs approach the time of hatching this color disappears and gives place to a dull, leaden hue.

The interval between the time of depositing and hatching of the eggs for the first brood varies considerably, and the latter may be greatly retarded by inclement weather.   Usually, however, not more than ten days are consumed in maturing the embryo within.   The eggs of the summer brood seldom require more than one week to hatch.

Without check the offspring of one female moth might in a single season (assuming one-half of her progeny to be female and barring all checks) number 125,000 caterpillars in early Fall—enough to ruin the shade trees of many a fine street.

THE LARVÆ (Plate X, Figs. 2a, 2b, and 2c).—The caterpillars just born are pale yellow, with two rows of black marks along the body, a black head, and with quite sparse hairs.   When full grown they generally appear pale yellowish or greenish, with a broad dusky stripe along the back and a yellow stripe along the sides; they are covered with whitish hairs, which spring from black and orange-yellow warts. The caterpillar is, however, very variable both as to depth of coloring and as to markings.   Close observations have failed to show that different food produces changes in the coloration; in fact, nearly all the various color varieties may be found upon the same tree.   The fall generation is, however, on the whole, darker, with browner hairs, than the spring generation.

As soon as the young caterpillars hatch they immediately go to work to spin a small silken web for themselves, which by their united efforts soon grows large enough to be noticed upon the trees. Under this protecting shelter they feed in company, at first devouring only the green upper portions of the leaf, and leaving the veins and lower skin unmolested. As they increase in size they enlarge their web by connecting it with the adjoining leaves and twigs; thus as they gradually work downwards their web becomes quite bulky, and, as it is filled with brown and skeletonized leaves and other discolored matter as well as with their old skins, it becomes quite an unpleasant feature in our public thoroughfares and parks. The caterpillars always feed underneath these webs; but as soon as they approach maturity, which requires about one month, they commence to scatter about, searching for suitable places in which to spin their cocoons. If very numerous upon the same tree the food-supply gives out, and they are forced by hunger to leave their sheltering homes before the usual time.

When the young caterpillars are forced to leave their web they do not drop suddenly to the ground, but suspend themselves by a fine silken thread, by means of which they easily recover the tree. Grown caterpillars, which measure 1.11 inches in length, do not spin such a thread. Both young and old ones drop themselves to the ground without spinning when disturbed or sorely pressed by hunger.

PUPA AND COCOON (Plate X, Figs. 2d and 2e).—Favorite recesses selected for pupation are the crevices in bark and similar shelters above ground, in some cases even the empty cocoons of other moths.* The angles of tree-boxes, the rubbish collected around the base of trees and other like shelter are employed for this purpose, while the second brood prefer to bury themselves just under the surface of the ground, provided that the earth be soft enough for that purpose. The cocoon itself is thin and almost transparent, and is composed of a slight web of silk intermixed with a few hairs, or mixed with sand if made in the soil.

The pupa is of a very dark-brown color, smooth and polished, and faintly punctuate. It is characterized by a swelling or bulging about the middle. It is 0.60 inch long and 0.23 inch broad in the middle of its body.

THE MOTH (Plate X, Figs. 1 a–j, and 2f).—The moths vary greatly, both in size and coloration. They have, in consequence of such variations, received many names, such as *cunea* Drury, *textor* Harr., *punctata* Fitch, *punctatissima* Smith. But there is no doubt, as proven from frequent breeding of specimens, that all these names apply to the very same insect, or at most to slight varieties, and that Drury's name *cunea*, having priority, must be used for the species.

The most frequent form observed in the vicinity of Washington is white, with a very slight fulvous shade. It has immaculate wings, tawny-yellow front thighs, and blackish feet. In some specimens the tawny thighs have a large black spot, while the shanks on the upper surface are rufous. In many all the thighs are tawny-yellow, while in others they have scarcely any color. Some specimens (often reared from the same lot of larvæ) have two tolerably distinct spots on each front wing, one at base of fork on the costal nerve and one just within the second furcation of the median nerve. Other specimens, again, have their wings spotted all over and approach the form *punctatissima*, described as the Many-spotted Ermine-moth of the Southern

---

* We have known the substantial cocoon of *Cerura* to be used for this purpose.

States. The wings of the moths expand from one inch and a quarter to one inch and three-eighths. The male moth, which is usually a little smaller, has its antennæ doubly feathered beneath, while those of the female possess instead two rows of minute teeth.

The pupa state lasts from six to eight days for the summer brood, while the hibernating brood, however, requires as many months, according to the latitude.

INJURY DONE IN 1886.

During the past year the city of Washington, as well as its vicinity, was entirely overrun by the caterpillars. With the exception of trees and plants the foliage of which was not agreeable to the taste of this insect, all vegetation suffered greatly. The appended list of trees, shrubs, and other plants shows that comparatively few kinds escaped entirely. The fine rows of shade trees which grace all the streets and avenues appeared leafless and covered with throngs of the hairy worms. Excepting on the very tall trees, in which the highest branches showed a few leaves too high for the caterpillars to reach, not a vestige of foliage could be seen. The trees were not alone bare, but were still more disfigured by old and new webs made by the caterpillars, in which bits of leaves and leaf-stems, as well as the dried frass, had collected, producing a very unpleasant sight. The pavements were also constantly covered with this unsightly frass, and the empty skins of the various molts the caterpillars had to undergo were drifted about with every wind and collected in masses in corners and tree-boxes. The parks fared a little better. Because of the great variety of trees planted there some escaped entirely, while others showed the effect of the united efforts of so many hungry caterpillars only in a more or less severe degree. The grassy spots surrounding the different groups of trees had also a protective influence, since the caterpillars do not like to travel over grass, except when prompted by a too ravenous hunger. The rapid increase of this insect is materially assisted by the peculiar method of selecting shade trees for the city. Every street has but one kind of shade tree; rows of them extend for miles, and the trees are planted so close together that their branches almost interlace. Thus there is no obstacle at all to the rapid increase and distribution of the caterpillars. If different kinds of trees had been planted so as to alternate, less trouble might be experienced. Plate XI shows a view of Fourteenth street, taken in late September, which illustrates the point, the Poplars on the west side being completely defoliated as far as the eye can reach, while the Maples on the east are almost untouched.

As long as the caterpillars were young and still small the different communities remained under cover of their webs and only offended the eye; but as soon as they reached maturity and commenced to scatter, prompted by the desire to find suitable places to spin their cocoons and transform to pupæ, matters became more unpleasant and complaints were heard from all those who had to pass such infested trees. In many localities no one could walk without stepping upon caterpillars; they dropped upon every one and every thing; they entered flower and vegetable gardens, porches and verandas, and the house itself, and became, in fact, a general nuisance.

The chief damage done to vegetation was confined to the city itself, although the caterpillars extended some distance into the surrounding country. There, however, they were more local and almost entirely confined to certain trees, and mainly so to the White Poplar and the Cotton-wood. Along the Baltimore and Potomac Railroad tracks these trees were defoliated as far as five miles from the Capitol. In Georgetown the caterpillars were equally noxious, but in the adjoining forests but very few webs could be seen.

The proportionate injury to any given species of tree is to some extent a matter of chance; and in some respects a year of great injury, as 1886, is not a good year to study the preferences of a species, because when hard pressed for food the caterpillars will feed upon almost any plant, though it is questionable whether they can mature and transform on those which they take to only under the influence of such absolute necessity. Again, the preference shown for particular trees is more the result of the preference of the parent moth than of its progeny in a case of so general a feeder as the Fall Web-worm. We had a very good illustration of this in Atlantic City last autumn. The caterpillars were exceedingly abundant during autumn along this portion of the Atlantic coast, especially on the trees above named. We studied particularly their ways upon one tree that was totally defoliated by September 11. The bulk of the caterpillars were then just through their last molt, though others were of all ages, illustrating different hatchings. There was an instinctive migration of these larvæ of all sizes, and the strength of their food-habit once acquired from birth upon a particular tree was well illustrated. At first the worms passed over various adjacent plants, like Honeysuckles, Roses, &c., the leaves of which they freely devour if hatched upon them; but as the migrating swarm became pressed with hunger they finally fell upon these, and even upon plants like the Peach and Ailanthus, which ordinarily are passed over. They would even pounce upon any food, and a rotten apple placed in their way was soon literally swarming with them and sucked dry.

In a general way it may be stated that conifers, grapes, and most herbaceous plants are free from their attacks, and it is very doubtful whether the species can mature upon them.

The list of plants which follows is arranged according to the relative damage to the foliage in the city of Washington. The three first named are most subject to attack, and in fact are almost always defoliated.

PROPORTIONATE INJURY TO DIFFERENT PLANTS AND SHADE TREES.

The damage done in the city of Washington was exceptional, but so was also the general damage throughout the New England States, if not throughout the country. In New England the greater predilection which the species showed for Poplar, Cottonwood, and the ranker growing Willows was everywhere manifest, and so much was this the case, that the destruction of the first brood on these trees would have substantially lessened the damage to other trees.

Plants marked 1 have lost from 75 to 100 per cent. of their foliage.
Plants marked 2 have lost from 50 to 75 per cent. of their foliage.
Plants marked 3 have lost from 25 to 50 per cent. of their foliage.
Plants marked 4 have lost from 1 to 25 per cent. of their foliage.
Plants marked with two figures have shown the relative immunity or injury indicated by both, the variation being in individual trees.

1. *Negundo aceroides* Mœnch.   (Box Elder.)
1. *Populus alba* L.   (European White Poplar.)
1. *Populus monilifera* Ait.   (Cottonwood.)

1-2. *Populus balsamifera* L.   (Balsam Poplar.)
1-2. *Populus tremuloides* Mich'x.   (American Aspen.)
1-2. *Fraxinus americana* L.   (White Ash.)
1-2. *Fraxinus excelsior* L.   (European Ash.)
1-2. *Sambucus canadensis* L.   (Elder.)
1-2. *Pyrus* species.   (Cultivated Pear and Apple.)
1-2. *Prunus avium* and *cerasus* L.   (Cherries.)
1-4. *Syringa vulgaris* L.   (Lilac.)
1-4. *Ilex* species.   (Holly.)
  2. *Platanus occidentalis* L.   (Sycamore.)
  2. *Salix* species.   (Willow.)
  2. *Tilia americana* L.   (American Linden.)
  2. *Tilia europaea* L.   (European Linden.)
  2. *Populus dilatata* Ait.   (Lombardy Poplar.)
  2. *Ulmus americana* L.   (American White Elm.)
2-3. *Ulmus fulva* Mich'x.   (Slippery Elm.)
2-3. *Prunus armenica* L.   (Apricot.)
2-3. *Alnus maritima* Muhl.   (Alder.)
2-3. *Betula alba* L.   (White Birch.)
2-3. *Viburnum* species.   (Haw or Sloe.)
2-3. *Lonicera* species.   (Honeysuckles.)
2-3. *Prunus americana* Marsh.   (Wild Red Plum.)
2-3. *Celtis occidentalis* L.   (Hackberry.)
2-3. *Rosa* species.   (Rose.)
2-3. *Gossypium album* Ham.   (Cotton.)
2-3. *Cephalanthus occidentalis* L.   (Button Bush.)
2-3. *Vitis* species.   (Grape-vine.)
2-4. *Convolvulus* species.   (Morning Glory.)
2-4. *Acer saccharinum* Wang.   (Sugar Maple.)
2-4. *Geranium* species.   (Geranium.)
  3. *Betula nigra* L.   (Red Birch.)
  3. *Tecoma radicans* Juss.   (Trumpet Creeper.)
  3. *Symphoricarpus racemosus* Mich'x.   (Snowberry.)
  3. *Larix europaea* Del.   (European Larch.)
  3. *Corylus americana* Walt.   (Hazel-nut.)
  3. *Quercus alba* L.   (White Oak.)
  3. *Diospyros virginiana* L.   (Persimmon.)
  3. *Carya* species.   (Hickory.)
  3. *Juglans* species.   (Walnut.)
  3. *Wistaria sinensis* Del.   (Chinese Wisteria.)
  3. *Wistaria frutescens*.   (Native Wisteria.)
  3. *Amelanchier canadensis* T. and G.   (Shad-bush.)
  3. *Cratœgus* species.   (Haw.)
  3. *Rubus* species.   (Blackberry.)
  3. *Spiræa* species.   (Spiræa.)
  3. *Ribes* species.   (Currant and Gooseberry.)
  3. *Staphylea trifolia* L.   (Bladder Nut.)
3-4. *Cydonia vulgaris* Pers.   (Quince.)
3-4. *Asimina triloba* Dun.   (Pawpaw.)
3-4. *Berberis canadensis* Pursh.   (Barberry.)
3-4. *Catalpa bignonioides* Walt.   (Indian Bean.)
3-4. *Catalpa speciosa* Ward.   (Bignonia.)
3-4. *Euonymus atropurpureus* Jaeg.   (Burning Bush.)
3-4. *Cupressus thyoides* L.   (White Cedar.)
3-4. *Juniperus virginiana* L.   (Red Cedar.)
3-4 *Cornus florida* L.   (Flowering Dogwood).

3-4. *Cornus alternifolia* L.   (Alternate-leaved Dogwood.)
3-4. *Carpinus americana* Mich'x.   (Hornbeam.) .
3-4. *Castanea americana* Mich'x.   (American Chestnut.)
3-4. *Castanea pumila* Mich'x.   (Chinquapin.)
3-4. *Ostrya virginica* Willd.   (Hop Hornbeam.)
3-4. *Quercus coccinea* Wang.   (Scarlet Oak.)
3-4. *Quercus phellos* L.   (Willow Oak.)
3-4. *Quercus prinus* L.   (Chestnut Oak.)
3-4. *Quercus rubra* L.   (Red Oak.)
3-4. *Diospyros kaki* L.   (Japan Persimmon.)
3-4. *Buxus sempervirens* L.   (Common Box.)
3-4. *Hamamelis virginica* L.   (Witch Hazel.)
3-4. *Sassafras officinale* Nees.   (Sassafras.)
3-4. *Cercis canadensis* L.   (Red Bud.)
3-4. *Hibiscus syriacus* L.   (Tree Hibiscus.)
3-4. *Rhamnus alnifolius* L'Her.   (Alder-leaved Buckthorn.)
3-4. *Prunus virginiana* L.   (Choke Cherry.)
3-4. *Persica vulgaris* Millan.   (Peach.)
3-4. *Æsculus hippocastanum* L.   (Horse Chestnut.)
3-4. *Paulownia imperialis* Seeb.   (Cigar-tree.)
3-4. *Ailanthus glandulosus* Daf.   (Tree of Heaven.)
3-4. *Maclura aurantiaca* Nutt.   (Osage Orange.)
3-4. *Ampelopsis quinquefolia* Mich'x.   (Virginia Creeper.)
3-4. *Clematis* species.   (Clematis.)
3-4. *Trifolium* species.   (Clover.)
3-4. *Helianthus* species.   (Sunflower.)
3-4. *Jasminum* species.   (Jessamine).
3-4. *Ficus carica* L.   (Fig.)
  4. *Rhus cotinus* L.   (Smoke Tree.)
  4. *Pinus* species.   (Pine.)
  4. *Taxus* species.   (Yew.)
  4. *Nyssa multiflora.* Wangerh.   (Sour Gum.)
  4. *Fagus ferruginea* Ait.   (Beech.)
  4. *Kalmia* species.   (Laurel.)
  4. *Rhododendron* species.   (Rhododendron.)
  4. *Ricinus communis* L.   (Castor-oil Plant.)
  4. *Liquidambar styraciflua* L.   (Sweet Gum.)
  4. *Gleditschia triacanthos* L.   (Honey Locust.)
  4. *Gymnocladus canadensis,* Lamb.   (Kentucky Coffee Tree.)
  4. *Robinia pseudacacia* L.   (Locust.)
  4. *Liriodendron tulipifera* L.   (Tulip Tree.)
  4. *Magnolia* species.   (Magnolia.)
  4. *Chionanthus virginicus* L.   (Fringe Tree.)
  4. *Ligustrum vulgare* L.   (Privet.)
  4. *Zanthoxylum americanum* M.   (Prickly Ash.)
  4. *Acer dasycarpum* Ehrh.   (White or Silver Maple.)
  4. *Acer rubrum* Wangert.   (Red Maple.)
  4. *Æsculus flava,* Ait.   (Sweet Buckeye.)
  4. *Æsculus glabra* Willd.   (Ohio Buckeye.)
  4. *Morus rubra* L.   (Red Mulberry.)

Trees in the vicinity of the White Poplar and Cottonwood suffer most. Even trees usually not injured, as, for instance, the Sugar Maple, are often badly defoliated when in such contiguity.

This list contains a number of plants not usually injured by these caterpillars. In some cases the injury was due to the fact that twigs containing the web with its occupants had been pruned from the tree and thrown near plants, instead of being burned at once or otherwise destroyed.

In other cases the injury is due to the peculiar position of the plant injured, *i. e.* under a tree infested by the caterpillars. These, when fully grown, commence to scatter, and dropping upon the plant underneath the tree, soon defoliated it without actually making their home upon it. The great number thus dropping from a large tree will soon defoliate any smaller plant, even if each caterpillar takes but a mouthful by way of trial. Thus Holly, a plant not usually eaten by these insects, soon became denuded. Other plants, unpalatable or even obnoxious to the caterpillars, are sometimes destroyed by the multitudes in their search for more suitable food.

Hungry caterpillars, leaving a denuded tree in search of food, wander in a straight line to the next tree, sometimes a distance of 25 feet, showing that they possess some keen sense to guide them. If such a tree offers unsuitable food, they still explore it for a long time before deserting it. In this manner two columns of wandering caterpillars are formed, which frequently move in opposite directions.

PECULIAR EFFECT OF DEFOLIATION UPON SOME PLANTS.

During the early part of October many trees, mainly Apple and Pear, which had been entirely denuded of their foliage by the caterpillars, showed renewed activity of growth. Some had a few scattered flowers upon them, others had one or two branches clothed with flowers, while in some few cases the whole tree appeared white. It looked as if the trees were covered with snow, since they lacked the green foliage usually seen with blossoms in spring. Some few flowers were also observed upon badly defoliated Cherry trees. Even as late as the middle of November, owing perhaps also to the pleasantly warm weather, some few flowers could be observed upon some imported plants belonging to the genus *Spiræa* and upon the Chinese Red Apple. All these plants usually flower early in spring. The caterpillars, having entirely defoliated the tree, produced thus an artificial period of rest, or winter, which was followed by unseasonable budding and flowering. Such a result often follows summer denudation by any insect, and we have referred to some remarkable cases in our previous writings.*

ENEMIES OF THE WEB-WORM OTHER THAN INSECTS.

The caterpillars have comparatively few enemies belonging to the vertebrate animals. This is not owing to any offensive odor or to any other means of defense, but it is entirely due to their hairiness. Chickens, and even the omnivorous ducks, do not eat them; if offered to the former they pick at these morsels, but do not swallow them.

The English Sparrow has, in this case at least, not proven of any assistance whatever. Indeed, as before stated, its introduction and multiplication have greatly favored the increase of the worms.

The "pellets" of a Screech-owl (*Scops asio*), found in the vicinity of Baltimore, Md.. and examined by Mr. Lugger, consisted apparently almost entirely of the hairs of these caterpillars, proving that this useful bird had done good service.

Perhaps the statement may be of interest, that this little owl is

*See Eighth Report on the Insects of Missouri, p. 121.

getting much more common in the vicinity of such cities in which the English Sparrows have become numerous, and that the imported birds will find in this owl as bold an enemy as the Sparrow-hawk is to them in Europe, and even more dangerous, since its attacks are made towards dusk, at a time when the Sparrow has retired for the night, and is not as wide awake for ways and means to escape.

If our two Cuckoos, the Black-billed as well as the Yellow-billed species, could be induced to build their nests within the city limits or in our parks, we should gain in them two very useful friends, since they feed upon hairy caterpillars.

The common Toad (*Bufo americana*) has eaten great numbers of these caterpillars, as shown by dissections made by Mr. Lugger, and it should be carefully protected, instead of being tormented or killed by boys, or even grown people. The Toad is always a useful animal, and ought to be introduced in all gardens and parks.

The following species of spiders were observed to eat the caterpillars, viz, *Marpessa undata* Koch, and *Attus* (*Phydippus*) *tripunctatus*. Neither species builds a web, but obtains its prey by boldly leaping upon it; they are, in consequence of such habits, frequently called tiger spiders. The former was exceedingly common last year, more so than for many previous years, thus plainly indicating that the species did not suffer for lack of food. This species is usually found upon the trunks of trees, and is there well protected by its color, which is like that of the bark. It hides in depressions and cracks of the bark, and, jumping upon the passing game, or, catlike approaching it from behind, it thrusts its poisonous fangs into the victim, which soon dies and is sucked dry. The *Attus* has similar habits, but is still more cautious; it usually hides under loose bark. Both spiders are wonderfully active and kill large numbers of caterpillars. Their large and flat egg-masses can be found during the winter under dead bark and in cracks. Both species hibernate in silken nests in similar localities.

PREDACEOUS INSECT ENEMIES.

The caterpillars of this moth have quite a number of external enemies, which slay large numbers of them. The well-known Rearhorse (*Mantis carolina*) seems to be very fond of the caterpillars. The so-called Wheel-bug (*Prionidus cristatus*) has proved to be one of our best friends in reducing the numbers of the caterpillars. This insect was formerly by no means very common in cities, but of late years it has greatly increased in numbers, and is now a well-known feature in all our public parks and such streets as possess shade trees. Outside of the city it is rarely met with; nor does it extend much farther North than Washington. It is, like the Mantis, in all its stages a voracious feeder upon insects, slaying alike beneficial and noxious ones. The bright-red larvæ and pupæ, also carnivorous, are seen in numbers during the summer; they usually remain together until hunger forces them to scatter. They assist each other in killing larger game, and are to this extent social. The Wheel-bug could be observed almost anywhere last summer, but usually motionless, stationed upon the trunks of trees, waiting for the approach of an insect. If one comes near, it quite leisurely inserts its very poisonous beak and sucks the life-blood of its victim. When this becomes empty it is hoisted up in the air, as if to facilitate the flow of blood, until eventually it is thrown away as a mere shriveled skin. The appetite of the Wheel-bug is remarkable, whenever chances offer to appease it to the fullest extent. Frequently, however, times go hard with it, and notwithstanding it is very loath to change a position once taken, it is sometimes forced to seek better hunting-grounds, and takes to its wings. The Wheel-bug has been observed to remain for days in the same ill-chosen position—for instance upon the walls of a building—waiting patiently for something to turn up. It is slow in all its motions, but withal very observant of everything occurring in its neighborhood, proving without doubt great acuteness of senses. It does not seem to possess any enemies itself, and a glance at its armor will indicate the reason for this unusual exemption.* During warm weather this bug possesses a good deal of very searching curiosity, and a thrust with its beak filled with poison is very painful indeed. Boys call it the "blood-sucker," a misnomer, since it does not suck human blood. Its eggs are laid during the autumn in various places, but chiefly upon smooth surfaces of the bark of tree trunks, and frequently in such a position as to be somewhat protected against rain by a projecting branch. The female bug always selects places the color of which is like that of the eggs, so that they are not easy to see, notwithstanding their large size.

Euschistus servus Say is another hemipterous insect that preys upon the caterpillar of *H. textor*, and in a similar manner to the Wheel-bug. It is a much smaller, but also a very useful insect.

Podisus spinosus, Dall., in all its stages, was quite numerous during the caterpillar plague. Its brightly-colored larvæ and pupæ were usually found in small numbers together, but as they grew older they became more solitary in their habits. All stages of this insect frequent the trunks and branches of trees, and are here actively engaged in feeding upon various insects. As soon as one of the more mature larvæ or pupæ has impaled its prey the smaller ones crowd about to obtain their share. But the lucky captor is by no means willing to divide with the others, and he will frequently project his beak forward, thus elevating the caterpillar into the air away from the others. The habit of carrying their food in such a difficult position has perhaps been acquired simply to prevent others from sharing it. A wonderful strength is necessary to perform such a feat, since the caterpillar is sometimes many times as heavy as the bug itself. The greediness of this bug was well illustrated in the following observation: A pupa of *P. spinosus* had impaled a caterpillar, and was actively engaged in sucking it dry; meanwhile a Wheel-bug utilized a favorable opportunity and impaled the pupa without forcing the same to let go the caterpillar. The elasticity of the beak of these bugs must be very great; they can bend it in any direction and yet keep it in sucking operation. The poison contained in the beak must act very rapidly, since the caterpillars impaled by it squirm but a very short time and then become quiet.

FUNGUS DISEASE OF THE WEB-WORM.

In our Fourth Missouri Entomological Report, p. 88, we called attention to the fact that the fungus disease of the domestic Silk-worm, called in France *Muscardine*, and supposed to be due to the development in the worms of the fungus *Botrytis bassiana*, or a disease which had not yet been distinguished from it, had made its appearance

---

*Its eggs, however, are pierced by a little egg-parasite—*Eupelmus reduvii* Howard.

among Silk-worms, both imported and wild, in some of the Eastern States, and that in the fall of 1870 it was so common around Saint Louis that we found hundreds of hairy caterpillars stiffly fastened to their food-plants and covered with the white efflorescence. On several occasions in Saint Louis we found the *Hyphantria* larvæ generally affected by it.

The latest authority upon this fungus (Saccardo) gives it as living upon Bombycid larvæ, particularly upon the Silk-worm of commerce, in France, Italy, and North America. *Botrytis tenella*, which he described in his "*Fungi Italicæ*" as a new species, he now considers as only a variety of *B. bassiana*. This variety is found upon dipterous larvæ and pupæ, upon wasps of the genus *Vespa*, and upon the larvæ of the coleopterous genus *Melolontha*. (P. A. Saccardo, *Sylloge Hyphomycetum omnium huscusque cognitorum*, Vol. IV, p. 119, Patavia, 1886.)

The first brood of the Web-worms at Washington in 1886 showed in some quite well-defined localities the indications of a fungus disease, which was probably only a variety of this *Botrytis*. It did not become, however, so general as later in the season, when it prevailed everywhere; yet it could be observed that the contagion had started from certain points. In such localities almost all the caterpillars were diseased and died, and large numbers of the dead were huddled together as in life. But when investigated their bodies were hard and dry, and would readily crumble to pieces when pressed, producing an odor like that of some mushrooms. Only full-grown, or rather caterpillars in their last larval skin, were thus affected. The dry remains had retained the original shape, and, if killed but recently by the fungus, their color as well. Before dying the caterpillars had fastened themselves very securely to trunks, twigs, and leaves of various trees, somewhat like the common house-fly, that dies by a similar disease in large numbers during September in our houses and produces around itself such a characteristic halo of white spores. Caterpillars infested by the incipient stages of this disease wander about aimlessly and at an irregular speed; often they halt for some time, then squirm about frantically to start again, and frequently in an opposite direction to the one they were going before. If such a diseased caterpillar is confined to a glass jar and observed, it is soon seen that a white mealy substance gradually grows out of all the soft spaces between the segments, which eventually covers the whole insect, leaving generally only the black head and tips of hairs visible. Before long many spores are scattered about, forming a circle of white dust around the caterpillar, and, if not arrested by an obstruction in its expulsion, the halo thus formed is quite regular and about 2 inches in diameter. Outdoors this white dust is but seldom observed, because even the slightest draft of air will carry it away and drift it about. Even the white mealy substance adhering to the caterpillar itself is usually swept away, and the victims look very much like healthy caterpillars; but they darken with time, and eventually drop to the ground. The magnifying-glass, however, still reveals some spores adhering to the hairs upon the under side and upon the bark or leaf of the tree in the immediate neighborhood.

This fungus kills caterpillars even after they have made their cocoons. Nor does the pupa escape. In the latter case the spores form a white crest over every suture of the thoracic segments; the abdominal segments, however, remain free from it. Evidently the caterpillars were nearly full-grown when attacked by the disease, and possessed vigor enough to transform into pupæ; later the fungus grew, and pressing the chitinous portion of the pupa apart, forced itself to the air to fructify.

Plants not usually eaten by the caterpillars, as well as others not eaten at all, have upon them the largest numbers of caterpillars killed by the fungus, provided that they grew in the vicinity of suitable food-plants. Perhaps unsuitable food, predisposing the caterpillars for any disease, is one of the causes of the innumerable host killed by this fungus.

The white cocoons of a parasite (*Apanteles hyphantriæ*) were in some cases observed to be covered with similar fungus spores. Opening such cocoons it was seen that the spores were not simply blown upon the silk and there retained, but that they came from the victim within, and had forced their way through the very dense silken mass.

EXPERIMENTS TO OBTAIN PERCENTAGE OF DISEASED CATERPILLARS.

Experiment I:

One hundred and twenty-five nearly grown caterpillars were gathered (October 7, 1886) at random in one of our public parks. They were imprisoned in large glass jars, and daily supplied with suitable food.

Result, October 18, 1886:

11 apparently healthy pupæ.
3 deformed pupæ.
18 yellow cocoons of *Meteorus hyphantriæ*.
9 dead pupæ, killed by fungus or otherwise.
84 dead caterpillars, killed by fungus or otherwise.

―――
125

In the earth of the jar were found 17 pupæ of Tachina flies, leaving 67 caterpillars and 9 pupæ killed by the fungus, or 61 per cent.

Experiment II:

One hundred and twenty-five nearly grown caterpillars were gathered (October 7, 1886) from a trunk of a soft maple (unsuitable food) and treated as above.

Result, October 18, 1886:

8 apparently healthy pupæ.
1 deformed pupa.
7 yellow cocoons of *Meteorus hyphantriæ*.
3 dead pupæ, killed by fungus or otherwise.
104 dead caterpillars, killed by fungus or otherwise.
2 cocoons containing Tachina larvæ.

―――
125

In the earth of the jar were found 28 pupæ of Tachina flies, leaving 76 caterpillars and 3 pupæ killed by fungus, or 63 per cent.

In both experiments it has been assumed that each Tachina fly had killed one caterpillar.

On November 15, 1886, the jars were again investigated and it was found that a number of the pupæ had been killed by the fungus since October 18, 1886, and that in fact all the remaining ones appeared diseased. The percentage of death by the fungus in the two experiments was thus increased to 63 per cent. in Experiment I and to 67 per cent in Experiment II.

34 AG—'86

TRUE PARASITES OF THE WEB-WORM.

Up to the present time no parasites of this insect have ever been recorded. On August 18, 1883, we bred a number of egg-parasites from a batch of eggs found upon a willow leaf at Washington, but unfortunately no description was made of them at the time, and, as they belonged to the soft-bodied genus *Trichogramma*, the specimens have now become so much shriveled and altered that they are unfit for descriptive purposes. We noticed after our return from Europe in September of this year that, at a number of points in New England, the worms were quite commonly attacked by parasites, and careful investigation at Washington by Mr. Lugger showed the presence of no less than five distinct species of primary parasites in addition to the *Trichogramma* just mentioned. These will be considered in some detail. The first was a new egg-parasite, which we have named *Telenomus bifidus;* the others were all parasitic on the larvæ, and consisted of a Braconid (*Meteorus hyphantriæ* n. sp.); a Microgaster (*Apanteles hyphantriæ,* n. sp.); an Ophionid (*Limneria pallipes* Prov.), and a Tachinid, which, though probably new, we shall not attempt to describe. These last four have been mentioned in about the order of their relative abundance and consequent importance. An astonishing number of Web-worms were killed by the four parasites, and so many died from this cause and from the fungus disease previously mentioned as to fully warrant the prediction of almost complete immunity for the summer of 1887.

In addition to these parasites found last Fall, the note-books of the Division show a prior breeding of another primary parasite, which will not be treated in detail here on account of insufficient material. It is an external feeder on the larva and belongs to the genus *Euplectrus*. It is closely related to *E. platyhypenæ,* described by Mr. Howard in Bulletin 5 of this Division.

We have found, however, that three of these primary parasites of the Web-worm, viz, the *Apanteles,* the *Limneria,* and the *Meteorus,* were killed off at a serious rate late in the season by secondary parasites, most of which belong to the family *Chalcididæ* with the exception of three species of the Ichneumonid genus *Hemiteles.* So extensive has been this killing off of the primary parasites by the secondary, that were not the fates of the three classes, viz, the plant-feeder, the primary and the secondary parasites so interwoven, the destruction of these beneficial insects might be considered a serious matter in dealing with the plant-feeder.

We have not taken time to determine these secondary parasites specifically, but give a little table showing the number of species concerned, mentioning them only by their genera:

SECONDARY PARASITES.

On *Apanteles:*
1. *Hemiteles* sp.
2. *Elasmus* sp.
3. *Eupelmus* sp.
4. *Panstenon* sp.
5. *Cirrospilus* sp.
6. *Pteromalus* sp.
7. *Pteromalus* sp.

On *Meteorus hyphantriæ:*
1. *Hemiteles* sp. (= 1 on *Apanteles*).
2. *Spilochalcis* sp.
3. *Hemiteles utilis* Nort.
4. *Eupelmus* sp. (= 3 on *Apanteles*).
5. *Hemiteles* sp.
6. *Pteromalus* sp. (= 6 on *Apanteles*).
7. *Pteromalus* sp. (= 7 on *Apanteles*).
Limneria pallipes Prov.:
1. *Eupelmus* sp. (= 3 on *Apanteles*).
2. *Tetrastichus* sp.
3. *Pteromalus* sp. (= 6 on *Apanteles*).
4. *Pteromalus* sp. (= 7 on *Apanteles*).
5. *Elasmus* sp. (= 2 on *Apanteles*).

THE TELENOMUS EGG-PARASITE.—A single egg of *H. cunea* is a very small affair, yet it is large enough to be a world for this little parasite, which undergoes all its transformations within it, and finds there all the food and lodgment required for the short period of its life. In several instances batches of eggs of this moth were parasitized, and instead of producing young caterpillars they brought forth the tiny insects of this species. The batches of parasitized eggs were found July 27 upon the leaves of Sunflower. Judging from this date, it was the second brood of moths which had deposited them. There can be no doubt, however, that eggs produced by moths emerging from their cocoons in early spring had been parasitized as well. The female *Telenomus* was also observed August 2, busily engaged in forcing its ovipositor into the eggs and ovipositing therein. The female insect is so very intent upon its work that it is not easily disturbed, and one can pluck a leaf and apply a lens without scaring it away. The eggs soon hatch inside the large egg of the moth, and the larvæ produced soon consume the contents. This egg-parasite is a very useful friend, nipping the evil in the bud, so to speak.

This parasite is new, and may be characterized as follows:

TELENOMUS BIFIDUS n. sp. ♂ ♀.—Average length, 0.75^{mm}; average expanse, 1.7^{mm}. Color of body, black throughout. *Head* three times as broad as long when seen from above; face, especially in the middle, lustrous and without sculpture; vertex polished and without a carina behind lateral ocelli; antennæ black, except bulla, which is honey-yellow. 11-jointed, joints 2 and 3 subequal in length. *Thorax:* Mesonotum very delicately punctulate and furnished with a moderately dense, fine, whitish pile; no parapsidal sutures; legs yellow, except coxæ, femora, and last joints of all tarsi, which are black or blackish; tibial spur of front legs bifid when seen under a high power, and corresponding first tarsal joint furnished with a fine and strong comb of bristles; fore wings with 11 costal bristles and with 3 cells visible in stigmal club. *Abdomen* with the second segment striate only at base.

Described from 5 ♀, 2 ♂, bred July 27, 1886, from eggs of *Hyphantria cunea* collected in the District of Columbia.

This species belongs nearest to *T. phalænarum* Nees, of Europe, which has been bred from the eggs of *Porthesia chrysorrhea* by Wachtl, from eggs of *Panolis piniperda* by Nördlinger, and from eggs of an unknown Noctuid on the leaves of *Æsculus hippocastanum* by Mayr. (See Mayr, " *Ueber die Schlupfwespengattung Telenomus*" Verh. d. k.-k. zoöl. Ges., Wien, 1879, p. 709.)

THE METEORUS PARASITE OF THE WEB-WORM (Plate X, fig. 4.)— This parasite has performed very good service during the caterpillar plague, and has done much to check any further increase of the Web-worm. During the earlier part of the summer this insect was not very numerous, but sufficient proofs in form of empty cocoons were observed to indicate at least one earlier brood. Towards the end of September, and as late as the 15th of October, very numerous cocoons of a second brood were formed; they could be found in all situations to which the caterpillar itself had access. But the great majority of them were suspended from the trunks* and branches of trees, and chiefly from near the base of the trunk. Each represents the death of one nearly full-grown caterpillar, since the latter harbors but one larva of the parasite. A careful watch was kept to see how such a suspended cocoon was formed, but in vain. Once a larva had just started to make a cocoon, but became detached, and dropped out of the orifice and commenced a new one. The larva, suspended by the mandibles, evidently spins at first loose, irregular, horizontal loops around its body, until a loose cradle is formed. The silk secreted for this purpose hardens very rapidly when exposed to the air. When secure inside this cradle it lets go its hold with the mandibles, and finishes the soft inside cocoon in the usual manner. If the larva has dropped to the ground, it still makes an outer loose cocoon, but the silken threads are thicker and much more irregular. In cocoons made during a high wind, the threads that suspend them are much longer, reaching sometimes the length of 4 inches; the more normal length varies from 1½ to 2 inches.

To find out the length of time which this insect occupies in maturing inside the cocoon 44 freshly made cocoons were put in a glass jar. With remarkable regularity, but ten days were consumed by the insect in changing from the larval to the winged form. The winged *Meteorus* issues through a perfectly round hole at the lower end of the cocoon by gnawing off and detaching a snugly fitting cap. The several secondary parasites of the *Meteorus* which we have mentioned all leave the cocoon of their host by smaller holes cut through the sides. Most of the adult *Meteorus* had issued by the 1st of November; but it is possible that some may remain in their cocoons until spring.

In order to obtain the proportion between the *Meteorus* raised from cocoons and its parasites (*i. e.*, secondary parasites of *Hyphantria*), 450 cocoons were confined in a glass jar the latter part of September. Up to the first week in November only 70 specimens were bred from these cocoons, the rest giving out secondary parasites, which continued to issue up to date of writing (December 20, 1886). Thus only 16 per cent. of the cocoons produced the primary, while 84 per cent. produced secondary parasites. The insect is new, and we submit the following description:—

METEORUS HYPHANTRIÆ n. sp.— ♀. Length, 5ᵐᵐ; expanse, 11ᵐᵐ. Comes nearest to *Meteorus communis* Cress., being, however, a larger species. Its cocoons are also larger and of a darker yellow-brown in color. General color, honey-yellow. The irregular reticulation of the metanotum shows less tendency to arrange itself in longitudinal carinæ, particularly into one median and two sublateral. The fine longitudinal impressed aciculations of the first abdominal segment are nearly parallel in *hyphantriæ*, while in *communis* the middle ones converge strongly towards the center behind. The general color is, as in *communis*, yellowish-ferruginous or honey-yellow. In general, *hyphantriæ* has more dark markings than *communis*. The antennæ are dusky at tip; the mandibles are brown at tip; the mesoscutum has two nearly black patches at sides and often a dusky stripe down middle; the metanotum is usually entirely dark, as is also the first joint of the abdomen above; the rest of the abdomen has two larger or smaller dark spots on each side; the sheaths of the

---

* In one instance only, the cocoon of this parasite was found inside that of its host.

ovipositor are dark, especially at base, and the ovipositor itself is honey-yellow; the legs are all honey-yellow except the tips of the hind tibiæ, which are dark.

♂.—Resembles the female, with the usual structural differences. Varies considerably in color, some specimens being almost immaculate, while others are marked like the female. Wing venation in both sexes varies in no way from that of *communis*, and but slightly from that in other species of the genus; in that the second submarginal cell is subquadrate, broadening slightly posteriorly, and in the first transverse cubital nervure being confluent with the recurrent nervure.

Described from 18 ♀, 9 ♂ specimens, all bred in District of Columbia from cocoons collected near remains of larvæ of *Hyphantria cunea*.

THE MICROGASTER PARASITE OF THE WEB-WORM.—This insect was about as numerous as the *Meteorus*, and did equally good service in preventing a further increase of the caterpillars. It appeared somewhat earlier in the season, and had killed only half-grown caterpillars. From the numerous old and empty cocoons in early summer it was plainly seen that a first brood had been quite numerous, and that from these cocoons mainly *Apanteles* had been bred, and not, as during the autumn, mostly secondary parasites. The white silky cocoon is formed almost under the middle of a half-grown caterpillar, and is fastened securely to the object its host happened to rest upon, and but slightly to the host itself, which is readily carried to the ground by wind and rain, and can therefore only be in position in the more sheltered places, such as cracks and fissures of the bark of trees. But one *Apanteles* is found in a caterpillar, so that each white cocoon indicates, like a tombstone, the death of a victim. In some places, and notably upon the trunks of poplars, these cocoons were so numerous as to attract attention; it seemed as if the trunk had been sprinkled with whitewash. But notwithstanding such vast numbers, but two specimens of the architects of these neat cocoons were raised; all the rest had been parasitized by secondary parasites. It is barely possible, however, that some specimens may hibernate in their cocoons, since numbers of them have as yet (December 20, 1886) not revealed any insects. The winged *Apanteles* leaves the cocoon by a perfectly round orifice in the front, by cutting off a little lid, which falls to the ground. Its parasites, however, leave by small holes cut through the sides. These secondary parasites were very common late in September and early in October, and busily engaged in inserting their ovipositors through the tough cocoon into their victim within. It seems as if the cocoons formed early in the season were on an average a little smaller than those formed later.

The cocoons of this *Apanteles* are of a uniform white color, but exceptionally a distinctly yellowish cocoon is found. From these yellow cocoons nothing has so far been bred, but since, as we have elsewhere shown,* the color of the cocoon may vary in the same species, it is probable that the variation here referred to is not specific.

Not quite one-half of 1 per cent of these cocoons produced the insect belonging to it; 99 per cent produced secondary parasites.

APANTELES HYPHANTRIÆ, n. sp.— ♀. Length, 3ᵐᵐ. Close to *Apanteles xylina*, Say, with which it may be compared. Differs as follows: Mesonotum without the faint median carina or polished posterior margin; scutellum not polished; first abdominal segment about as broad as long, with a quite distinct median carina, the apex of which is polished, and its posterior margin broadly bilobed. In *A. xylina* the first abdominal segment is rather slender, and longer than wide, without distinct carina and with the apex almost straight. A quite distinct carina on the second segment, wanting in *xylina*. Third abdominal segment coarsely pitted at base,

* Notes on North American Microgasters, &c., Trans. Saint Louis Acad. Sciences, vol. 4, author's separate copy, p. 7.

the rest quite distinctly shagreened; in *xylina* the basal punctuation is less pronounced and the rest of the segment smooth. All coxæ black (in *xylina* the apical half of lower edge of posterior coxæ is reddish); the first joint of metatarsi perceptibly stouter than the other joints (almost like the other joints in *xylina*). Cocoon white and single (in *xylina* the cocoons are enclosed in wooly masses).
Described from two ♀ specimens.

THE LIMNERIA PARASITE OF THE WEB-WORM.—In addition to the two Hymenopterous parasites treated of, a third one has been very numerous, and has done much good in reducing the numbers of caterpillars. This, an Ichneumonid, and a much larger insect, does not form an exposed cocoon like that of the other parasites described. Yet a little attention will soon reveal large numbers of them. Upon the trunks of various trees, but chiefly upon those of the Poplar and Sugar Maple, small colonies of caterpillars, varying in number from 4 to 12, could be observed, which did not show any signs of life. When removed from the tree they appeared contracted, all of the same size, and pale or almost white. A closer inspection would reveal the fact that the posterior portion of the caterpillar had shrunken away to almost nothing, whilst the rest was somewhat inflated, and covered with an unchanged, but bleached skin, retaining all the hairs in their normal position. Opening one of these inflated skins, a long, cylindrical, brown cocoon would be exposed; this is the cocoon of the *Limneria* under consideration. As numbers of such inflated skins would always occur together, it was clearly seen that the same parent *Limneria* had oviposited in all of them. Most of the cocoons were found in depressions of the rough bark, or other protected places. Single ones were but rarely met with. The Hyphantria larvæ in dying had very securely fastened all their legs into the crevices of the bark, so that neither wind nor rain could easily dislodge them. Only half-grown caterpillars had thus been killed. Many of these inflated skins showed in the early part of October a large hole of exit in their posterior and dorsal ends, from which the Ichneumons had escaped. Trying to obtain winged specimens of this parasite, 140 of these cocoons—and only such as were not perforated in any way—were collected and put in a glass jar. Only a single female was produced from all up to time of writing, whilst very large numbers of secondary parasites issued from October 11 to November 20, and doubtless others will appear during the spring of 1887, because some of these inflated skins show as yet no holes of exit.

This parasite is, according to Mr. Cresson, unnamed in the Philadelphia collection, and, after close study of all accessible descriptions, we have decided that it should be placed, temporarily at least, with Provancher's *Limneria pallipes*. The specimens which we have bred correspond with his variety, in which the four anterior femora are pale red. The species is not unlike *L. lophyri* Riley, which we described in our Ninth Missouri Entomological Report from a large series of specimens bred from the larvæ of Abbott's White Pine Worm (*Lophyrus abbottii*), but is smaller and has certain colorational differences.

THE TACHINA PARASITE OF THE WEB-WORM.—The parasites of *H. textor* described so far belong to the order *Hymenoptera*, which furnishes the greatest number of them; but the fly now to be treated is fully as useful as any of the others. We have not named and described this species, on account of the fact that the family to which it belongs has not been worked up and because the characters are not well understood.

Tachina flies are very easily overlooked, because they resemble large house-flies both in appearance and flight, and their presence out of doors is not usually noticed on that account. Yet they play a very important rôle, living as they do in their larval state entirely in insects. During the caterpillar plague such flies were often seen to dart repeatedly at an intended victim, buzz about it, and quickly disappear. If the caterpillar thus attacked was investigated, from 1 to 4 yellowish-white, ovoid, polished, and tough eggs would be found usually fastened upon its neck, or on some spot where they could not readily be removed. These eggs are glued so tightly to the skin of the caterpillar that they cannot easily be removed. Sometimes as many as 7 eggs could be counted upon a single caterpillar, showing a faulty instinct of the fly or flies, because the victim is not large enough to furnish food for so many voracious maggots. If the victim happens to be near a molt, it casts its skin with the eggs, and escapes a slow but sure death. But usually the eggs hatch so soon, that the small maggots have time to enter the body of the caterpillar, where they soon reach their full growth, after which they force their way through the skin and drop to the ground, into which they enter, to shrink into a brown, tunlike object (known technically as the coarctate pupa), which contains the true pupa. The caterpillar, tormented by enemies feeding within it, stops feeding, and wanders about for a long time until it dies. As a rule, not more than two maggots of this fly mature in their host, and generally but one. The caterpillar attacked by a Tachina fly is always either fully grown or nearly so.

Tachina flies abounded during the whole term of the prevalence of the caterpillars, but it is impossible to state positively whether they were all bred from them or not, since the many species of this genus of flies resemble each other so closely, that a very scrutinizing investigation would have been necessary to settle such a question. But there is no doubt that they were very numerous during the summer. Some maggots obtained from caterpillars kept for this purpose in breeding jars changed to flies in six days, others appeared in twenty-three days, and still others, obtained at about the same time, are still under ground, where they will hibernate. The maggots of these flies do not, however, always enter the ground, as some were found inside cocoons made by caterpillars among rubbish above ground.

REMEDIES.

PRUNING AND BURNING.—The old and well-tried remedies of pruning or burning, or pruning and burning, will answer every purpose against this insect in ordinary seasons, where it is thoroughly done and over a whole neighborhood. It must, however, be done upon the first appearance of the webs on the trees, and not, as was done by the Parking Commission of this city last season, after the first brood of worms had attained their full growth and many had already transformed to pupæ. The nests at that time had assumed large proportions, and their removal entire injured the appearance of many young trees. Then, too, they were piled upon an open wagon, which was dragged for many hours around the streets, permitting a large proportion of the worms to escape.

On the first appearance of the webs, which should be looked for with care, they should be cut off or burned off; and if cut off, they should be burned at once. The "tree-pruners," manufactured for the trade and well known to all gardeners, answer the purpose admirably.

The customary method of burning the nests is by means of rags saturated with kerosene or coal tar and fastened to the tip of a long pole. An old sponge has been substituted to advantage for the rags, but probably the best substitute for this purpose is a piece of porous brick. In a pointed communication published in the *Evening Star* of August 21, Major Key, agent of the Humane Society, thus describes the making of a "brick-torch:" "Take a piece of soft brick, commonly termed salmon brick, trim it to an egg shape; then take two soft wires, cross them over this brick, wrapping them together around the opposite side so as to firmly secure it; now tie this end to a long stick, such as the boys get at the planing-mills, by wrapping around it; then soak the brick in coal-oil, light it with a match, and you are armed with the best and cheapest weapon known to science. Holding this brick torch under the nests of caterpillars will precipitate to the sidewalk all the worms on one or two trees at least from one soaking of the brick, and it can be repeated as often as necessary. Then use a broom to roll them under it, and the work will be done, the controversy ended, and the trees saved."

A little thorough work with a simple torch like this, *at the right time,* will in nearly every case obviate the necessity of the more expensive remedies later in the season, when the worms of the first brood have grown larger, or when the second brood has appeared.

MULCHING.—After a bad caterpillar year a little judicious raking together of leaves and rubbish around the trunks of trees which have been infested, at the time when the worms of the second brood are about full-grown and before they commence to wander, will result in the confinement of a large proportion of the pupæ to these limited spaces, where, with a little hot water or a match, they can readily be destroyed during the winter. Many of the caterpillars of course reach the ground by dropping purposely or falling accidentally from the branches, but the great majority descend by the trunk, and finding the convenient shelter for pupation ready at the foot of the tree, go no farther. This has been tested on the Department grounds the past season, and is mentioned as a method of riddance supplementary only to others.

ARSENICAL POISONS.—It is seldom, however, that individuals, and still more rarely that corporations, can be brought to the use of remedies until damage is plain, and when this time comes nothing is better than the application of some one of the arsenical mixtures. We have already treated of the methods for applying such mixtures to shade trees on a large scale in our report as Entomologist to the Department for 1883, and in Bulletin 6 of this division, in both cases in connection with the treatment of the Imported Elm Leaf-beetle (*Galeruca xanthomelæna*).

The most economical and convenient apparatus consists of a large barrel, provided with a force-pump and mixer, mounted on an ordinary cart. A long hose, a metallic pipe, and a cyclone nozzle, arranged for elevation by means of a bamboo pole, complete the outfit.

Detailed descriptions of the apparatus having already appeared in the reports just mentioned, it is unnecessary to repeat them here.

A somewhat similar apparatus is used in the California orange groves against the Cottony Cushion-scale, and is illustrated in operation on Plate V. In this case a tank made especially for the purpose is mounted in the high wagon-box and secured by cleats, and supports a small hose-reel. The so-called "San José nozzle" (a direct-discharge nozzle) is used. A feature of the illustration is the long, portable ladder, which can be handled by one man. Such an apparatus as this would be well adapted for use against the Web-worm. It could be readily constructed and kept for years by the parking authorities of any city liable to the attacks of this or other leaf-eating shade-tree pests.

In the use of arsenical poisons a number of points were brought out by the series of experiments upon the Elm Leaf-beetle which are important, and which may be briefly adverted to here:

Certain trees are more susceptible to the corrosive effects of the arsenic than others. The 1883 experiments were confined to Elms, and we have no reliable data as to the relative susceptibility of other shade trees; so that we can simply mention the probability that those trees which are most liked by worms are more apt to be affected by the poison than trees which are distasteful to the worms.

"After each rain the poison takes a new effect upon the plant and the pest, which indicates that the poison is absorbed more or is more active when wet, and that it acts by dehydrating thereafter. Where the tree is too strongly poisoned each rain causes a new lot of leaves to become discolored by the poison or to fall. On some of the trees the discoloration appears in brown dead blotches on the foliage, chiefly about the gnawed places and margins, while in other instances many of the leaves turn yellow, and others fall without change of color. * * *

"The poison not only produces the local effects from contact with the parts touched by it, but following this there appears a more general effect, manifested in that all the foliage appears to lose, to some extent, its freshness and vitality. This secondary influence is probably from poisoning of the sap in a moderate degree. When this is once observable no leaf-eater thrives upon the foliage. Slight over-poisoning seems to have a tonic or invigorating effect on the trees."

In the case of the Elm Leaf-beetle it was found that a *preventive* application of the poison was valuable. It was made while the eggs were being deposited and before the young larvæ were hatched, in order to prevent the worms from getting a·start. It had the additional advantage of injuring the tree less than when applied later in the season, as the caustic effect of the poison is greater when it comes in contact with the sap at the gnawed edges and surfaces of the leaves.

It was found advisable in 1883 to mix a certain amount of flour with the Paris green or London purple used, in order to render the mixture adhesive to the leaves. Three quarts of flour were used to the barrel (40 gallons) of water. Where London purple was used it was noted that the minimum amount per barrel of water was one-fourth of a pound and the maximum three-fourths of a pound. Less ·than the minimum did not kill the larvæ and more than the maximum injured the foliage. Three-eighths of a pound was recommended. With Paris green the quantity was somewhat greater, ranging from a minimum of one-half of a pound to a maximum of one pound.

In mixing the poison, flour and water, a large galvanized iron funnel of thirteen quarts capacity, having a cross septum of fine wire gauze, and having also vertical sides and a rim to keep it from rocking on the barrel, was used. The flour was first placed in the funnel and washed through the wire gauze with water. This caused it to diffuse in the water without forming in lumps. The same process was followed with the London purple or the Paris green, according to which substance was to be used.

London purple has the advantage over Paris green in cheapness, better diffusibility, and visibility upon the foliage, and experience showed that the green seemed to injure the foliage more than the purple.

It was noticed with the Elm Leaf-beetle that the effect of a poisoning was slow in appearing; good effects are not expected before the third or fourth day. Impatience which would lead to a repoisoning on the second or third day would be apt to result in the burning and fall of the leaves.

EMULSIONS OF KEROSENE.—We have had occasion for the last few years to many times recommend the use of emulsions of kerosene against different injurious insects. We need not repeat the advantages of these preparations here, but simply state that when the Web-worms are abundant, a thorough spraying with a dilute emulsion will doubtless destroy the majority of them. On account of our absence last summer no experiments were made upon the effect of applying such an emulsion upon the foliage of the commoner shade trees, but the result of experiments detailed in Bulletin No. 11 of the Division would augur the destruction of the worms. These experiments (made by Mr. Webster at La Fayette, Ind.) were not performed upon this species, however, but upon the somewhat similar larvæ of *Pieris rapæ* and *Datana ministra*. Colonel Bowles, as we shall soon show, rejected the emulsion of soap and kerosene as not effective against the worms when reduced so as not to injure the plants; but, as he has not given us the details of the experiments, we still consider the matter open to proof. The formulæ for several emulsions are given in the article on the Cottony Cushion-scale (*Icerya purchasi*). One of the most serviceable is that which we call the "Hubbard formula," and which was used most extensively by Mr. Hubbard in his work on the scale insects of the Orange, and which has been repeatedly given in the publications of the Division.

NAPHTHA.—Some experiments were undertaken in the height of the Web-worm season by Col. John Bowles, of Washington, which possess a certain interest on account of the substance used and on account of the manner of its application. It is, however, more expensive than the arsenical poisons and the kerosene emulsions, and the spray from the atomizer is not so far-reaching as from the force-pump and cyclone nozzle. We append Colonel Bowles's condensed account of his experiments, with the remark that the experiments with the oil doubtless failed of satisfactory results because of imperfect emulsifying and application:

In accordance with your request I send herewith a concise statement of experiments made by myself in exterminating caterpillars, web-worms, &c., which destroy the beautiful foliage of our shade trees.

My experiment commenced with an effort to save the shrubbery of my yard and garden from the rapacious caterpillars that seem almost to germinate in the poplar trees, one of which stood in our front yard. After denuding this tree and literally raising an army of conquest and invasion, they broke camp and set forth as a huge foraging party, consuming everything in their way, save the rough bark of the trees and the fences.

I opposed them first with kerosene oil, which was equally fatal to the plants and worms.

Then a simple emulsion of soap in proportion of 1 to 4 was made with the oil and finally abandoned, not being effective against the worms when reduced so as not to injure the plants.

Lighter oils of the same character were resorted to and applied with a spray. This killed the vermin, yet injured the plant. Still lighter oils were used, but, when sprayed on, the foliage was materially injured. A vaporizer by means of compressed air was substituted for the spray, and with use of very light oil or naptha, known in commerce as 88, in half a second froze the worm and plant alike, with this difference, that in ten or fifteen minutes the vermin revived, but the tender leaves and twigs wilted and turned black as though struck by Jack Frost in January.

The grade of oil was reduced until the proper gravity of, say, 77 was found to kill the vermin and still leave the plant essentially unharmed.

The mechanical devices for vaporizing the oil and applying it to the upper branches of trees and shrubbery alike, as demonstrated to the Commissioners of the District some time since, and to which you kindly refer, have been since perfected, and so reduced in cost as to make the management easy by any common day laborer and the whole cost within the reach of all interested, whilst the oil costs less than 10 cents per gallon.

JOINT WORMS.

Order HYMENOPTERA; Family CHALCIDIDÆ.

THE COMMON JOINT WORM.

(*Isosoma hordei*, Harr.)

This old and well-known species has for the past few years been increasing in numbers and importance in certain sections of the country, while for a number of years previously it had been almost lost sight of. Since 1881 its work has been quite noticeable in portions of Louisa, Albemarle, Goochland, Orange, and Fluvanna Counties, Virginia, or, in other words, in just the locality where it was observed and studied thirty-five years ago by F. G. Ruffin, Professor Cabell, and Mr. Rives. Through the courtesy of Mr. F. C. Brooke, of Cuckoo, Louisa County, we have been kept informed of the progress of the pest and have been supplied with specimens from time to time.

In June, 1885, wishing to learn definitely the state of affairs in this section, and more particularly on Mr. Brooke's farm, we sent one of our assistants, Mr. Pergande, accompanied by Mr. A. Stewart, a member of the Entomological Society of Washington, to Cuckoo to make a few days' observations. The reports made by these gentlemen showed that the damage done to the wheat crop by this and other wheat insects was very great. Mr. Brooke's crop for 1884 averaged less than 5 bushels to the acre, which did not pay expenses.

The Joint Worm was not alone concerned in accomplishing this result, although an important factor. The Hessian Fly (*Cecidomyia destructor*), the Wheat Midge (*Diplosis tritici*), the Wheat Isosoma (*Isosoma tritici*), the Tarnished Plant-bug (*Lygus lineolaris*), and quite a number of other hemipterous insects were present in force, and almost every straw had been injured by one or more of these species. In the portions of the field most injured the plants were often scarcely a foot in height, few in number, and many were bent near the ground, so that frequently six or eight out of a bunch of twelve were prostrate. The ears of these straws were, however, better developed and fuller of sound grain than those which stood erect. On examination the prostrate stalks were found to be badly infested by Joint Worms above the first or second joint, but almost entirely free from Hessian Fly and Wheat Midge, while the standing stalks frequently had both of the others in addition to *Isosma tritici* and *I. hordei*. Of all these the Wheat Midge undoubtedly did the greatest and most direct damage, and many ears were found white and blasted from its work. In the most flourishing parts of the field, where the stalks were green and 4 feet high, the Joint Worm was also found, although not in such numbers as before.

The larvæ of *Isosoma tritici* were often found in the same stalk with *I. hordei*, often boring just alongside of the galls of the latter. *I. hordei*, however, were quite uniformly found just above the first or second joint, and in such position that the cutting of the grain would not disturb them, while *I. tritici* was found in all parts of the stalk from near the ground to above the upper joint.

In spite of the great abundance of the Joint Worms at this time they were less numerous than in 1884, and in 1886 they were still more reduced in numbers, owing, in great measure, to the prevalence of Chalcid parasites in 1885. The most abundant of these was *Semiotellus chalcidiphagus* Walsh, the larvæ of which were found in nearly every swelling examined. The larvæ of *Eupelmus allynii* (French) were also found, but in smaller numbers.

A study of the comparative injury done by the four principal insects found in this field would rank them in the following order: *Diplosis tritici, Cecidomyia destructor, Isosoma tritici, Isosoma hordei*, yet *I. hordei* alone had been complained of.

In parts of Ohio, too, the Joint Worm has been abundant. Mr. Elliot Luse, of Barry, Cuyahoga County, writing under date of May 4, 1885, complained that the previous Fall, while threshing, bits of hard straw from half an inch to three inches in length would come through with the wheat. When cleaned with a hand-mill he would get a bushel of these bits to 20 bushels of grain. The real nature of the small pieces was not discovered by Mr. Luse until spring, when, after feeding stock with chopped straw and ground feed and making them sick, the straw was examined and the insects found and sent to us for determination.

This case formed the text for an article which we wrote for the *Rural New Yorker* of June 20, 1885 (vol. 44, p. 418), in which we pointed out the necessity of cleaning with a hand-mill all wheat thrashed with a steam-thrasher from infested straw, and of burning not only the galls thus separated, but also the straw itself, as its loss can be well afforded to lessen the injury the ensuing year.

Specimens were also received from Chagrin Falls, a few miles south from Barry, in October, 1885, from Miss E. J. Phillips, who stated that the wheat straw had been badly infested in that vicinity for two years past, but that the yield did not seem to have been affected, as she knew of several fields which yielded 30 and 35 bushels per acre, and which were at the same time badly infested. The only trouble was that the little pieces of straw came through the separator with the wheat.

In Central New York the Joint Worm has also done some damage, as we learn from correspondence with Dr. Lintner, the State entomologist. Here, as in Ohio, the worms were often found higher in the stalk than was customary in Virginia. In Ohio this is shown by the fact that so many galls were found in the harvested straw, while Dr. Lintner writes us that his correspondent informed him that the worms were found "in every joint." From this he argued that it might be *Isosoma tritici*, instead of *I. hordei*, but its identity with the latter species was settled by breeding the adults at the De-

partment from straws received from Dr. Lintner, who has referred to this matter publicly in the *Country Gentleman*, vol. 49, p. 857.*
In Michigan the same insect appeared in 1884, working in the same way. In the *Rural New Yorker* for May 9, 1885 (vol. 44, p. 314), Prof. A. J. Cook described it in all stages at some length under the name of "The Black Wheat-stalk Isosoma" (*Isosoma nigrum*, n. sp.). He stated that he had received it from Wayne and Washtenaw Counties, and that at a "farmers' institute" held at Plymouth, Wayne County, in January, he found hardly a farmer who had not been vexed by the small pieces of straw, but that not one had discovered the cause.
On the appearance of Professor Cook's article we wrote to him for specimens, strongly suspecting that his new species would turn out to be the Common Joint Worm. He kindly complied with our request, and our suspicions were at once verified, and, as stated in our article in the *Rural New Yorker* (*loc. cit.*), they proved to be well-marked examples of Fitch's *tritici* form of *I. hordei*. Professor Cook is still, we believe, inclined to insist that his species is a good one, but without going into the details of our rather extensive correspondence with him in this matter, we reassert the correctness of our conclusion and pronounce the Michigan insect to be *I. hordei.*†
In conclusion we may extract a few facts from our notes bearing on the dates of transformations and the prevalence and habits of the parasites:
December 9, 1884.—Eight straws which were received from Louisa County, Virginia, July 30, were examined, with the following result: No. 1. Two parasites had issued, and the straw still contained three pupæ of Isosoma and seven larvæ of a Chalcid parasite. No. 2. Five parasites had issued, and seven parasitic larvæ still remained. No. 3. Ten parasites had issued, and one pupa of Isosoma; one living and three dead larvæ of the parasite remained. No. 4. Two parasites had issued, and six pupæ of Isosoma, and one parasitic larva. No. 5. One parasite had issued, and three Isosoma pupæ and four parasitic larvæ remained. No. 6. Two parasites had issued, and three pupæ of Isosoma and two parasitic larvæ remained. No. 7. Contained four Isosoma pupæ and three parasitic larvæ. No. 8. Five Isosoma pupæ and five parasitic larvæ. Isosoma was found only in the pupa state.
On December 17 the adult Isosomas began to issue, and they continued to appear in small numbers through January, February, March, and April, issuing most abundantly the first week in May. On May 28 straws were received from Louisa County which contained eggs nearly ready to hatch.
The breeding of 1885–'86 was very similar to this, and indicates that the periods mentioned are about normal. The adults of both sexes

---

* In the *American Agriculturist* for December, 1884, vol. 43, p. 531, what is evidently the same insect is treated as having been received from "Central New York," and which is there determined as *Isosoma tritici*, a reproduction of our figure of that species being also given.
† Professor Cook later republished the bulk of his first article on the subject as an original contribution to the *American Naturalist* for September, 1885 (pp. 804–808). Here he seems to be in some doubt as to the validity of his species and expresses the opinion that it will take time to "clear all this up," and says: "As species are only venerable varieties which by age have been run into the mold of variability, it really makes no great difference. Practically the matter remains the same in either case." Such reasoning would justify unlimited species-making from any one species known to be quite variable.

began to issue in numbers from Virginia straws December 19. December 31 another large lot issued, as also on January 5, January 8, and February 1.

From our breedings it becomes doubtful whether the principal parasite of the Joint Worm (*Semiotellus chalcidiphagus*, Walsh) has one or two annual generations. A few specimens were swept in the field by Messrs. Pergande and Stewart as early as June 13, while in the Department breeding-jars they issued in large numbers through July and on until August 22. Then no more were noticed until October 10, when a number were found in the jars.* During the winter straws cut open showed the presence of many of these parasites still in the larval state. April 9 a large number issued, and none after this date.

From these facts it seems that this species winters both in the adult state and as larvæ in the straws, the latter issuing in early spring. They undoubtedly oviposit in growing grain infested with *Isosoma* in the spring, and some individuals develop and issue in July and August, while others winter in the straw and stubble as larvæ. What becomes of the adults which issue so early in the season we can only surmise. It is after harvest when they appear, and to parasitize Joint Worm larvæ they would have to pierce the hard stubble or work their way into their own holes of exit or into the cut ends of the stubble; not a very likely proceeding. These early individuals may oviposit in some other host, or they may live and hibernate without ovipositing before spring.

The common *Eupelmus allynii* (French) is also, as we have elsewhere stated,† a parasite of *Isosoma hordei*, as well as of *Isosoma tritici* and the Hessian Fly (*Cecidomyia destructor*). From the Joint Worm it has also been bred from Virginia specimens, and on three dates, viz, August 22, 1884, October 11, 1884, and April 9, 1885. Although a considerable number issued on each of these dates, it appears to be only about one-tenth as numerous as the *Semiotellus*.

THE WHEAT-STRAW ISOSOMA.

(*Isosoma tritici*,‡ Riley.)

In our annual report for 1884, in describing the larger Wheat-straw Isosoma, we called attention (p. 358) to the possible relationship between this species and *I. tritici* in the following words:

"It may be here stated as an interesting fact that of the specimens so far reared both of *tritici* and *grande*, all are females, and whether or not there is any dimorphic relationship between these two forms is a question which future observations alone can decide. The probabilities are, however, that there is no connection between them, for,

---

* There is a possibility that some of these issued several days prior to this date.

† On the Parasites of the Hessian Fly, by C. V. Riley, Ph. D., Proceedings of the U. S. National Museum, 1885, pp. 413–422.

‡ As the object of this article is to show that the two species which we have described as *Isosoma tritici* and *I. grande* are in reality but seasonal dimorphic forms of one and the same species, it may be well to state that we retain the species name "*tritici*" as having priority, and because it represents the bisexual form of the species. We retain this name in preference to "*grande*" because, in addition to these reasons, it is an eminently appropriate name, and, as we have previously shown, Fitch's *Eurytoma tritici* is but a variety of *Isosoma hordei*, and cannot even be looked upon as entitled to a varietal name, since there is no constancy in the characters upon which it is based.

on the assumption that they represent alternate generations, we should expect the one or the other to comprise both sexes."

The history of our experiments with the two forms, in order to ascertain whether or not the relationship suggested in the above paragraph has any real existence, is briefly as follows:

Grande was first found by Mr. Webster in the summer of 1884. He observed it, and indeed bred it, early in June in Illinois, and on June 6 found females ovipositing in wheat at Oxford, Ind. On the 7th he found a pupa and a fully developed adult in wheat-stalks. The adults continued abundant until the 18th, when they began to decrease in numbers, and the last one was noticed June 27. A number of the straws in which these females were observed to oviposit in the field were sent to the Department, and a number were retained by Mr. Webster himself. From the straws sent to the Department *tritici* issued very abundantly in January and February, 1885. With Mr. Webster two premature individuals issued in October, 1884, and others issued in December, 1884, and January, and February, 1885; but all attempts to induce oviposition proved failures. No specimens of *grande* made their appearance. From straws left outdoors *tritici* issued in March and April, and again no specimens of *grande* were seen, although the straws were cut open and thoroughly examined.

This predisposed us to the conclusion that *tritici* had developed from eggs laid by *grande,* and although none of the specimens of *tritici* thus bred could be induced to oviposit in confinement, the hypothesis of an alternation of the two forms thus received strong support.

On the 2d of June, 1885, *grande* was once more observed in considerable numbers in a wheat plot, and examination showed this form present in nearly all stages of growth in the stalks. On August 12, 1885, stalks were isolated in which *grande* alone were observed to oviposit, and from these *tritici* began to issue at Washington January 7, 1886, and continued to issue on the following dates: January 15, 20, 21, 22, 23, 26, 27, and February 3, 4, 6, and 8, 1886. These all refused to oviposit, as was the case the previous winter. Mr. Webster was sent South the first of March on another investigation, and on his return to La Fayette in April found a limited number of *tritici,* which had emerged much later (probably during the latter part of March), still alive in his breeding-cages.

These specimens he at once transferred, as he states in his report, on the 12th of April, to young wheat plants grown and kept continuously under cover in a corner of his garden. These plants were carefully protected from outside insects, and on the 2d of June, 1886, the reverse of the former breeding was accomplished, and *grande* was bred from wheat in which indubitably nothing but *tritici* had oviposited! Several specimens issued in the next few days, and all immediately began to oviposit in the now nearly full-grown straw in other portions of the same stools from which they had issued.

The next step was then carried out, and these straws, in which the *bred* specimens of *grande* had oviposited from June 2 to June 12, were divided, and part sent to Washington and part retained at La Fayette, Ind., by Mr. Webster. On February 4, 1887, two female *tritici* were bred at Washington, and on the same day, as we subsequently learned, two were bred at La Fayette.

Thus the complete alternation of the two forms has been established. It will be remembered that the entire absence of a male among the many specimens of both forms bred and collected was a stumbling-block to our acceptance of this hyphothesis in 1884 before the alternation had been proven, and it so remained until January 6, 1886, when a male Isosoma was bred by us from the same straws in which *grande* was observed ovipositing by Mr. Webster at La Fayette August 12. 1885, and which had since been isolated, and from which female *tritici* were being bred and were subsequently bred in numbers. On February 4 another of these males was bred from this lot of straw, and on February 6 still another, making three in all. In size these males were slightly smaller than the females of *tritici*, and of course much smaller than *grande*. They were all three fully winged, and could have been nothing else than the males of *tritici*. Attempts were made while they were yet alive to establish this beyond all peradventure by placing them with living females of *tritici* bred from the same straws and also with living females bred from straws received from California. The result was unsatisfactory. The males were lively and ran actively about in the breeding-jars, but made no attempt to pair. As soon as they came in contact with the females they either flew away or dropped as if startled. They were watched, however, only during the daytime from 9 a. m. until 4 p. m., and were in confinement in breeding-jars in the Divisional laboratory. All males died after three or four days, and none of the males issued on the same day with the females, so that one or the other was weak when watched with the opposite sex. It is also probable that the artificial conditions of a vivarium are unfavorable to proper development or maturity of the specimens, and that freedom and sunlight are essential to coition.

This breeding of the males, although not perfectly satisfactory, removes the last obstacle to the acceptance of the fact of alternation of generations with this species; for we must now call it a single species. The summary of its life-history in Indiana is as follows:

In March and April there issue from old last year's straws, either stubble or volunteer, wingless females of the *tritici* form, with, in some seasons, males. These oviposit in growing wheat. In June the winged females of the *grande* form issue from this same wheat, with, so far as known, *no* males. These oviposit in the now nearly grown straws of wheat, and from these eggs hatch larvæ which mature before winter and give forth adults of the *tritici* form early the ensuing spring.

From this summary it will be seen that it is the *grande* form alone which does the damage in Indiana; and supposing this relationship to hold wherever the species occurs, it effectually relieves those northern regions where only spring wheat is grown from any anticipation of injury, and indicates the obvious remedy of destruction of stubble and volunteer grain in the cultivation of winter wheat. In localities where both winter and spring wheat are grown we should expect to find the insect the most numerous.

Bearing out this suggestion, we may state that we have received the insect from no portion of the country in which spring wheat exclusively is grown.

We have used the above qualifying clause as to the alternation of generation in these two forms in all sections where the species occurs, for the reason that while *grande* has been found only in Bloomington and Normal, Ill., and Oxford and La Fayette, Ind., *tritici* has been sent to us from Virginia, Indiana, Illinois, Tennessee, Missouri, Kansas, California, and Washington Territory.

Mr. J. F. Donkin, of Grayson, Stanislaus County, California, wrote us under date of May 23, 1885, sending specimens, and again on June 19. Mr. Coquillett, writing from Atwater, Merced County, California, June 29, sent similar specimens. Mr. Donkin, in his first letter, said: "They are killing a large percentage of our wheat. The heads turn yellow and die long before the wheat ripens." In his second letter he supplemented this as follows: "I send you by this mail samples of wheat-straw taken from different fields several miles apart. I am told by friends who have been growing wheat for years on the same land that the worms are in all the wheat this year. They have found it in the wheat of every field examined. There is a difference of opinion about the damage done by it. Some say that when we have plenty of rain and the wheat is thrifty it does no harm. One told me that he had noticed pieces of about one-eighth of an acre in extent where about one-eighth of the heads had no wheat. Last year was the first that I saw any myself."

That this insect has existed in California for a number of years there can be no doubt from the evidence of correspondents. It is probably the same insect which was sent to Dr. Packard through the *Pacific Rural Press* in September, 1879, from Healdsburg, Sonoma County, California, and which was identified by him as a wingless Joint Worm. Other specimens were received by him the same year from Madison, Yolo County. It was also received by us in September, 1882, from Mr. J. A. Starner, of Dayton, Columbia County, Washington Territory, in stalks which contained larvæ and pupæ. Although the work and early stages were precisely similar to those of *tritici*, the great difference in locality led to the presumption that it might be a different though related species, but subsequent breeding of the adults settled the question of identity.*

The presence of this insect in the other States mentioned has already been placed on record, with the exception of Kansas. From this State we received specimens in July, 1885, from Mr. Warren Knaus, of Salina. The straws contained larvæ which were dried up on receipt, so that it was impossible to say to which form they belonged. The work in the straws indicated either *tritici* or *grande*, while the date of collecting (July 5) rendered it more probable that they were *grande*. As this is the first recorded finding of *Isosoma* in Kansas, we may quote briefly from Mr. Knaus' account:

"I mail you to-day a box containing specimens of what I take to be *Isosoma tritici*. The joints infested are all the second from the ground, and are the only ones in the stalk of wheat containing the worm. Stalks from various fields are almost all infested, many containing three larvæ. I have taken a number of larvæ from immediately above the joint next the head. My observation is that these worms have caused more damage to the wheat in this part of the State than the Hessian Fly fully 50 per cent. of the heads in many fields of wheat showing their work in a very marked manner."

In a letter dated August 16 he gives the following:

"I have just returned from a trip through Northwest Kansas, and find that the Wheat-straw Worm has seriously damaged the wheat in the counties of Ottawa, Cloud, Osborne, Rooks, and Phillips; also in Saline, McPherson, and Dickinson Counties. It has really done more damaged than the Hessian Fly."

In order to compare the customary situation and abundance of the larvæ in the straw in California with Mr. Knaus' statement and with

* See *American Naturalist*, December, 1882, p. 1017.

Mr. Webster's table in our last Annual Report (p. 386), we give the result of an examination of ten straws received May 23 from Mr. Donkin, of Grayson, Cal.:

Above fourth knot from ear 3
Above third knot from ear.. 12
Above second knot from ear.. 15
Above first knot from ear.. 5
In second knot from ear.. 2
In third knot from ear 6
In fourth knot from ear 1

Total number of larvæ in ten stalks................................... 44

PARASITES.—By far the most numerous parasite bred during the season from both the bisexual and unisexual forms has been *Eupelmus allynii* (French). But one specimen (female) of *Stictonotus isosomatis* Riley, which we described in our Annual Report for 1881–'82 (p. 186), has been reared since the original description, which was drawn up from one female and two males. We have, however, bred a most interesting parasite of the Proctotrupid genus *Dryinus* from the *grande* form and a new Pteromalid from both forms.

SILK CULTURE.

In our last Annual Report we reiterated the recommendations which we had several times made that means be given for the establishment in Washington of an experimental silk filature, and expressed the hope that we should be able to obtain a certain number of Serrell automatic reels with which to carry out any experiments which might be authorized.

In pursuance of this recommendation Congress, at its last session, appropriated $10,000 in aid of silk culture, and, among other things, authorized "experiments with automatic machinery for reeling silk from the cocoon at some point in the District of Columbia." The experimental reeling station at New Orleans had been closed at the beginning of the calendar year, and on the 30th of June that at Philadelphia was also closed and its appurtenances loaned to the Women's Silk Culture Association, in aid of which Congress also appropriated $5,000.

In pursuance of this act (June 30, 1886) an experimental silk filature has been set up in one of the Department buildings in Washington. It consists of a battery of six Serrell automatic reels and an automatic cocoon-brushing machine, invented partly by the same engineer.

Several objects will be held in view in operating this establishment. Among them we shall endeavor to settle conclusively the commercial value of Osage Orange as a silk-worm food, and, more important still, as foreshadowed in our last report, will be the determination of the question as to whether silk can be reeled with profit in the United States by means of the most improved machinery.

OSAGE ORANGE VS. MULBERRY.

In reference to the first object, the work already done justifies the statement that cocoons raised from Maclura-fed worms produce as good a silk as when the worms are fed on Mulberry. The difficulty found when these cocoons were reeled in France was that the rendi-

tion * was too great, being in the neighborhood of 5, while 4 is only
a fair result with white-mulberry cocoons.

The second week's work in the Washington filature on Osage Orange
cocoons gave a rendition of 3.69, and subsequently a result as low as
3.65 has been attained. This result was reported to Mr. Serrell, the
inventor of the reels used, who, though living abroad, has always
taken a lively interest in American silk culture, and his comments
thereon are so encouraging that their substance is presented here:

The rendition from Osage Orange cocoons at the Washington filature is astonishing. So far as I know, the only time they have been reeled in France they gave
a rendition of nearly 5. That is to say, as reeled in France it took a pound and a
third more cocoons to produce a pound of silk than in the work done in Washington. It is fair to say, however, that in France they were reeled in a filature accustomed to only the best French cocoons.

" Be that as it may, the result attained is extremely remarkable, and makes me
foresee a prompter outcome from American cocoons than I had supposed was possible.

Of the silk mentioned several skeins were taken to New York and
submitted to the most rigorous tests at the Silk-conditioning Works
in that city. It is needless to go into the details of the technical report made by its manager, but it will suffice to say that this Osage
Orange silk gave excellent results, the faults being such as can be
cured as our silk-raisers gain in experience.

The use of Osage Orange as a food-plant has now become quite
general in the States where it is plentiful. Some observations which
have been made on cocoons raised therefrom may be of service to
the raisers who employ it. If two batches of cocoons be taken,
raised from the same eggs, the one on the Mulberry and the other on
the Osage, they will to the ordinary eye possess no distinct characteristics. The expert, however, can at once and almost unerringly designate the food used in either case, and this on account of the greater
degree of satinage observable in those produced by the Osage Orange-
fed worms. It was explained in the last edition of our manual that
this satinage consisted of an inferior gumming together of the layers
of the cocoon, and is made apparent to the eye by the coarser texture
of its surface. As a result, the water penetrates to the interior, and
causes them to sink to the bottom of the basin in reeling, and thus
to break off the filament. Although this difficulty has not been
proved to be the result of any given cause, still it is generally believed to be due to the insufficient feeding of the worm during the
last days of its life. At this time almost all of its food goes to the
formation of silk, and though a worm may make its cocoon if the
feeding is stopped five days after the last molt, still it will be weak
and commercially useless. In order that it should be strong and well
garnished, no food should be spared at this time. The almost universal difference found between the cocoons raised on Osage Orange
and Mulberry in this particular leads to the opinion that a greater
quantity of the former food is required than of the latter, and that
our people have not learned to supply their silk-worms with enough
liberality during the days which precede the spinning.

What has been said above must not be construed as a serious ob-
jection to the use of such food, but simply as an indication of how
it may be used with greater advantage than at present. On the con-

* By " rendition " is meant the number of pounds of dry cocoons required to produce a pound of reeled silk.

trary, though nothing definite can be said as to the result of the limited experiments already made, the indications point to Osage Orange as at least the equal of Mulberry as silk-worm food, and confirm in continuous reeling the conclusions arrived at in previous years, and which we have reiterated in past writings.

THE SERRELL REEL—COST OF WORK UP TO THE PRESENT TIME.

In regard to the more important feature of our experiments we have not yet gone far enough to be willing to venture any opinion upon the probable outcome of the work. The limited appropriation prevented the setting up of more than six reels, though we had hoped to obtain twelve. Even with these six it has been somewhat slow work to train the young girls employed in their operation, and the consequent sale of the silk produced has been delayed longer than we anticipated. But at the best we cannot this year hope for results which will be more than indicative of the future prospects of the industry; for there are so many items of loss in the operation of a small establishment, which would not occur in a larger one worked under what we may call factory conditions, that it is impossible to make altogether accurate estimates. We shall be able, however, to show the silk manufacturers of the country what quality of silk can be made from American cocoons, and to give capitalists some indications of the probable profit to be realized or loss to be suffered in working a filature supplied with the best machines. We hope to be able to give in our next annual report the result of at least nine months of work under as favorable conditions as are possible with a small establishment.

The expenses of the operation of the experimental filature have been so far as follows:

	Per week.
1 forewoman	$8 65
5 operatives	23 08
Total	31 73

Or of each of the five reeling days, $6.35.

It has been found best to reel forty hours per week, and employ the time Saturday in sorting cocoons, so that the above sum ($6.35) includes the total expense for productive labor employed in making one day's product.

Only five of the reels have been in operation. The best product made on the five reels mentioned has been 850 grams per diem (1.87 pounds).

This silk has cost us:

For labor as above	$6 35
For cocoons	7 29
Total	13 64

The value of the product would be, at minimum figures (1.87 pounds of silk, at $5)	9 35
Waste	1 50
Total	10 85

This will show a daily loss of $2.79, or a loss of approximately $1.50 per pound of silk produced, not including interest on capital involved or cost of superintendence. It is not a very good showing, and we quote Mr. Walker's conclusion as to the chances of improving it:

"I am of the opinion that saving can be made in the following ways: In the present machines the two threads of each basin are so dependent upon each other that when one thread breaks the reels of both threads stop. Judging from the result of carefully noted experiments within the past week, I am of the opinion that if these threads were made independently of each other the daily production would be increased by 125 grams without increase of the labor employed. Again, the two girls at the reels, owing to their slight experience, are unable to keep the threads sufficiently free from almost exhausted cocoons, and as a result bunches run up into the *croisure* and cause the rupture of the filament. By careful noting of the time lost by these breakages I found that it amounted to 20 per cent. of the working day. I put Mrs. Vaccarino in the place of the two girls, and by her superior ability in taking out exhausted cocoons she diminished the loss of time to slightly over 6 per cent. It is probable that with properly constructed *purgeurs* the ratio of time lost would be reduced as low as 10 per cent. And I am now experimenting with some devices which justify, I think, my hopes of arriving at such a result. If I do succeed, I shall, without increasing my labor, increase my production from 1.87 pounds to 2.37 pounds.

"This silk will require in its production:

For labor	$6 35
For cocoons	9 24
Total	15 59

"The product will be worth:

Silk..	$11 85
Waste..	2 00
Total	13 85

"This would reduce the daily loss to $1.74, or the loss per pound of silk produced to 74 cents."

THE DISTRIBUTION OF EGGS.

In 1885, as stated in our last report, a quantity of silk-worm eggs were purchased of American silk-raisers and 150 ounces were distributed to applicants in different parts of the country. The general result was so unsatisfactory as to prevent the repetition of the experiment. There were but few of the sellers who had the slightest idea of the care to be taken in egg production, and it has not been thought wise to continue the encouragement of this kind of work. There is, too, undoubtedly, evidence of the existence in the country of much "seed" of inferior races, and it is our aim to prevent the use of this as much as possible by the gratuitous distribution of choice qualities. In 1885 our distribution was confined to the class of races commonly called the large Milan, and the same policy will be followed in 1887. Silk-raisers who have had cause to be dissatisfied with their stock, either from failure in their education or from poor prices received for their product, will do well to apply to the Department for a new supply.

The reason for confining the distribution of eggs to the large Milan

races is one dictated by the necessities of the case. They have, as a
rule, been submitted to the Pasteur microscopical selection, which is
not true of Asiatic stock. This would have been of little importance
some years ago, but now there is good evidence of the existence of
the pebrine in Japan and China, and the only means of guarding
against it is by avoiding the purchase of such material.

Of the Milan races, then, stock of assured purity may be obtained.
The worms are hardy and the cocoons give excellent results in reeling. The few reeling establishments now existing or likely to exist
in the United States in the near future can consume but a comparatively small quantity of cocoons and produce but a small quantity of
silk. In order to find a ready market for such silk it must be of good
quality, a term which includes among other things evenness of color.
To produce this evenness we must have not only cocoons of the same
color, but as much as possible of the same shade. The use of the
many races now in vogue in this country prevents the attaining of
this desirable end, and the cocoons that are offered at the filature are
not all that can be desired in this direction. It is true that we might
choose some of the other European races that are as carefully selected,
such, for example, as the Bionne, but taking everything into consideration, the conditions sought for are best found in the large Milan
varieties.

Last spring some of this sort of eggs, produced by the house of
Darbrousse, in France, were sent to us by a gentleman in New Or-
leans, and a few of them were raised in the Department building, the
food employed being Osage orange. There were almost no deaths in
the batch, and about 4 pounds of cocoons were produced. It took
256 of these to make a pound, while 300 is considered an extremely
good result. Part of the best of these were selected for reproduction, and were found to weigh a pound to each 216. Such cocoons as
these are what silk-reelers want and are willing to pay extra prices
for, but unfortunately there are few of them offered.

IMPROPER CHOKING OF COCOONS.

Our experience in the filature, too, has shown us that our people
are sadly deficient in their knowledge of the art of stifling cocoons,
and many lots have been received which were of otherwise excellent
quality, but which had been burned by the employment of improper
means for destroying the life of the chrysalis. It is the custom in
Europe for the silk-raiser to dispose of his cocoons at the filature as
soon as they are raised and before they have been stifled. The raiser
then has the advantage of getting payment for his work as soon as
it is completed, and the silk-reeler is enabled to stifle his cocoons in
large quantities and by the most approved process. This scheme,
however, has thus far been found impossible in the United States, as
the silk-raisers are as a rule located so far from the available markets,
that there would be danger of the moths piercing the cocoons before
they could be choked. American buyers have therefore been obliged
to purchase only stifled cocoons which have been thoroughly dried,
and as this process of drying requires several months, silk-raisers have
not received the proceeds of their season's labor until well into the
autumn. And again, through inability to purchase apparatus or
through lack of knowledge on the subject, they have resorted to such
means of stifling as were at their command, and have destroyed in
many cases an otherwise excellent crop. This burning of the cocoons

may always be obviated by using steam in their stifling and afterwards thoroughly drying them to prevent molding. A very efficient though simple piece of apparatus for thus stifling cocoons was purchased last spring by this Department of the New York Silk Exchange, and is within the means of most silk-growers. A sketch of it, in a slightly modified form, is given at Fig. 1. It consists of a tin reservoir, A, which, when in use, is about one-third filled with water. Slightly above the surface of the water is a movable perforated partition, B, intended to prevent spattering during ebullition. The uppe rportion contains a perforated pan for holding the cocoons, while all is tightly closed by a cover. Cocoons may be thoroughly stifled by exposure in this apparatus over boiling water for twenty minutes. It will be seen, too, that much the same apparatus can be contrived by the use of a deep kettle, into which is set an ordinary colander full of cocoons. It is well to avoid, however, so filling the kettle with water that it will splash upon the cocoons in boiling, as they should only be subjected to the action of steam. The apparatus owned by the Department is 12 inches in diameter and 13 inches deep, and will stifle from 3 to 4 pounds of cocoons at a time.

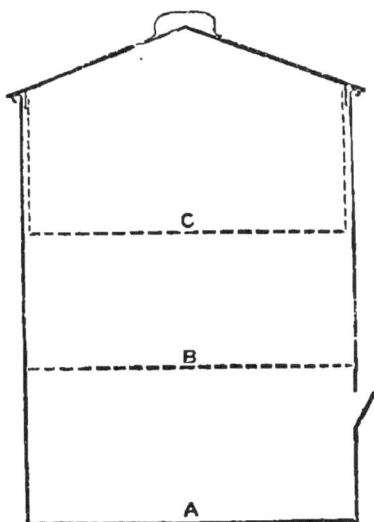

COCOONS PRODUCED IN THE UNITED STATES IN 1886.

Desirous of getting some statistics as to the amount of silk produced during the year in this country, and believing that the result could be approximately obtained by summing up the receipts at Washington and Philadelphia, we applied to Mrs. Lucas, who has kindly furnished the data from the Women's Silk-Culture Association of Philadelphia, of which she is president. These receipts are for the first half of the fiscal year, or from October 1, 1886, to the end of the year. They do not include whatever silk was raised in California, and will probably be materially increased by receipts during the first quarter of 1887. The result is, however, quite interesting, and the more so that no impetus was given to the raising of the cocoons by the establishment of the filature at Washington (and the same may be said in a great measure of Philadelphia), since the appropriation did not become available until after the silk-raising season was over.

Figures show that during the time stated there have been purchased at the Washington filature 1,313 pounds 15 ounces, valued at $1,272.04, and by the Women's Silk Culture Association at Philadelphia, 3,801 pounds 9 ounces, valued at $2,720.88. This makes a total of 5,115 pounds 8 ounces, for which there was paid the sum of $3,982.96, or nearly 78 cents per pound. These were obtained, as will be seen by the following table, from twenty-six States and Territories. It is probable that the table is not a just indication of the production of those States, as there have been certain cases where lots of cocoons have been received at the filature which were the results of collections made from many different raisers and which were possibly not raised in the State from which they were purchased.

State.	Philadelphia.				Washington.				Total.				Average value per pound.
	Quantity.		Value.		Quantity.		Value.		Quantity.		Value.		
	Lbs.	*oz.*	*Dollars.*		*Lbs.*	*oz.*	*Dollars.*		*Lbs.*	*oz.*	*Dollars.*		*Dollars.*
Alabama	1	12	0	70	5	10	6	04	7	6	6	74	0 91
Arkansas	30	1¼	15	40	5	1	3	54	35	2¼	18	94	54
District of Columbia	.....		.....		3	12	3	32	3	12	3	32	885
Florida	56	2¼	52	24	8	2	4	05	64	4¼	56	29	88
Georgia	18	6¼	11	38	0	12		78	19	2¼	12	16	63
Illinois	780	2	622	33	249	7	241	12	1,029	9	863	45	838
Indiana	140	13	100	80	85	8	81	70	226	5	182	50	805
Iowa	165	2	111	68	3	2	3	59	168	4	115	27	685
Kansas	596	7	351	85	57	5	61	08	653	12	412	93	63
Kentucky	67	10	38	80	5	12	6	11	73	6	44	91	61
Louisiana	9	0¼	8	72	162	8	172	54	171	14¼	181	26	89
Massachusetts	4	6	3	41	.....		.....		4	6	3	45	788
Michigan	241	12	223	18	4	12	5	46	246	8	228	64	92
Mississippi	3	10	1	27	111	2	86	49	114	12	87	76	76
Missouri	267	13	194	45	125	12	129	04	393	9	323	49	82
Nebraska	71	3	32	18	116	11	125	78	187	14	157	96	84
New Jersey	8	8¼	8	14	3	4	3	25	11	12¼	11	39	966
New York	3	5	2	81	3	3	2	86	6	8	5	67	87
North Carolina	95	7	49	36	37	3	41	23	132	10	90	59	68
Ohio	1,063	11	780	13	121	5	113	13	1,185	0	893	26	75
Pennsylvania	54	4½	40	55	144	4	115	40	198	8½	155	95	78
South Carolina	9	4	4	77	.....		.....		9	4	4	77	515
Tennessee	37	0	13	56	2	3	2	18	39	3	15	74	40
Texas	11	12¼	6	99	40	10	39	97	52	6¼	46	96	89
Virginia	60	10½	42	80	15	4	11	95	75	14½	54	75	72
West Virginia	3	0	3	38	1	7	1	43	4	7	4	81	1 08
Total	3,801	9¼	2,720	88	1,313	15	1,262	04	5,115	8¼	3,982	96	772

REPORTS OF AGENTS.

REPORT ON REMEDIES FOR THE COTTONY CUSHION-SCALE.

By D. W. Coquillett, *Special Agent.*

LETTER OF TRANSMITTAL.

SIR: The following pages comprise my report upon the experiments to destroy the Cottony Cushion-scale (*Icerya purchasi*, Maskell).

In accordance with your letter of instruction I proceeded to Los Angeles on the 9th of February, 1886, and had a conference with the County Horticultural Commission relative to the best place for me to to locate in order to study to the best advantage the life-history and habits of the Cottony Cushion-scale, and they assured me that they could find such a location in the city of Los Angeles, but wanted time to enable them to make the necessary arrangements. Accordingly I returned to Anaheim, and on the 15th of February again visited Los Angeles, and was shown several orchards, in either of which I could carry on my investigations. I chose the Wolfskill orchard as offering the best opportunities for my studies, and was not a little influenced in my choice by the fact that I would thereby secure the aid of the superintendent of this orchard, Mr. Alexander Craw, whom I found to be a most careful and accurate observer of the habits of insects in general, and who has had considerable experience in combating scale insects of various kinds.

In this orchard I carried on my experiments with various remedies for the destruction of the Cottony Cushion-scale, and it was here that the greater number of my observations upon the history and habits of this insect were made; but I also studied it in many of the other orchards and yards in various parts of this city.

On the 18th of June, 1885, the board of supervisors of Los Angeles County passed an ordinance relating to the destruction of insect pests. In accordance with this ordinance the office of County Board of Horticultural Commissioners was established, and Messrs. J. R. Dobbins, George Rice, and S McKinley were appointed to the board. It is the duty of this commission to divide the county into districts and appoint an inspector for each district. When trees or plants are found to be infested with the Cottony Cushion-scale or other injurious insect the owner is notified of this fact and is requested to disinfect such trees or plants, and if he fails to do so within due time his premises are deemed a public nuisance, to be proceeded against as any ordinary nuisance until abated.

On the 4th of August, 1885, the city council of the city of Los Angeles passed an ordinance declaring trees and plants infested with the Cottony Cushion-scale within the city limits a public nuisance immediately, and it also established the offices of inspectors of fruit pests, whose duty it was to see that the provisions of this ordinance were enforced.

On the 13th of November, 1885, the board of supervisors of Los Angeles County offered a reward of $1,000 for a perfect exterminator of the Cottony Cushion-scale, and the horticultural commission and myself were appointed by the board to act as a committee for determining the efficacy of the various remedies presented by the different applicants for the above reward. Up to the present writing there have been eleven applicants for this reward, and these have made thirty-eight tests, but none of these remedies have been deemed worthy of the offered reward.

In the prosecution of my studies I have been not a little aided by the above commission and their able corps of inspectors, to all of whom my warmest thanks are due. Mr. Albert Koebele, one of the agents of the United States Division of Entomology, has been with me part of the time, and has aided me much in the mechanical part of my experiments.

Respectfully, yours,

D. W. COQUILLETT.

Prof. C. V. RILEY,
United States Entomologist.

GENERAL CONSIDERATIONS.

The great desideratum in a remedy for scale insects is that it shall kill all of the insects and their eggs without producing any injury whatever to the tree or fruit, and to this must be added the additional qualification that it must be reasonably cheap. A wash costing from 1 to $1\frac{1}{2}$ cents per gallon would be cheap enough to be extensively used, while if it should exceed 3 cents per gallon it would be beyond the reach of the majority of the fruit-growers.

It is no difficult task to discover a wash possessing any two of the above qualities; but to discover one which possesses the three properties combined is a far more difficult matter.

The remedies in common use in Southern California for the destruction of the Cottony Cushion-scale consist of various liquid solutions applied to the infested trees in the form of a spray. The usual appliances for performing this operation consist of a force or spraying pump mounted upon a barrel or tank; to the pump is attached from one to four pieces of rubber hose from 15 to 20 feet in length, and to the end of each is attached an iron tube measuring from 4 to 10 feet in length. The nozzle commonly used is known as the "San José" nozzle, and is fastened to the outer end of the iron tube above described.

This nozzle consists of a short brass tube, upon the outer end of which is screwed a brass cap having a large opening in the top. This cap holds in place a circular piece of brass, in the center of which is a small slit, through which the solution is forced in the form of a fan-shaped spray. Sometimes a piece of rubber is substituted for the circular piece of brass in the nozzle; it has the advantage of not becoming clogged so easily as the brass one, but is far less durable.

The Cyclone nozzle, which has been fully described in previous reports of this Department, has been used by a few different persons here, but these, with one accord, prefer the San José nozzle. For thorough work, however, the Cyclone nozzle is to be preferred, as it does not become clogged so easily as the San José nozzle, and it also permits the operator to spray the leaves from all directions, the spray issuing from the side of the nozzle instead of from the outer end, so that by simply turning about the iron tube carrying the nozzle the spray can be thrown in all directions.

This defect in the San José nozzle is overcome to a certain extent by means of a ladder, by the use of which the tree can be sprayed both from above and from below. For this purpose an improved ladder, mounted upon wheels, is now coming into use. This can be wheeled from one tree to the other, and being provided with the proper supports, does not rest against the tree itself. In this way the operator can move up and down the ladder without being hindered by the branches of the tree he is operating upon. (See Plate V.)

Even the most skillful operator, however, when equipped with the best of appliances, will find it to be absolutely impossible to spray the solution upon *every* insect on the tree, as a few are quite certain to escape, protected, it may be, by a curled leaf or similar object. Much can be done to aid in properly spraying the trees by first removing from the tree, especially from the inside of the top of it, all of the branches that can possibly be spared. This will not only greatly expedite the task of spraying and make it more efficient, but will make a great saving in the quantity of the solution required, thus lessening the cost of spraying in proportion to the number of branches removed.

Another item of importance is to prevent the great waste of that portion of the solution which ordinarily falls upon the ground after having been sprayed upon the trees. This can be accomplished by using some simple contrivance for catching the solution in such a manner that it can be made to flow into a tub or other vessel, being in the mean time strained from all extraneous substances; it can then be emptied into the tank or barrel to which the spraying-pump is attached and thus be used over again. It has been ascertained that fully *two-thirds* of the quantity of the solution first used could in this way be saved and with but very little additional labor.*

As illustrating the extreme tenacity of life with which the female Cottony Cushion-scale insect is endowed, I may state a fact that I have frequently witnessed, namely, that an adult female, with her egg-case attached, when sprayed with a solution so caustic that her back was burned black and was hard and wrinkled, still retained the use of all of her organs three weeks after the application of the solution had been made. In such instances the cottony egg-sac had been hardened and discolored by the solution, and the addition to it which the female had excreted after the application of the solution was very conspicuous by its whiteness.

Several persons have succeeded in clearing their trees of the Cottony Cushion-scale by simply spraying them with pure cold water thrown upon the trees with considerable force, repeating the operation once or twice each week until all of the insects have been removed from the trees.

When once these insects have inserted their beaks into the bark of the tree it is quite impossible to extract them from the bark by any forcible means that we may employ, as the beak is very brittle and easily broken off short to the body. It is doubtless owing to this fact that the water remedy referred to above is so effective when employed against these insects, as the beaks are broken off in dislodging them from the tree, and the insects, thus deprived of the organ through which their food is obtained, must necessarily perish of starvation.

This method is practicable only in places where but few trees are to be treated; it is much too laborious and requires repetition too frequently to be used on a large scale.

Following is a summary of the experiments which I have made with various remedies for the destruction of the Cottony Cushion-scale. For spraying these solutions upon the trees I used a Johnson pump and a Cyclone nozzle.

In making these experiments it has been my aim to discover a remedy that would prove fatal not only to the insects in their various stages of development but also to the eggs, as it will be easily seen that if the latter are not destroyed they will in due time hatch out, and thus again stock the tree with these pernicious pests.

Of course a remedy that merely destroys the insects could be used with good success by making a second application at an interval of about two months after the first one, thus giving the eggs time to hatch out; but this would require double the labor and cost of a single application and the risk of injuring the tree would also be much greater.

CAUSTIC POTASH.

The crude potash was dissolved in water and the solution then sprayed upon the trees. The cost of the potash at wholesale is about 7 cents per pound.

One Pound of Potash dissolved in one Gallon of Water.—An hour after the application the leaves upon the newest growth on the tree had sensibly withered; nine days later about one-half of the leaves had dried up and fallen from the tree. Two months after making the application one-tenth of the smaller lateral branches had become dead and dry, while upon the other branches a new growth had started. About 95 per cent. of the insects and 60 per cent. of the eggs were killed; the insects which es-

---

* Such a drain-table has already been made and used at San José for the purpose indicated. It is described in the first report of the State Board of Horticultural Commissioners, 1882, p. 83, in Mr. Chapin's report, as follows: "The table is made of sheet-iron and zinc, fixed upon a frame in halves, which are placed against the trunk of the tree on either side, thus forming a circular basin 14 feet in diameter, and requiring but one minute for transfer from one tree to another. * * * The saving caused by this was at least two-thirds of the material."

caped injury were those in the adult stage, both before and after excreting the egg-mass.

One Pound of Potash and two Gallons of Water.—This killed about one-tenth of the leaves upon the tree and several of the smaller branches. All of the insects in the first and second stages were killed, but only about one-half of the adult females, one-fourth of the females with egg-masses, and one-tenth of the eggs were killed.

One Pound of Potash and four Gallons of Water.—This killed about 5 per cent. of the leaves and burned brown spots of various sizes in many of the others. Nearly all of the insects in the first and second stages were killed, but not more than one-fourth of the adult females before secreting the egg-masses were killed, while the females with these egg-masses were scarcely affected by the application; eggs uninjured.

CAUSTIC SODA.

The crude caustic soda was used; the present price of the soda is 5 cents per pound when purchased in large quantities.

One Pound of caustic Soda dissolved in two Gallons of Water.—This killed all of the leaves upon the tree and burned the bark brown, but later in the season the tree put forth a new growth on some of the larger branches. All of the insects were killed, with the exception of about one-tenth of the adult females before secreting the egg-masses and one-eighth of those with egg-masses; eggs scarcely injured. (In one of the egg-masses situated upon a spot where the bark had been burned brown I found three recently hatched larvæ five days after making the application.)

One Pound of caustic Soda to four Gallons of Water.—This killed about four-fifths of the leaves and one-third of the smaller branches, and burned the bark brown in large spots. With the exception of about one-sixth of the adult females before secreting the egg-masses and one-fourth of those with egg-masses, all of the insects were killed; eggs uninjured.

One Pound of caustic Soda to six Gallons of Water.—This killed about one-third of the leaves upon the tree, while the bark was not injured. A slightly larger number of the adult females escaped injury than in the preceding experiment; eggs uninjured.

Several egg-masses were immersed in a solution composed of 1 pound of caustic soda dissolved in 1 gallon of water; this killed about one-third of the eggs thus treated.

HARD SOAP.

This was a brown laundry soap, manufactured by the Los Angeles Soap Company, under the name of "Our Favorite German Chemical Soap," and I am informed by one of the members of the above firm that this soap is composed of tallow, caustic soda, a little sal-soda, and resin. It is retailed at the rate of 5 cents per bar, weighing somewhat less than a pound, but it could probably be obtained at wholesale at the rate of 3 cents per pound. It was first dissolved in hot water and afterward diluted with cold water, and sprayed upon the trees when quite cold.

One Pound of Soap and two Gallons of Water.—This left a whitish coating upon the leaves and bark of the tree, but did not appear to injure the latter. It killed all of the insects with the exception of about 1 per cent. of the females with egg-masses, and hardened the outside of the egg-masses to such a degree that the insects after hatching were unable to make their way to the outside world. Fully four-fifths of the eggs were thus virtually destroyed.

One Pound of Soap and three Gallons of Water.—This also left a whitish coating upon the leaves and bark. All of the insects were killed with the exception of about 4 per cent. of the adult females, before secreting the egg-masses and 8 per cent. of the females with egg-masses. About three-fourths of the eggs were destroyed in the manner related above.

Several of the egg-masses were immersed in a solution composed of 1 pound of the soap to 1 gallon of water, and not a living insect issued from either of the egg-masses thus treated.

It is necessary to spray these solutions when quite hot, since the cold solutions are of such a thick consistency that it is very difficult to force them through a spraying nozzle.

SOFT SOAP.

This was made by dissolving 1 pound of refined potash and 1 of concentrated lye in 3 gallons of water, to which was added one-half gallon of fish-oil. This was boiled for about one hour, when 4½ gallons of water were added. The cost of these materials when purchased in large quantities is about as follows: Potash and concentrated lye, each about 10 cents per pound; fish-oil, 35 cents per gallon. The materials used in making the soap above described made about 66 pints of soap, at a cost of 37 cents, being a trifle over half a cent per pint.

Two Pints of Soap in one Gallon of Water.—This proved fatal to all of the insects with the exception of about 10 per cent. of the adult females. About three-fourths of the eggs were destroyed, the solution having the property of hardening the egg-masses.

One Pint of Soap in one Gallon of Water.—This proved fatal to all of the insects with the exception of about one-third of the adult females, but not more than one-third of the eggs were destroyed.

KEROSENE EMULSIONS.

An emulsion was made by dissolving half a pound of hard soap in 1 gallon of water, and adding it, boiling hot, to 2 gallons of the best grade of kerosene (150° fire-test), and forcing this through a spraying-pump back again into the vessel containing the solution. This was continued for about twenty minutes, when a very good emulsion was formed.

This emulsion was used in various proportions from 1 part of the emulsion to 6 parts of water, to 1 part of the emulsion to 18 of water. Neither of these solutions produced an injurious effect upon the trees operated upon.

One Part of the Emulsion to six Parts of Water.—This proved fatal to all of the insects with the exception of about 6 per cent. of the females before secreting the egg-masses and 10 per cent. of those with egg-masses. Nearly all of the eggs were killed.

One Part of the Emulsion to nine Parts of Water.—This was fatal to only about one-third of the adult females and a somewhat larger proportion of the young ones. About four-fifths of the eggs were destroyed.

A number of the egg-masses were immersed in the undiluted emulsion, and none of the eggs thus treated hatched out.

An emulsion of the same grade of kerosene as that used above was formed of 2 gallons of kerosene and 1 gallon of sweet milk. This formed a better and more stable emulsion than the one made with soap-suds, but its effects upon the insects were not as good as those produced by the latter emulsion.

A solution composed of 1 part of this emulsion to 6 parts of water killed nearly all of the young insects, but proved fatal to only 10 per cent. of the adult females with egg-masses. About one-half of the eggs were killed.

A third emulsion was formed by emulsifying 2 gallons of the same grade of kerosene as that used above with 1 gallon of soft soap dissolved in 2 gallons of water. Considerable difficulty was experienced in forming a stable emulsion with these ingredients.

This emulsion was diluted with water to such an extent that each 5 gallons of the diluted wash contained 1 gallon of kerosene. This proved fatal alike to the insects in all of their stages and also to their eggs.

It was also used in such proportions that each 7 gallons of the diluted wash contained 1 gallon of kerosene; this was fatal to all of the insects with the exception of a small number of the adult females with egg-masses; all of the eggs were killed.

Even the strongest solution, containing 1 gallon of kerosene in each 5 gallons of the diluted solution, produced no injurious effect either upon the trees or fruit; the trees experimented on were small orange trees about four years old.

Unlike the soap solutions, which penetrate the egg-masses and afterward harden, thus preventing the escape of the young insects after hatching out, the kerosene deprives the eggs of their vitality by penetrating first the egg-sacs and then the eggs themselves.

The cost of the kerosene (150°) is about 20 cents per gallon when purchased in large quantities.

TOBACCO.

Two pounds of tobacco leaves and stems were boiled in water until the strength of the tobacco had been extracted; the solution when cold was diluted with water and used in various proportions.

When used in the proportion of 1 pound of the tobacco to each 2 gallons of water, all of the insects were killed; about 3 per cent. of the eggs escaped injury.

When used in the proportion of 1 pound of the tobacco to each 4 gallons of the solution, it proved fatal to all of the insects with the exception of about 10 per cent. of the adult females with egg-masses; about 95 per cent. of the eggs were killed.

The strongest solution used, 1 pound of tobacco to each 2 gallons of water, produced no injurious effect upon the tree.

Several egg-masses were immersed in a solution containing a pound of tobacco to

1¼ gallons of water, and this proved fatal to about one-half of the eggs. As this is out of all proportion as compared with the other experiments made by spraying the egg-masses upon the trees with the tobacco decoction of various strengths, I am led to believe that when the egg-masses are simply immersed in any solution, except when held in the solution for some time, they do not become so thoroughly saturated with it as when the latter is sprayed upon them: and I have proved beyond a doubt that a solution thrown upon the insects in the form of a fine spray will have a better effect than if thrown upon them in a coarser spray, just as a heavy fog or mist will more thoroughly wet a tree than a heavy shower of rain in large drops will do.

The cost of the tobacco at wholesale is about 10 cents per pound, but sometimes refuse tobacco can be obtained from cigar manufactories at from 1½ to 2 cents per pound.

SHEEP DIP.

This was the "Gold-leaf" brand, manufactured at Louisville, Ky., and said to be a pure extract of tobacco; it costs about $1.75 per gallon when purchased in large quantities.

It was diluted with water in various proportions, but even when used in the proportion of 1 gallon of the dip to 80 gallons of water it proved fatal to only about four-fifths of the young insects and one-fourth of the adult females with egg-masses, while the eggs were scarcely affected by it.

Several egg-masses were immersed in the pure dip, and none of the eggs thus treated hatched out.

TOBACCO SOAP.

Samples of this soap were received from the manufacturers. the Rose Manufacturing Company, of 17 South William street, New York City. The soap was first dissolved in hot water and afterward diluted with cold water.

One Pound of the Soap to nine Gallons of Water.—This proved fatal alike to the insects in all stages of development and also to their eggs.

One Pound of the Soap to twenty-one Gallons of Water.—This was fatal to all of the insects with the exception of about one-third of the adult females before secreting the egg-masses and a slightly larger number of those with egg-masses.

The cost of this soap has heretofore been 50 cents per pound, but I am informed by the agent here, Mr. J. B. Francisco, that the price of the soap has been recently reduced one-half.

VINEGAR.

A small branch of a lemon tree upon which were a number of Cottony Cushion-scales was immersed in pure grape vinegar, but it had very little effect upon the adult females and their eggs, and produced no perceptible injury to the leaves. It likewise had but little effect upon the insects when used in the proportion of 1 gallon of vinegar to 8 gallons of water in which 4 pints of soft soap had been dissolved.

PARIS GREEN.

One-half an Ounce of Paris green was thoroughly stirred into two Gallons of Water.—The whole was sprayed upon a small orange tree growing in the shade of some large eucalyptus trees. This proved alike fatal to the insects and the tree. In many places upon the tree the sap had exuded from the bark in considerable quantities, and remained adhering to the bark in the form of a brownish gum.

One-third of an Ounce of Paris green to two Gallons of Water.—This was sprayed upon all parts of a small orange tree, the greater part of it being sprayed upon the trunk and bases of the larger branches. In these places all of the insects were killed, but fully one-third of those situated upon the outer ends of the branches were not killed. In several different places the sap had exuded from some of the branches.

One-fourth of an Ounce of Paris green to two Gallons of Water.—This also killed all of the insects upon the trunk and bases of the larger branches. where the greater part of the solution had been sprayed, but only about one-half of the insects situated upon the outer ends of the branches were killed. This solution did not cause the sap to exude from any part of the tree.

One-fourth of an Ounce of Paris green to two Gallons of Water and one Pint of the Kerosene Emulsion.—The emulsion was formed by emulsifying 2 gallons of kerosene in 1 gallon of hot water in which had been dissolved half a pound of soap. A pint of this emulsion was diluted with 2 gallons of water. after which the Paris green was added; but it was impossible to keep the green incorporated in the solution, as it would rise to the surface the moment the stirring ceased. The effect of the solution upon the tree and insect was about the same as in the preceding experiment, with the exception that only about one-third of the insects situated upon the outer ends of the branches were killed.

REPORT UPON SUPPLEMENTARY EXPERIMENTS ON THE COTTONY CUSHION-SCALE; FOLLOWED BY A REPORT ON EXPERIMENTS ON THE RED SCALE.

By ALBERT KOEBELE, *Special Agent.*

LETTER OF TRANSMITTAL.

ALAMEDA, CAL., *December* 1, 1886.

SIR: I herewith submit a report of continued experiments on the Cottony Cushion-scale (*Icerya purchasi*), made at Los Angeles, Cal., after the expiration of the appointment of D. W. Coquillett, with whom I worked previously, as directed by you in letter of January 28.

My warmest thanks are due to Mr. August Buschbaupt, of the Los Angeles Soap Company, for kindly assisting me in preparing the various soaps.

Very respectfully,

ALBERT KOEBELE.

Prof. C. V. RILEY,
  U. S. Entomologist, Washington, D. C.

INTRODUCTORY.

The chief object of my work has been to find a wash as low in price as possible, and at the same time one which all the fruit-growers can prepare themselves. This, as is shown below, is not a difficult matter.

In March and April, while at work with Mr. Coquillett, and after witnessing various experiments, especially with soaps, I concluded that these, if tried in all their varieties, would prove good agents in destroying the scales, and that they also could be produced at a very reasonable cost. Up to this day, in my limited intercourse with orange-growers, I have seen nothing cheaper for killing the Cottony Cushion-scale.

It has always been a difficult matter to know just how much of the article used should be taken to a certain quantity of water to be effective on the scales and not injure the trees. Very often the spraying is done by inexperienced hands, and in such cases no good results can ever be expected even with the best washes. Naturally it will be used in stronger doses at the next operation, and the consequence will often be that there is more injury done than good. Experienced hands should always be engaged in this work to secure good results. I have myself witnessed a pair of inexpert operators, and was much amazed at the rapid progress of the work; yet when examining the trees a week later it was hard to find "dead scales."

No wash will be effective on *Icerya* unless penetrating the cottony mass, and for this purpose I found soap, or washes of soapy nature, the best. In most cases the majority of the young scales are found among the egg-masses, and unless these are destroyed the labor is of little value.

SOAP SOLUTIONS.

Almost any soap, if used in right quantity, will be destructive to both the eggs and the insects of *Icerya*, and, aside from resin compounds, will best penetrate the cottony mass. The egg-masses should always, and immediately after the tree has been sprayed, be completely penetrated by the wash. Unless this is the case the wash has not the effect of destroying everything. In some of the washes used, especially such as contained resin, the egg-masses, if not reached in the center, became so hard that rarely one of the young scales was able to leave its place of birth. Often one or more newly hatched scales will be found under the body of the mother scale at the point where the beak is inserted. Here, too, the mother scale exudes a little of the cottony substance, on which the body rests close to the bark. After light spraying and with weak wash this place remains dry and the young scales uninjured. Therefore a strong spray is of value, by which the scale is raised or somewhat removed from its firm place. Soaps 144 and 152, which I have made, will do as well at ¼ cent with a strong and thorough spraying as at ¼ cent by weak spray. Never have I observed eggs that were completely wetted by any of the washes used to hatch; in every instance they were destroyed.

For applying solutions there is nothing better than a cyclone nozzle for thorough work, especially if the exit hole be made considerably larger, to save time, and this is easily done.

The cyclone nozzle used in my experiments had been eaten out opposite the exit hole to a depth of about 6ᵐᵐ, and three additional plates of 2ᵐᵐ thickness had been put on successively; a circular cavity formed in the chamber, and last the cap containing the outlet fell off. This also had been eaten nearly through. Not more than 1,000 gallons of wash had been sprayed with the nozzle. This may be largely due to the impure and sandy water used.

PREPARATION OF SOAP.

At the beginning of my work, in preparing whale-oil soap, I used chiefly Babbitt's potash or lye, which is sold in boxes of 4 dozen 1-pound cans, at from 9 to 10 cents per pound. To 1 pound of potash 2 gallons of water were added and placed over fire. After all the potash had been dissolved, 2 pints of fish-oil were added and contents cooked until the soap had formed; then 2 gallons more water were added and well mixed together. This formed a soft soap, and would, after cooling, readily mix with cold water.

The cost of this soap is about ⅓ cent per pint, and 2 pints are required to 1 gallon of water to destroy eggs and insects of *Icerya*. This would be 1 cent for 10 pints of wash. Fish-oil is sold generally at Los Angeles at about 32 cents per gallon, wholesale price.

Later, however, instead of using Babbitt's potash, I obtained caustic soda from the Los Angeles Soap Company. This is sold at wholesale by the same firm at 5 cents per pound, and it is equally as good as Babbitt's potash. To 1 pound of this caustic soda 3 pounds of grease, or part of that and resin to the full amount, should be taken, as will be shown in the experiments. Three pounds of tallow and resin to 1 pound of soda did much better work than did 4 of the first to 1 of the last. Tallow is sold by the same firm at 3 cents per pound and resin at 1¼ cents, wholesale price. Almost any grease would answer in making soap, and much could be saved for this purpose which otherwise would not be made use of.

In making soap 152, 1 pound of caustic soda is dissolved in 1¼ gallons of water; then the 2 pounds of resin and 1 pound of tallow is dissolved in 1 quart of the lye; after the resin is all well dissolved by moderate heat the lye is added slowly, while cooking, under continued stirring. The mixture, if good, will become dark brown and thick. Should it become whitish and flocky (this is caused by too much and too strong lye), water should be added and it will become right again. This will make 22 pints of soap—for water should be added to make that amount after all the lye is in—at a cost of 11 cents, excluding fuel and labor in preparing it, which amount to but little, and will be sufficient for 44 gallons of wash if sprayed well. This is for *Icerya*. I would not recommend it stronger than ⅓ cent for a gallon of the wash.

The same rule is to be observed in preparing soap No. 144. This has been tried also on two large trees by Messrs. Wolfskill and Craw, at ⅓ cent per gallon of the wash. All eggs and insects were destroyed and the tree left in excellent condition.

In preparing these soaps the resin and tallow should never be dissolved without the additional lye. It will become so hot, that if a little lye is added a good part of the contents of the kettle will boil over. All this is avoided by adding the lye as said above, and the resin will dissolve the quicker.

In making tallow soap for experiment 77 the caustic soda should be dissolved in somewhat less water. One gallon is used. After the tallow and resin are dissolved together (in this soap it can be done without the lye) the lye should be added slowly while boiling, and afterward the required water added. Thirty-seven pints of soap were made in experiment 77 at ⅓ cent per pint. In using caustic soda the cost of same quantity—i. e., 1 pound of soda, 5 cents; tallow, 2¼ pounds, 7.5 cents; resin, ⅓ pound, 0.73 cent—would be only 13¼ cents; and in making 40 pints of soap this would be ⅓ cent per pint. One pint of soap to 7 pints of water would be sufficiently strong to kill the scales and their eggs.

A soap emulsion prepared cold is used extensively in and around Los Angeles. I have not seen any good results from it. If mixed with water free oil would float on the top, and trees treated with it would lose half their leaves and be arrested in growth for weeks. The fruit would be burned and marked from the excessive caustic it contains. I have seen several hundred trees in such condition in the Wolfskill orchard. The consistency of this particular mixture I could not learn. Never, and I have been assured so by experienced soap-men, can a proper soap be made except by cooking. Although my experiments 35 and 71 show good results, I would not recommend them.

RESIN COMPOUNDS.

Those I found excellent for destroying *Icerya*, and the few experiments made on the Red Scale (*Aspidiotus aurantii*) showed promising results; yet further experiments are required to be positive. The resin compound will penetrate the cottony mass of *Icerya* as well as, or even better than, soap. Yet its actions are slower, and if not used sufficiently strong, even if all the eggs are destroyed, some of the mother scales will not be killed by it, or if so, only after they have left a few fresh eggs, which will in due time hatch. Such eggs, if few, are brought forth loose, *i. e.*, without the usual protection of cottony exudation, and either drop to the ground or lie free above the destroyed egg-mass and under the dead mother. No doubt, many of these eggs never hatch, especially in hot weather.

It is quite different with eggs which are deposited by females that really survive treatment; the usual cottony mass is exuded, and thus the eggs are protected as usual and hatch always.

Its action on Red Scale is very promising, either mixed with soap or in simple emulsion, as experiments will show. Experiment 132, $\frac{1}{2}$ pint of compound to 1 gallon of water, although costing only $\frac{1}{4}$ cent per gallon of the wash, destroyed a large number of the scales; and a few days after application the covering became loose from the insect, so much so that some of them could be blown off and leave the insects exposed, affording an excellent opportunity for the mites, with which the tree was swarming, and which do not seem to be harmed by the wash.

A strong application of this emulsion will form a coating over everything on the tree, will exclude the insects from air for a few days, and will have entirely disappeared in a week in warm weather, as shown in experiment 134.

LYE SOLUTION.

A few experiments were made on hedges of young orange plants. Experiments 108–118 will show the results. While in every case the plant was more or less injured, the insects alone were killed, or part of them, and the contents of egg-sacs were not in the least affected, even with so strong an application that the plant was destroyed entirely.

BISULPHIDE OF CARBON.

A few experiments were made in fumigating with this article, but its action is too slow to be of value on large trees. Messrs. Wolfskill and Craw have made several experiments, and on trees of about 8 feet in diameter all the scales were destroyed in twenty-four hours. The trees were greatly benefited by it, as I am informed by these gentlemen.

KEROSENE EMULSION.

The cost of this article is too high for general use as a remedy for the Cottony Cushion-scale. An emulsion of "kerosene 1 gallon, soft soap $\frac{1}{2}$ gallon, and water 1 gallon" (see experiment 41), cost about 24 cents for $2\frac{1}{2}$ gallons of the emulsion. This is wholesale price. Three pints of this emulsion is required to 1 gallon of water to destroy both the *Icerya* and its eggs. This would be about 18 cents for 7 gallons of the wash.

In all the experiments made with this emulsion I have not seen the slightest injury done to the trees, as is the case with some of the soaps if used too strong.

Made in this way with soap, it penetrates the cottony mass more easily than if emulsified with some other substance.

Very good results were had with emulsion of petroleum. As this could be bought at from 6 to 7 cents per gallon in large quantities and combined with soap, it makes a reasonably cheap wash. The orange trees are left in an unsightly condition even for a month or six weeks after application, and it could therefore not be used on maturing fruit; yet if properly tried it may do good work on other scales on deciduous trees in the dormant state.

EXPERIMENTS.*

I now give in some detail an account of the more instructive of the experiments made, noting results in each case.

Experiment 18. Sheep-dip.

Sheep-dip, 1 pint; water, 15 pints. Applied July 9. On examination, July 16, found but few of the smaller scales killed; contents of egg-sacs not affected. Mr. Coquillett reported on other experiments with same mixture.

---

* It will be noticed that the numbers of the experiments are not perfectly consecutive; but the omitted numbers will be found under the head of the "Red Scale", in the last section of the report.

Experiment 19.   Emulsion of crude petroleum.

One gallon of crude petroleum; ¼ gallon of soap of experiment 13 (consisting of whale-oil, 4 pints; potash, 1 pound; concentrated lye, 1 pound; and water, 7½ gallons), and ¼ gallon of water. Applied May 4, and reported on by Mr. Coquillett. Soap and water were heated together first and petroleum added. This made a good emulsion after working for half an hour with hand pump, and remained stable for the next three weeks.

Emulsion, 1 pint; water, 1 gallon. Applied July 16. Will settle in drops on tree and not penetrate egg-masses. August 9, only a few of the smaller insects dead. Leaves spotted, but not injured.

Experiment 20.   Emulsion of crude petroleum.

Emulsion, 2 pints; water, 1 gallon. Applied July 17. Will not penetrate egg-sac. August 9, found nearly all insects dead on trunk and large branches; young hatching numerously. The trunk and large limbs of tree remained free from scales for a long time after.

Experiment 21.   Emulsion of crude petroleum and soap 13.

Emulsion, 1 pint; soap, 1 pint; water, 1 gallon. Applied July 17, and penetrated nearly all egg-masses. August 9, all insects killed and dry; a few of the eggs have hatched.

Experiment 22.   Whale-oil soap and lime water.

Made of fish-oil, 3 pints; potash, 1 pound; water (in which 1 pound of slaked lime had stood for twenty-four hours*), 4 gallons.

Soap, ¼ pint; water, 1 gallon. Applied July 31. Only a small part of scales killed and a few of the smaller egg-masses destroyed. Killed about half of the young Black Scale (*Lecanium oleæ*).

Experiment 23.   Soap 22.

Soap, 1 pint; water, 1 gallon. Applied July 31. Will not penetrate all the larger egg-masses. August 8, a few of the mother scales still living; some young hatching. September 14, insects were not numerous.

Experiment 24.   Soap 22.

Soap, 1½ pints; water, 1 gallon. Applied July 31 on lemon tree, with trunk and branches completely covered with scales. Penetrated all egg-masses. One hour after spraying, many dead Coleoptera, Hemiptera, and lace-wing flies were found on ground. August 8, occasionally a single living insect was found. August 33, insects few; very few young hatched; tree healthy and blooming.

Experiment 25.   Whale-oil soap.

Made of fish oil, 9 pints; crude potash, 3 pounds; caustic soda, 1 pound; lime, 3 pounds; and water, 9½ gallons.

Soap, ¼ pint; water, 1 gallon. Applied July 31. Will penetrate only smaller egg-masses. August 9, only a small part of scales killed. August 14, scales numerous; egg-masses covered with fungus.

Experiment 26.   Soap 25.

Soap, 1 pint; water, 1 gallon. Applied July 31. Will penetrate all egg-masses. August 9, nearly all scales killed; a few newly hatched young on tree. September 14, scales few; tree in good condition.

Experiment 27.   Soap 25.

Soap, 1½ pints; water, 1 gallon. Applied August 2. August 10, a few eggs found uninjured. August 14, some of the mother scales have produced fresh eggs before dying; others still living. September 14, scales quite numerous; tree healthy.

Experiment 28.   Soap 25.

Soap, 2 pints; water, 1 gallon. Applied August 5 on lemon trees. Nearly all the scales were dry the following day. August 14, no living scales could be found; tree not injured.

---

* Whenever lime was used, only the clear water was taken after the lime had settled to the bottom.

Experiment 29. Soap 22.

Soap, 2 pints; water, 1 gallon. Applied August 6. August 10, found all scales and egg-masses hard: tree not injured. September 15, many scales have come on tree again; it is healthy and blooming.

Experiment 30. Soap 25 and crude carbolic acid.

Soap, 6 pints; crude carbolic acid, emulsified, ¼ pound; water, 6 gallons. Applied August 7. Did not penetrate egg-masses well. August 23, living scales quite numerous.

Experiment 31. Soap 25 and petroleum emulsion.

Soap, 2 pints; emulsion, 1 pint; water, 3 gallons. Applied August 8. August 10, scales nearly all dead but not dry, having an inflated appearance. August 14, a few scales have recovered. September 14, tree clean; scales very few.

Experiment 32. Soap 25. Petroleum emulsion.

Soap, 2 pints; emulsion, 1 pint; water, 2 gallons. Applied August 9. Destroyed all scales and eggs. September 14, occasionally one scale on branches only; none on stem. Tree healthy; fruit not injured or spotted.

Experiment 34. Soap 25. Petroleum emulsion.

Soap, 3 pints; emulsion, 1 pint; water, 2 gallons. Applied August 9. Found scales and egg-masses hardened the following day and many dead insects on ground. September 14, very few scales; stem and large branches entirely free; tree healthy and growing.

Experiment 35. Soap made cold. Soap emulsion.

One pound of potash was dissolved in 1 quart of water; 2 pints of fish-oil made lukewarm, and the lye slowly added under continued stirring; then ¼ gallon of water, in which 1 pound of slaked lime had been, was added. After two days water was added to make 36 pints, and in a week it had become an emulsion or imperfect soap. One pint of this (costing 1 cent) to 1 gallon of water. Applied August 11. Will penetrate all egg-masses well. August 14, found all scales and eggs destroyed. August 17, black sticky drops remained on fruit and leaves had begun to drop. September 14, occasionally one young scale; black drops had disappeared from fruit, not leaving any mark. About one-quarter of the leaves have fallen.

Experiment 36. Emulsion 35.

Heated emulsion to cooking-point; then took 1 pint to 1 gallon of water. This did not penetrate egg-masses well, and many of the larger remained dry inside. Destroyed all of the scales, but some of the eggs hatched and young became numerous. Many leaves dropped.

Experiment 37. Whale-oil soap.

Made of potash, 1 pound; fish-oil, 2 pints; and water to make 36 pints of soap, costing ½ cent per pint.
Soap, 2 pints; water, 1 gallon. Applied August 13. This penetrated all egg-masses well, and all the scales were found dead the next day. August 17, scales and egg-masses hard.

Experiment 38. Soap 37.

Soap, 1 pint; water, 1 gallon. Applied August 13. Will not penetrate egg-masses well. About half of the eggs and scales killed.

Experiment 39. Soap 37. Petroleum emulsion.

Soap, 5 pints; emulsion, 1 pint; water, 42 pints. Applied August 13. Tree well sprayed. All the scales were found dead the next day. Only a few of the eggs hatched, but scales were numerous again September 14.

Experiment 40. Soap 37. Petroleum emulsion.

Soap, 5 pints; emulsion, 1 pint; water, 4 gallons. Applied August 16. On the 18th all the scales killed; egg-masses hard. August 23, a few scales on stem again. September 14, scales increasing, especially on stem; tree and fruit not injured or discolored.

Experiment 41.   Kerosene emulsion.

Kerosene, 1 gallon: soap, 37½ gallons: water, 1 gallon. Soap and water heated and all worked together for half an hour with pump. This formed a cream-white emulsion and became as thick as cream on cooling.
One pint of this emulsion to 1 gallon of water. Applied August 16. Did not penetrate egg-masses; killed only a small part of young scales. September 14, tree full of scales.

Experiment 42.   Kerosene emulsion 41.

Emulsion, 2 pints; water, 1 gallon. Applied August 16. Did not penetrate egg-masses well. Found next day about half of the eggs destroyed, also about half of the scales were dead; several dead Coleoptera on ground. August 23, a few of the scales still living; eggs hatching. September 14, a few of the mother scales still living; young hatching numerously.

Experiment 43.   Kerosene emulsion 41; soap 37.

Emulsion, 1 pint; soap, 1 pint; water, 1 gallon. Applied August 16. Tree well sprayed; penetrated nearly all the egg-masses. August 23, a few insects still living. September 14, scales numerous; Black Scale (*L. oleæ*) not all dead.

Experiment 44.   Kerosene emulsion 41; soap 37.

Emulsion, 1 pint; soap, 3 pints; water, 4 gallons. Applied August 16. Tree sprayed well, and nearly all egg-masses were found wet. August 18, about half of the scales dry, the others still soft but inflated; some of the egg-masses dry in center. August 23, young hatching occasionally. September 14, scales numerous again.

Experiment 45.   Kerosene emulsion 41; soap 37.

Emulsion, 1 pint; soap, 3 pints; water, 2 gallons. Applied August 17. Had penetrated all egg-masses well after spraying; found 3 dead larvæ of *Tortrix* on stem, destroyed by wash. August 23, occasionally one living insect; no young hatching. September 14, few insects on branches, but stem full.

Experiment 46.   Kerosene emulsion 41; soap 37.

Emulsion, 1 pint; soap, 5 pints; water, 6 gallons. Applied August 17 on lemon tree. Did not penetrate egg-masses well; killed one-half of the eggs and three-fourths of the scales. In a short time the tree was full again.

Experiment 47.   Kerosene emulsion 41; soap 37.

Emulsion, 1 pint; soap, 5 pints; water, 4 gallons. Applied August 18. Occasionally one of the mother scales survived, but very few young hatched.

Experiment 51.   Kerosene emulsion 41.

Emulsion, 3 pints; water, 1 gallon. Applied August 25. Tree full of *Icerya* and Red Scales. Penetrated all egg-masses well; killed eggs and insects of *Icerya*. Only a few young of Red Scale hatched; old all destroyed.

Experiment 63.   Tar soap.

Made of fish-oil, 2 pints; pine tar, 1 pint; potash, 1 pound; water, 4 gallons.
Soap, 1 pint; water, 1 gallon. Applied August 31. September 10, some of the mother insects still living and producing fresh eggs. September 18, all insects covered with fungus; some of the mother scales living; young hatching.

Experiment 64.   Tar soap 63.

Soap, 2 pints; water, 1 gallon. Applied August 31. Penetrated all egg-masses well, and all scales and eggs were destroyed; tree not injured.

Experiment 65.   Tar soap 63.

Soap, ½ pint; water, 1 gallon. Applied August 31. Killed only a small part of young scales and small egg-masses.

Experiment 68.   Tobacco soap.

Made of tobacco, ½ pound; fish-oil, 2 pints; potash, 1 pound; and water to make 42 pints of soap.*

* The tobacco is placed in a bag and well cooked with part of the lye, and this is added after the soap is complete.

Soap, 1 pint; water, 1 gallon. Applied September 2. Penetrated only smaller egg-masses well. September 6, occasionally one scale living; no young as yet have hatched. September 11, scales still dying; large females, although yet soft and sickly; noticed many walking down on trunk of tree. No newly hatched young could be found. November 4, scales few; tree in good condition.

Experiment 69. Tobacco soap 68.

Soap, 1¼ pint; water, 1 gallon. Applied September 2. Will not penetrate egg-masses well. November 6, no living insects found. November 11, occasionally one moving scale; nearly everything dry. September 14, a few of the mother scales are depositing fresh eggs, but without cottony mass, lying exposed. November 4, scales very few; tree healthy.

Experiment 70. Tobacco soap 68.

Soap, 2 pints; water, 1 gallon. Applied September 2. Will penetrate all egg-masses if sprayed well. Pump broke and tree was not sprayed well. September 6, all eggs destroyed and nearly all the insects; a few were observed leaving the tree. September 18, quite a number of living scales on tree; some still dying. November 4, scales few; tree healthy.

Experiment 71. Soap emulsion 35.

Another trial of this emulsion was made; contents same as in 35. The mixture was stirred every day and used on the tenth day.
One pint of this emulsion to 1 gallon of water. Applied September 2 on large tree; 10 gallons of the wash used. Penetrated all egg-masses. September 6, all eggs and scales destroyed. Result about the same as in 25, but not quite as many leaves fell. October 7, tree remarkably clean, growing well; fruit not marked.

Experiment 74. Whale-oil soap.

Made of whale-oil, 3 pints; potash, 1 pound; water to make 40 pints of soap; costing about ¼ cent per pint. This was not as perfect as when only 2 pints of oil were used.
Soap, 1 pint; water, 1 gallon. Applied September 6. Result, about three-fourths of scales and eggs killed.

Experiment 75. Soap 74.

Soap, 1¼ pints; water, 1 gallon. Applied September 6. Result: Will destroy eggs and scales, but also tips and budding leaves or tender shoots; the older leaves did not fall.

Experiment 76. Soap 74.

Soap, 2 pints; water, 1 gallon. Applied September 6. Killed scales and eggs; result on tree about the same as in 75.

Experiment 77. Tallow soap.

Made of tallow, 2½ pounds; resin, ½ pound; potash, 1 pound; and water to make 34 pints of soap; costing ½ cent per pint.
Soap, 1 pint; water, 1 gallon. Applied September 9. Wash will penetrate all egg-masses well. September 10, eggs and insects destroyed; nearly everything hard. Nothing escaped this wash, and the tree was not in the slightest injured or arrested in its growth.

Experiment 78. Soap 77.

Soap, 1½ pints; water, 1 gallon. Applied September 9. Killed scales and eggs; tree not injured.

Experiment 79. Soap 77.

Soap, ½ pint; water, 1 gallon. Applied warm, September 9. Penetrated only smaller egg-masses well. About half of the scales and eggs destroyed.

Experiment 84. Soap of fish-oil, tobacco, and resin.

Made of fish-oil, 2 pints; resin, ½ pound; tobacco, ¼ pound; potash, 1 pound; and water, 3 gallons.
Soap, ½ pint; water, 1 gallon. Applied September 11. Many of the scales survived, and only small part of the eggs were destroyed.

Experiment 85. Soap 84.

Soap, 1 pint; water, 1 gallon. Applied September 11. September 18, some of the scales hardened and others became inflated. One of the mother scales deposited 6 more eggs before dying and one of the young hatched. On September 22 all had hardened. October 5, no young scales; tree covered with fungus. November 4, fungus loose; scales very few; tree in good condition.

Experiment 86. Soap 84.

Soap, 1½ pints; water, 1 gallon. Applied September 11. On the 18th some of the insects were still dying. On the 30th all were hard. October 5, tree full of fungus·

Experiment 87. Soap 77.

Soap, ½ pint; water, 1 gallon. Applied September 11. Tree well sprayed, and most of the egg-masses were penetrated by wash. Result: Nearly all the eggs destroyed; only a few mother scales survived and produced fresh eggs.

Experiment 88. Resin soap.

Made of resin, 2 pounds; tallow, 1 pound; potash, 1 pound; and water to make 20 pints of soap; costing ⅔ cent per pint.
Soap, ¼ pint; water, 1 gallon. Applied September 13. Penetrated all egg-masses well. September 18, some of the scales began to dry up; no fresh eggs. September 22, all dead, but not hard. October 4, occasionally one young scale; tree in fine condition.

Experiment 89. Soap 88.

Soap, 1 pint; water, 1 gallon. Applied September 13. The scales were all dead on the 22d, but not hard. October 5, scales and eggs destroyed; tree in good condition.

Experiment 90. Soap 88.

Soap, 1½ pints; water, 1 gallon. Applied September 13. Destroyed scales and eggs, although they were not hard on the 22d. October 5, no living scales; tree in good condition.

Experiment 92. Tobacco soap.

Made of tobacco, ½ pound; tallow, 1½ pounds; resin, 1½ pounds; potash, 1 pound; and water to make 40 pints of soap; costing ⅓ cent per pint.
Soap, ¼ pint; water, 1 gallon. Applied September 15. Tree well sprayed. Result: Nearly all the scales and eggs destroyed; scales die very slowly; some Hemiptera and Coccinellids found dead on ground.

Experiment 93. Soap 92.

Soap, ⅔ pint; water, 1 gallon. Applied September 15. September 17, all eggs and scales seem to be destroyed. September 22, insects not yet all dry, but dead; tree in very good condition. Wash sufficiently effective.

Experiment 94. Soap 92.

Soap, 1 pint; water, 1 gallon. Applied September 15. Penetrated all egg-masses well and destroyed everything. September 22, scales not hardened; nothing living.

Experiment 99. Resin soap.

Made of resin, 3 pounds; tallow, 1 pound; potash, 1 pound; and water to make 32 pints of soap; costing ¼ cent per pint.
Soap, ¼ pint; water, 1 gallon. Applied September 20 on large and dirty tree full of fungus, almost covering some of the egg-masses. Nearly all the eggs were destroyed. Some of the mother scales recovered and produced fresh eggs.

Experiment 100. Soap 99.

Soap, ⅔ pint; water, 1 gallon. Applied September 20. Had penetrated all egg-masses after spraying. September 22, nearly all scales killed. October 12, occasionally one living scale.

Experiment 101. Soap 99.

Soap, 1 pint; water, 1 gallon. Applied September 22. Some of the mother scales were still living on the 24th, yet all had died on September 30, but were not dry. November 2, tree nearly clean of scales. It was also thickly infested with Red Scale, but all these were killed.

Experiment 102. Soap 77 and lime water.

One pound of slaked lime in 20 pints of water. After the water became clear ½ pint of this was taken with ½ pint of soap to 7½ pints of pure water. Applied September 24. Result: All eggs destroyed and scales all dead after six days, although a few fresh eggs were left. Tree not injured. The trees were very thoroughly sprayed. The result would not have been so good with a light spraying.

Experiment 103.   Tobacco soap 92; lime water 102.

Soap, ½ pint: lime water, ¼ pint: water, 7½ pints. Applied September 24. Result not as good as in 102, as a number of mother scales survived. October 5, found a number of living scales, fresh eggs, and newly hatched young.

Experiment 104.   Resin soap 99; lime water 102.

Soap ¼ pint: lime water, ¼ pint; water, 7½ pints. Applied September 24. Result as in 102; very few living scales October 4.

Experiment 108.   Babbitt's potash lye.

Potash, 1 pound; water, 2 gallons. Applied September 29. Result; Killed all insects, but did not injure contents of egg-sacs; nearly all leaves dropped; tender shoots killed and bark burned.

Experiment 109.   Babbitt's potash lye.

Potash, 1 pound; water, 4 gallons. Applied September 29. Result: Killed scales; did not injure contents of egg-sacs; tips of plant destroyed; leaves badly burned in spots.

Experiment 110.   Babbitt's potash lye.

Potash, 1 pound; water, 6 gallons. Applied September 29. Killed all free young and nearly all of the mother scales, contents of egg-sacs uninjured; tips of plant broken off; leaves spotted in parts.

Experiment 111.   Babbitt's potash lye.

Potash, 1 pound; water, 8 gallons. Applied September 29. Only part of scales killed; contents of egg-sacs uninjured; tips of plant injured; leaves spotted in parts.

Experiment 112.   Babbitt's concentrated lye.

Concentrated lye, 1 pound; water, 2 gallons. Applied September 29. Scales all killed; contents of egg-sacs uninjured; all leaves dropped; tips of plant killed; bark burned in parts.

Experiment 113.   Babbitt's concentrated lye.

Concentrated lye, 1 pound; water, 4 gallons. Applied September 29. Killed all scales, not injuring contents of egg-sacs; tips of plant killed; one-third of the leaves dropped, remainder all spotted.

Experiment 114.   Gillett's concentrated lye.

Concentrated lye, 1 pound; water, 1 gallon. Applied September 29. Scales all killed; contents of egg-sacs uninjured; plant entirely killed.

Experiment 115.   Gillett's concentrated lye.

Concentrated lye, 1 pound; water, 2 gallons. Applied September 29. Killed all scales; contents of egg-sacs uninjured. Some of the shoots killed near ground; only a few leaves remaining near the ground.

Experiment 116.   Gillett's concentrated lye.

Concentrated lye, 1 pound; water, 4 gallons. Applied September 29. Killed scales, not injuring contents of egg-sacs; tips of plant destroyed; leaves spotted.

Experiment 117.   Gillett's concentrated lye.

Concentrated lye, 1 pound; water, 6 gallons. Applied September 29. About half of the mother scales survived; contents of egg-sacs not injured; tips of plants destroyed.

Experiment 118.   Gillett's concentrated lye.

Concentrated lye, 1 pound; water, 12 gallons. Applied September 29. Only a few of the scales killed; contents of egg-sacs not injured; tips of plants destroyed.

Experiment 119.   Lime water.

One pound of slacked lime in 20 pints of water. Applied September 29. Killed only a few of the scales; all became completely covered by fungus. This had disappeared again November 4, and insects were in good condition.

Experiment 120.   Resin soap.

Made of resin, 3 pounds; tallow, 1 pound; caustic soda, 1 pound; and water to make 25 pints of soap; costing ¼ cent per pint.

Soap, ½ pint; water, 1 gallon. Applied October 4 on large tree. Three gallons of wash were required; only lightly sprayed. Scales died slowly; mother scales left a few fresh eggs. October 14, occasionally one young scale found.

[All experiments after 120 only lightly sprayed.]

Experiment 121. Soap 120.

Soap, 1 pint; water, 3 gallons. Applied October 4. Will penetrate egg masses in about 3 minutes. A few of the scales recovered and produced fresh eggs.

Experiment 122. Resin compound.

Made of resin, 4 pounds; soda ash (pure carbonate of soda), 1 pound; water to make 36 pints of compound; costing 11 cents.

Compound, 1 pint; water, 3 gallons. Applied October 4. Only penetrated smaller egg-masses. Killed only a few of the smaller scales, and a few eggs only were destroyed.

Experiment 123. Resin compound 122.

Compound, 1 pint; water, 2 gallons. Applied October 4; did not penetrate egg-masses well, and only about half of them were destroyed. Many mother scales survived.

Experiment 124. Resin compound 122.

Compound, 1 pint; water, 1½ gallons. Applied October 4. Penetrated all but the largest egg-masses well. Some of the mother scales and some eggs escaped.

Experiment 125. Resin compound 122.

Compound, 1 pint; water, 1 gallon. Applied October 4. Penetrated all egg-masses well. A few of the mother scales survived and produced fresh eggs. None of the eggs sprayed have hatched.

Experiment 126. Resin soap 120.

Soap, 1 pint; water, 4 gallons. Applied October 4. Penetrated only smaller egg-masses. Killed most of the smaller scales, but only a few of the smaller egg-masses were destroyed.

Experiment 129. Resin compound.

Made of resin, 4 pounds; common washing soda (carbonate of soda), 3 pounds; water to make 36 pints of compound; costing ¼ cent per pint.

Compound, 1 pint; water, 2 gallons. Applied October 7. Will penetrate only smaller egg-masses. A few young scales only and small portion of eggs destroyed.

Experiment 130. Resin compound 129.

Compound, 1 pint; water, 1½ gallons. Applied October 7. Did not penetrate larger egg-masses. Destroyed all smaller ones and a few of the mother scales. November 4, scales numerous on tree.

Experiment 131. Resin compound 129.

Compound, 1 pint; water, 1 gallon. Applied October 7. Penetrated all egg-masses well on slight spraying. October 11, a few mother scales, which were protected by fungus, still living. October 14, all scales dead; occasionally a few eggs left among fungus.

Experiment 134. Resin compound 129.

Half compound and half water, to see effect on plants. Applied October 7. Will penetrate egg-masses instantly on application. All scales and egg-masses hard on examination two days after; plant as if varnished and sticky. This had disappeared on October 13, leaving the plant in excellent condition, not a leaf having dropped.

Experiment 135. Resin compound.

Made of resin, 4 pounds; caustic soda, 1 pound; and water to make 33 pints of compound; costing ¼ cent per pint.

Compound, 1 pint; water, 2 gallons. Applied October 8. Will penetrate only smaller egg-masses on light spraying; many of the mother scales survived and young were numerous November 4.

Experiment 136. Resin compound 135.

Compound, 1 pint; water, 1½ gallons. Applied October 8. Did not penetrate larger egg-masses well on light spraying; many of the mother scales survived, and October 25 occasionally a single young could be found.

Experiment 137. Resin compound 135.

Compound, 1 pint: water, 1 gallon. Applied October 8. Will penetrate all egg-masses well on light spraying in about two minutes. October 11, some of the mother scales still living, but no fresh eggs could be observed. October 14, scales all dead. November 4, no young have hatched; tree not injured.

Experiment 138. Resin soap.

Made of resin, 2 pounds: tallow, 2 pounds: caustic soda, 1 pound; and water to make 28 pints of soap: costing ½ cent per pint.
Soap, 1 pint; water, 2 gallons. Applied October 14. Did not penetrate egg-masses: killed most of smaller scales, but had no effect on contents of egg-sacs.

Experiment 139. Soap 138.

Soap, 1 pint; water, 1½ gallon. Applied October 14. Will penetrate only the smaller egg-masses well. October 16, all scales are dead. November 4, no young had hatched.

Experiment 140. Soap 138.

Soap, 1 pint; water, 7 pints. Applied October 14. Will penetrate all egg-masses well on light spraying. October 16, no living scales could be found.

Experiment 141. Resin compound.

Made of resin, 4 pounds; washing soda, 3 pounds; and water to make 24 pints of compound. This is somewhat thick, and will not so readily mix with water as 129, especially after cooling.
Compound, 1 pint; water, 1½ gallon. Applied October 15. Penetrated all egg-masses and destroyed them; some of the mother scales produced fresh eggs before dying. Found no living scales October 25.

Experiment 142. Resin compound 141.

Compound, 1 pint; water, 1 gallon. Applied October 15. Will penetrate all egg-masses well in about 2 minutes with light spraying. Found no living scales October 16.

Experiment 143. Resin compound 141.

Compound, 2 pints; water, 1½ gallons. Applied October 15. Will penetrate immediately. October 16, nothing living. October 28, scales still soft, but rotten. November 4, no living scales on tree, which was left in fine condition, with the wash still visible.

Experiment 144. Resin soap.

Made of resin, 1½ pounds; tallow, 1½ pounds; caustic soda, 1 pound; and water to make 23½ pints of soap; costing ½ cent per pint.
Soap, 1 pint; water, 2 gallons. Applied October 18. Penetrated all but a few large egg-masses well with light spraying. October 23, all scales dead; no fresh eggs. October 28, found occasionally one newly hatched larva.

Experiment 145. Soap 144.

Soap, 1 pint; water, 1½ gallons. Applied October 18. Destroyed all eggs and insects.

Experiment 146. Soap 144.

Soap, 1 pint; water, 1 gallon. Applied October 18. All egg-masses well penetrated after spraying; destroyed all eggs and scales; not the slightest injury done to the tree.

Experiment 152. Resin soap.

Made of resin, 2 pounds; tallow, 1 pound; caustic soda, 1 pound; and water to make 25 pints of soap; costing 11 cents.
Soap, 1 pint; water, 2 gallons. Applied October 27. Will penetrate nearly all egg-masses with light spraying. November 1, all scales dead; no fresh eggs left; a few of the old eggs will hatch.

Experiment 153. Soap 152.

Soap, 1 pint; water, 1½ gallons. Applied October 27. Will penetrate all egg-masses well in about two minutes after a light spraying. Next day some of the mother scales were still living, but all were dead October 30, and no fresh eggs were left. November 4, nothing living; fungus loosening and coming off; tree in fine condition.

Experiment 157.   Resin compound.

Made of resin, 30 pounds; caustic soda, 3 pounds; and water to make 230 gallons of wash; at a cost of 60 cents. Sprayed by Mr. Alexander Craw, and reported in letter of November 22. White Scale when well saturated die, but when only lightly sprayed form new wax. Black Scale all dead. As a wash for Black Scale in the fall and winter it will be admirable, but for the most thorough work only 180 gallons of water should be taken.

Experiments on Fumigation with Bisulphide of Carbon.

Experiment 1.—September 29. One and a half fluid ounces in 1-pound tin can were set on the ground near young shoots of orange, and a 50-gallon cask placed over this for three hours. After removing cask only half of the carbon had evaporated; scales seemed to be dead. On examining next day found all of them living.

Experiment 2.—September 29. Poured three-fourths fluid ounce into bottom of cask; placed this over young plants at 3 p. m.; left until 1 p. m. next day. All the insects were found dead, and had changed their color to a light hyacinth red. October 4, leaves began to drop. October 7, nearly all eggs had changed to straw color. About three-fourths of the leaves dropped, and the plant had not recovered November 1.

Experiment 3.—September 30. One and a half fluid ounces in 1-pound tin can set under cask and left for 20 hours. Destroyed all scales and eggs. About one-third of the leaves dropped.

Experiment 4.—October 1. One and a half fluid ounces poured into cask and placed over plants for 3 hours. Killed all scales and eggs. No leaves dropped, and the plant has not in the least been injured.

Experiment 5.—October 14. Made on tree about 7 feet high and 5 inches in diameter, under tent. Two fluid ounces in shallow tin pan placed in middle of tree from 11 a. m. until 3 p. m. Destroyed all the scales except those on a few of the lowest branches, where the eggs also remained uninjured. Tree not injured; no leaves dropped.

Experiment 6.—October 22. On tree about 8 feet in diameter, under tent. Six fluid ounces in shallow tin pan set in middle of tree at 3.30 p. m. and left until 6.30 p. m. Had no effect whatever on scales.

EXPERIMENTS ON RED SCALE (*Aspidiotus aurantii*).

Experiment 33.   Soap 25.

Soap, 2 pints; water, 1 gallon. Applied August 5. August 14, nearly all scales killed; a few mother scales with eggs and young living. October 5, only a few newly formed scales could be found.

Experiment 48.   Kerosene emulsion and soap 37.

Kerosene emulsion, 1 pint; soap, 5 pints; water, 4 gallons. Applied August 18. Tree full of scales; some of the branches already destroyed. August 23, many young scales have hatched; only part of large scales dead. September 24, about one-fifth of old scales living; many young on tree.

Experiment 49.   Soap 37.

Soap, 3 pints; water, 1 gallon. Applied August 18. Tree thickly infested with *Icerya* and Red Scales. August 23, scales nearly all dead and dry; a few young. September 24, a few of the old scales still living; occasionally a young larva found; tree in good condition.

Experiment 50.   Soap 37.

Soap, 3 pints; water, 1 gallon. Applied August 18. Tree thickly infested with scales; half of the branches killed. August 23, about half the leaves have dropped. September 6, leaves have ceased dropping; tree recovering; occasionally one young scale found. September 18, tree pushing out new shoots. November 4, tree growing vigorously; young scales very few.

Experiment 52.   Kerosene emulsion 41.

Emulsion, 4 pints; water, 1 gallon. Applied August 25 on tree infested with *Icerya* and Red Scale. August 28, *Icerya* all destroyed, Red Scales apparently so. September 24, a few gravid females still living; occasionally a single newly formed scale.

Experiment 53.   Kerosene emulsion 41; soap 37.

Emulsion, 2 pints; soap, 1 pint; water, 1 gallon. Applied August 25. August 28, many young scales forming. September 7, about 10 per cent. of old scales living; many young forming. November 4, tree swarming with scales.

Experiment 54.   Kerosene emulsion 41; soap 37.

Emulsion, 1 pint; soap, 2 pints; water, 1 gallon; Applied August 25. September 7. found two mother scales living; young forming quite numerously. October 5, tree full of young scales.

Experiment 55.   Kerosene emulsion 41; soap 37.

Emulsion, 3 pints; soap, 1 pint; water, 1 gallon. Applied August 25 on small and faded tree. September 7, leaves nearly all off; many young scales forming. September 22, branches all dead; many young scales on stem; no living adults.

Experiment 56.   Kerosene emulsion 41; soap 37.

Emulsion, 1 pint; soap, 3 pints; water, 1 gallon. Applied August 25. August 28, found a few living young under mother scale. September 7, many newly formed scales. September 24, old scales all dead; young quite numerous. October 5, scales very few; tree doing well.   -

Experiment 57.   Kerosene emulsion 41.

Emulsion, 5 pints; water, 1 gallon. Applied August 31 on small and sickly tree· September 7, no living old scales; only two living young could be found. September 24, leaves all off; scales few. October 5, tree pushing out new shoots on stem; some branches still living. November 4, tree growing; scales few.

Experiment 58.   Kerosene emulsion 41.

Emulsion, 6 pints; water, 1 gallon. Applied August 31. Tree lightly sprayed. September 22, a few of the mother scales still living; young forming quite numerously. October 5, no living old scales; young few; tree in good condition.

Experiment 59.   Kerosene emulsion 41.

Half emulsion and half water. Applied August 31. Tree sickly and thickly infested with *Icerya* and Red Scale; also many Black Scales; many branches already dead. On very careful examination September 7 found one gravid female still living and some young scales forming. September 24, tree bringing forth new shoots on stem; young scales quite numerous. October 5, upper part of tree all dead, although growing well below; scales few.

Experiment 60.   Soap 37.

Soap, 4 pints; water, 1 gallon. Applied August 31 on small and faded tree thickly infested with *Icerya* and Red Scale. September 7, found two moving young; leaves remaining only on lower branches. September 24, tree nearly dead; trunk again covered with *Icerya*. October 5, tree shooting out below; scales few.

Experiment 61.   Soap 37.

Soap, 6 pints; water, 1 gallon. Applied August 31 on small and withered tree full of *Icerya*, Red and Black Scales. September 7, all scales destroyed; occasionally one young forming. September 24, a few young scales; tree shooting out again. October 5, hardly any Red Scales, yet the tree is covered again with Cottony Cushion-scale.

Experiment 62.   Soap 37.

Half soap and half water. Applied August 31. September 7, scales all destroyed; on careful examination only one moving young could be found; only a few leaves had dropped. October 5, tree shooting out everywhere. November 4, tree almost free from scales and growing vigorously.

Experiment 66.   Tar soap 63.

Soap, 2 pints; water, 1 gallon. Applied September 2 on tree that had been nearly killed by the scales. September 6, scales not all killed; young hatching numerously. October 5, some of the older scales still living; young numerous; tree nearly dead.

Experiment 67.   Tar soap 63.

Soap, 4 pints; water, 1 gallon. Applied September 2 on large tree covered with scales. September 22, found only a very few young; old scales all dead; tree not injured by wash. November 4, on careful examination only a few young scales could be found.

Experiment 72. Tobacco soap 68.

Soap, 2 pints; water, 1 gallon. Applied September 3 on thickly infested and nearly dead tree. September 22, only about three-fourths of the scales killed. October 5, living scales of all sizes present, but not abundant.

Experiment 73. Tobacco soap 68.

Soap, 4 pints; water, 1 gallon. Applied September 3 on small and sickly tree; some of the branches already killed by scales. September 7, scales not yet all dead; tips of young shoots somewhat injured, and a few of the old leaves dropping. September 22, no living scales; tree recovering. October 5, not a single scale could be found on most careful examination; tree in fine condition, growing vigorously.

Experiment 82. Soap 77.

Soap, ½ pint; water, 1 gallon. Applied September 9. September 18, only a small part of the scales killed. October 5, about four-fifths of the scales dead.

Experiment 83. Soap 77.

Soap, 1½ pints; water, 1 gallon. Applied September 9. September 18, all scales killed; not the slightest injury done to tree by wash. October 5, not a living scale could be found; tree in fine condition.

Experiment 95. Tobacco soap 92.

Soap, 1 pint; water, 1 gallon. Applied September 18. October 5, scales nearly all killed; young hatching quite abundantly. October 28, no living adults; young numerous.

Experiment 96. Tobacco soap 92.

Soap, 2 pints; water, 1 gallon. Applied September 18. October 5, a few gravid females living; a few young hatching. October 28, only young scales could be found, but these were quite numerous; tree in good condition.

Experiment 97. Tobacco soap 92.

Soap, 3 pints; water, 1 gallon. Applied September 18. September 24, tree not injured. October 11, all scales dry; no young could be found.

Experiment 98. Resin soap 88.

Soap, 1 pint; water, 1 gallon. Applied September 18. September 24, scales dying slowly; blossoms and budding leaves not injured. October 5, occasionally one gravid female living; very few young.

Experiment 105. Resin soap 99.

Soap, 1 pint; water, 1 gallon. Applied September 27. October 5, scales apparently all killed; found two newly-formed young. October 11, old scales all dead; young quite numerous.

Experiment 106. Resin soap 99.

Soap, 2 pints; water, 1 gallon. Applied September 27. October 5, scales apparently all dead; have changed in color; a few leaves dropping. October 11, scales all killed; not a single young scale could be found; tree not injured.

Experiment 107. Resin soap 99.

Soap, 4 pints; water, 1 gallon. Applied September 27. October 5, all scales discolored; not yet dry; leaves dropping. October 7, leaves still dropping. October 11, leaves have ceased dropping; all scales dead; no young. October 28, not a living scale could be found; tree in good condition.

Experiment 127. Resin soap 120.

Soap, 1 pint; water, 1 gallon. Applied October 4. October 11, all young and nearly all old scales dry; found two moving young. October 16, scales all dead. November 4, occasionally one young scale.

Experiment 128. Resin soap 120.

Soap, 2 pints; water, 1 gallon. Applied October 4. October 11, all scales dead and dry; tree not in the least injured. On the most careful examination, October

16 and 22, and November 1 and 4. I was unable to find any living scales; tree was growing nicely at last-mentioned date.

Experiment 132.   Resin compound 129.

Compound, ½ pint; water, 1 gallon. Applied October 7. October 12, all young scales dry; old scales all loose and changed in color. October 15, old scales seem to be dead, yet not dry; found many dead young under mother scales. November 4, about three-fourths of the scales killed; they became firm again on the leaves after two weeks; mites very numerous.

Experiment 133.   Resin compound 129.

Compound, 1 pint; water, 1 gallon. Applied October 7. October 12, nearly all scales dead and dry and changed in color; all the scales on insects that were not dry loose and easily removed; mites very numerous. October 15, no living scales could be found. October 22, found three newly formed scales. November 4, very few young and no living old scales could be found; tree not in the least injured; no leaves dropped.

Experiment 147.   Resin soap 144.

Soap, 1 pint; water, 2 gallons. Applied October 23. October 28, found several moving young and a few newly formed scales. November 4, a few gravid females still living; young increasing.

Experiment 148.   Resin soap 144.

Soap, 1 pint; water, 1 gallon. Applied October 23. October 28, all scales killed; found one moving young. November 4, occasionally one young; no old scales could be found.

Experiment 149.   Resin soap 144.

Soap, 2 pints; water, 1 gallon. Applied October 23. October 28, budding leaves destroyed; old leaves dropping. November 1, a few leaves still dropping; tree had been in poor condition, and this experiment was made chiefly to see result of wash.

Experiment 154.   Resin soap 152.

Soap, 1 pint; water, 1½ gallons. Applied October 27. November 3, nearly all scales killed; some of the mother scales not yet dry.

Experiment 155.   Resin soap 152.

Soap, 1 pint; water, 1 gallon. Applied October 27. November 3, found all scales dead; no young could be found.

Experiment 156.   Resin compound 141.

Compound, 3 pints; water, 1 gallon. Applied November 2. November 4, all scales have changed on tree as well as on fruit. Mr. Craw examined the tree again for me September 22, and he writes that all the young scales were dead, but many of the old scales were living.

Experiments 154 and 155 were made at a late date, and the results perhaps would vary a little if examined a month later; yet the soap will do excellent work on *Icerya* at ¼ cent per gallon with strong spray. I believe that the wash of experiment 154 would not kill all the Red Scales. The soap of experiment 120 is but little different, yet this destroyed all the Red Scales, at ¼ cent per gallon of the wash, as sprayed by Messrs. Wolfskill and Craw.

In regard to experiment 156. Mr. Craw's statement is contrary to my expectations. Although I had at the time of spraying a poor pump, and the tree had not been sprayed well, yet the spray would miss the young as well as the old scales.

I examined tree of Experiment 133 often and carefully. In eight days nearly all the scales were dry. This is the same wash as that of 156, but costs only ¼ cent for 9 pints of the wash, while in experiment 156 the cost would be 1 cent for 10 pints of the wash.

Resin compound is a good remedy in destroying *Icerya* and its eggs, and further experiments will show the value of it on Red Scale.

The best results so far on the Red Scale were had with soaps 120, 144, and 152, and these last two are also best for *Icerya*.

The fact that there are nearly always, even with the strongest washes, young scales found afterward may be largely due to the fact that the ground below thickly infested trees is always covered with infested leaves which have dropped, and naturally most of the young will crawl back upon the tree again after the spraying. They will also come from surrounding plants.

INSECTS AFFECTING SMALL GRAINS AND GRASSES.

By F. M. WEBSTER, *Special Agent.*

LETTER OF TRANSMITTAL.

LA FAYETTE, IND., *November 2, 1886.*

SIR: I herewith transmit my annual report for the current year, containing a continuation of my studies of the Wheat Isosoma, and a new pest, the Companion Wheat-fly; notes on *Meromyza americana*, and some insects affecting Barley; a list of insects frequenting or depredating upon Buckwheat; notes upon the destruction of timothy meadows by the Glassy Cut-worm; and two enemies of the White Clover.

As usual, I am under obligation to yourself and assistants for the determination of material, and numberless other favors.

Respectfully submitted,

F. M. WEBSTER,

Special Agent.

Dr. C. V. RILEY,

Entomologist.

INSECTS AFFECTING FALL WHEAT.

THE WHEAT-STRAW ISOSOMA.

(*Isosoma tritici* Riley.)

Up to June of the present year matters remained very much as they were left in my previous report, so far as obtaining any additional facts relative to the habits of this species is concerned. Straws, in which *grande* only had oviposited, failed to furnish adults of any sort, and straws taken from the fields gave only wingless females of *tritici*, which, as usual with those reared in mid-winter, refused to oviposit on wheat plants grown and kept indoors for that purpose. On returning from the South in April, however, we found a limited number of these *tritici*, which had emerged much later, probably in March, alive in the breeding-cages, and at once transferred them to young wheat plants grown and kept continually under cover, in a corner of our garden, at least three-fourths of a mile from any field of either wheat, rye, or barley. This was on the 12th of April.

From this time forward until the grain and straw were fully ripened, early the following July, the utmost caution was observed in keeping the plants thoroughly protected from outside insects, and, with the exception of a single Tipulid, which appeared during spring, no insects whatever were at any time observed within the inclosure except the *Isosoma*.

On the 2d of June, fifty-one days after the *tritici* had been placed in the inclosure, a female of *grande* was observed in the act of ovipositing in the now nearly full-grown straw, and within the next few days several others were noticed similarly occupied, placing their eggs not only in the upper joint, but in the one below also. Previous to this, and, in fact, since the 21st of May, the latter species had been observed continually in the fields, and the belated appearance of these in the inclosure is perhaps due to the fact that their progenitors, the *tritici*, were of the last to emerge in the spring. Absence from home for two months previous to the date of their removal from the breeding-cage to the young wheat made it impossible to secure them earlier, as it was difficult to get enough then living to carry on the experiments, the numerous dead in the cage indicating that the species had been emerging for some time.

As before stated, the *tritici* placed in the inclosure were all of them females. Neither could any males be found among those that had previously died, and, moreover, all of the *grande* were females apparently, as all that were observed at all in the inclosure were ovipositing. Hence the males of either form, if there are any, are still unknown to me.*

A winged form of *Isosoma*, seemingly intermediate between *tritici* and *grande*, was taken with the latter in considerable numbers about Bloomington, Ill., during May, 1884, and has since been found in the vicinity of La Fayette, Ind., in both grain fields and grass lands, but in too limited numbers to permit of successful

---

* As shown on page 544, we have been more successful in this respect than has Mr. Webster, and three males of *tritici* were bred in January, 1886.—C. V. R.

rearing in confinement, and hence what affinities it may have with other forms or species is not known.

A small form of *hordei* also occurred about La Fayette during the latter part of May, 1885, on blue grass and timothy, growing up intermixed, and also to a very limited extent on wheat; but this also refused to oviposit in the latter in the breeding-cages, and disappeared from the field of both grain and grass altogether in a few days.

The same locality was repeatedly swept over during the present season, but no *hordei* could be found. *Grande* were, however, obtained in considerable numbers from grass lands, but the most careful search failed to reveal any indication that they emerged from these grasses or that they oviposit in them.

It may be proper to state here that in the three years during which I have had these Isosomas under observation they have never been observed ovipositing in chess, nor has an instance been noticed where the straws of this grass have been affected by them. This discrimination on the part of these insects, whereby the stools of wheat are prevented from heading, while those of the grass continue to flourish, may perhaps in part account for the unexpected preponderance of the latter during some seasons, a phenomenon which so sorely taxes the science of the unbotanical farmer.

There is, however, a species of larva infesting the stems of timothy from the latter part of July to the following spring whose method of work is very similar to that of the wheat-straw worms, but which nevertheless belongs to a different order of insects. It is probably the larva of a species of *Languria*,* and may readily be distinguished by the form of the head, by the more slender and less smooth body, and by the presence of well-developed legs on the thoracic segments.

THE AMERICAN MEROMYZA.

(*Meromyza americana* Fitch.)

Full-grown larvæ of this species were observed by us on June 18 of the present year in a field of rye near Kentland, Newton County, Indiana, and we bred adults from straw grown near La Fayette about July 21, and again from volunteer wheat in the same field from which the straw had been taken from September 3 to 21. A previous examination of this field made August 31 had revealed the fact that the volunteer wheat plants growing upon a space 1 foot square contained 11 puparia, 1 empty case, and 1 two-thirds grown larva.

On October 5 we found adults in great numbers (and also adults of a parasite, *Cœlinius meromyzæ* Forbes) engaged in ovipositing on wheat in a field sown September 22, and on going to another field, which had been sown much earlier, we found adults there also, but in less numbers, although the former field had been sown on oat stubble, while the latter field had last produced a crop of wheat.

In view of these observations and the results of your own breedings from volunteer wheat sent you from Oxford, Ind., on September 6, 1884, there seems little reason to doubt the existence of a third brood of flies, originating, largely at least, in volunteer grain, and emerging therefrom during the month of September.

As we have elsewhere shown,† the observations of Fitch, Riley, Lintner, Forbes, and ourself in no case have indicated that a third brood was improbable, but in some instances strongly presage its existence.

THE COMPANION WHEAT-FLY.

Oscinis (?) sp.

During the latter part of June, 1884, while examining wheat straws in which the larvæ of *Meromyza americana* were at work, we often found several smaller larvæ, also dipterous, and so closely associated with the former that we at first suspected them of being parasites. They were almost invariably found among the juicy mass of substance that had been displaced by their larger consort.

Securing a supply of affected straws, we cut from each a section about 3 inches

---

*Specimens of this larva were forwarded to us by Mr. Webster, but the adult beetle was not bred. The larva was indistinguishable from that of *Languria mozardi*, described by Professor Comstock in the Annual Report of this Department for 1879 under the popular name of "The Clover-stem Borer," as he had reared it from stems of Red Clover at Washington. Mr. Webster's larvæ probably belong to this species, which is figured on Plate I, Fig. 6, of the report just cited, and described on page 199.—C. V. R.

† Bulletin No. 9, Purdue University, issued October, 1886.

long, including the upper joint, but excluding the head, and placed them in a breeding jar. The result was, when the adult *Meromyza* emerged from these sections, July 18 to 23, there appeared among them quite a number of a much smaller black species, closely resembling those of the genus *Oscinis*, but, however, being quite distinct.

Early in the following September larvæ, seemingly like those observed in the straw, were found feeding within the stems of young volunteer wheat plants, and later the same thing was observed to destroy young plants in a field of early sown wheat.

From this volunteer wheat adult flies of the species now under consideration emerged from September 7 to October 1. The present season they began to emerge August 30, in both cases being the most numerous about the 10th of September. We have also reared adults from larvæ in wheat sown during the last week of August, these emerging as late as the 3d of October. The adults are common in wheat fields after about September 10 until the 1st of October, and hover about the young plants, doubtless for the purpose of ovipositing, as they are often observed pairing.

We have never observed them during late fall or early spring. They are sometimes attacked by a fungous parasite very similar to, if not identical with, that attacking the house-fly.

The larvæ are much smaller than those of *Meromyza*, but in a general way resemble them in form and color, particularly when the latter are only partly grown.

The puparia are, however, very different, being only about 2.5^{mm} long and 0.8^{mm} broad. The color is never like that of *Meromyza*, being at first of a yellowish-white, with tinge of green, but later changing to a uniform brown. They are readily distinguished from those of the Hessian fly by being cylindrical and by the segments being well defined.

From the foregoing it will be observed that, so far as we have been able to study the species, its cycle is exactly parallel with that of the *Meromyza*, and besides, there is a strong probability that while in young wheat the larvæ work independently, in the full-grown straws, where the tissue is too tough for their less rugged mouth parts, they become the mess-mates of their stronger consort, and feed from the vegetable juices by which it is surrounded. It is this characteristic that suggested the common appellation selected.

The damage done to young wheat in the fall by this species must be considerable, the credit thereof falling upon the *Meromyza*, as the effect of the two larvæ is exactly the same.

INSECTS AFFECTING BARLEY.

On account of the limited area sown, we have had but little opportunity to study the insect enemies of this cereal, but it is extremely probable that the species do not differ greatly from those depredating upon the closely allied grains—wheat and rye.

The two species here mentioned were observed in a small plot of this grain on the University experiment farm, which had produced nothing but barley for the last five or six years.

THE WHITE GRUB.

(*Lachnosterna fusca* Fröhl.)

These well-known depredators were observed during the present season engaged in cutting off the roots of the full-grown and fully-headed grain. As late as the 28th of June they were causing whole stools of the straw to wither and dry up before the kernels had filled.

THE BARLEY ROOT-LOUSE.

(*Schizoneura* sp.)

Both winged and apterous individuals were found clustering on the roots of barley in this same plot on the 12th of June, 1885, and at that time seemed to be doing considerable injury, but we were unable to secure an above-ground form.

The present season we found the same species in the same place but several days earlier, and watched them continuously until the 15th of July, when a few individuals might still be found upon the roots, although the grain was fully matured. Again we failed to secure an aereal form, although the grain was kept under careful inspection until harvest, nor could we rear any such in a breeding-cage, to which we had transferred infested barley plants.

In the fields the lice were all attended by ants, as usual, and, when placed in the breeding-cage without their protectors, seemed to be well-nigh helpless.

THE GRAIN APHIS.

(Siphonophora avenœ Fab.)

This species was observed infesting the heads of barley in considerable numbers, and, when the grain was fully ripe and the winged adults ready to forsake the barley heads, we placed some of them in cages in which growing timothy, blue-grass, and red-top had been transplanted, with the hopes of learning where the species passed the summer or until the young wheat appeared in the fall. The grasses were kept alive, but the insects died, and no trace of a following generation was observed.

INSECTS FREQUENTING OR DEPREDATING UPON BUCK-WHEAT.

So many reports of the aversion of insects for this plant are going the rounds of the press, nearly all of which are unaccompanied by generally accepted authority, that some exact data relative to the matter seems very desirable. It was with a view of obtaining this information that, under Dr. Riley's instructions, we began a series of observations, selecting as a basis one of the experiment plots of the University farm, which for the past five years has grown nothing but buckwheat, thereby eliminating at the start any insects that might have been attracted by a previous crop of grain or grass or remained over in either the adult or adolescent stages.

As the object of the observations was a twofold one, *i. e.*, to learn both the repulsive and the direct and indirect attractive properties of the growing plant, what may at first appear to be overexactness will at once be seen to be quite essential, as the occurrence of an insect but once or twice during several weeks is strongly indicative of a repugnance for the locality.

Observations began as soon as the plants were well above the surface of the ground, and, until they were high enough to sweep with an insect-net, consisted of careful inspection only, but later the entire plot was swept over at intervals of a few days and a record kept of all captures. As some species visit the plants at one time of day and others at another, the time of sweeping was varied, in order to preclude the possibility of any escaping notice in that way. These observations were carried on until frost destroyed the plants.

In the table the symbol "A" signifies abundant; "C," common. Where only very few examples occurred their number is indicated numerically. Unless otherwise stated the adult stage is intended, and where a * follows the name of insect the larval state only is intended; if a †, the pupal. When these follow the other symbols, A or C, it is to be understood that all states occur, adults preponderating. If they precede the letter, all states occurred in numbers indicated. Thus A * †, adults abundant, larvæ and pupæ; * † C, all stages common.

List of insects.

Insects.	Aug. 4, p. m.	Aug. 17, p. m.	Aug. 18, a. m.	Aug. 20, 9.30 a. m.	Aug. 24, 4 p. m.	Aug. 28, 4 p. m.	Aug. 31, 10.30 a.m.	Sept. 3, 1.30 p. m.	Sept. 7, 10 a. m.	Sept. 11, 3.30 p. m.	Sept. 14, 9.15 a. m.	Sept. 20, 12 m.	Sept. 25, 2.30 p. m.	Oct. 1, 2 p. m.
Apis mellifica Linn				C			A		A		A	A		
Bombus sp									1		2			
Cerceris compactus Cr.	1													
Halictus flavipes (Fabr.)		C					2			1	1			
Halictus sp. ? (No. 19)		C	A	A			C		C		2			
Sphex pennsylvanicus Linn	1						1		1		2			
Ammophila uruaria Dahlb					1					2		1		1
Pompilus sp									1					
Tiphia (near) inornata Say						1								
Tiphia sp. ?		C	C	C		C	1					2		
Myzine harnata Say		1		2			2		A		1	3		
Mutilla (near) fenestrata St. F		1					1				1			
Lasius flavus	C	C	C	C	C	C	C		C	A	A	A		2
Perilampus (near) hyalinus Say				2	C	2	A	A	A	A	A	A	C	1
Formica schaufussii	3	C	C	C	C	C	A	3	A	A	A	C		3
Caliopsis andreniformis Say		C	C	1			1		C	C				
Cynipid sp. ?					C	C	A		C	C				
Agathis sp. ?			1							2				
Mesograpta marginata Say										C				
Pieris protodice Bd.				2			2	1	C	C	A	A	C	
Colias eurytheme Bd.							C		C		1	2		
Danais archippus Fab.							1		1					
Pyrameis atalanta Linn							1		1			1		
Pyrameis cardui Linn							1		1					
Deilephila lineata Fab.*							1		3		1	2	2	

List of insects—Continued.

Insects.	Aug. 4, p. m.	Aug. 17, p. m.	Aug. 18, a. m.	Aug. 20, 9.30 a. m.	Aug. 24, 4 p. m.	Aug. 28, 4 p. m.	Aug. 31, 10.30 a. m.	Sept. 3, 1.30 p. m.	Sept. 7, 10 a. m.	Sept. 11, 3.30 p. m.	Sept. 14, 9.15 a. m.	Sept. 20, 12 m.	Sept. 25, 2.30 p. m.	Oct. 1, 2 p. m.
Acronycta oblinita A. & S.*											1			
Acontia crastoides Guen				2	C	A	C	C	C	C	C	C		
Geometrid larva				1										
Crambus (near) fuscicostella Zell. (No. 13)	1													
Dichelia sulphureana Clem.*					2	1	1	1						
Eurycreon rantalis Guen				C	A	A	A	A	A	A	A	C	2	
Cicindela punctulata Fab	C	C	C	C	C	C	C	C	C	C	3	1	1	1
Harpalus pennsylvanicus Dej								1	1					
Tachyporus brunneus Fab.				1		1		1			C			
Sylvanus advena Wald.											1			
Corticaria pumilis Mels.				2				C	C	1	C	C	C	
Hippodamia convergens Guen.								1						
Hippodamia parenthesis Say									1		2			
Cycloneda sanguinea Linn							1				1			
Coccinella 9-notata Hb							1				1			
Chauliognathus pennsylvanicus Först				2	C	C	C	C	A	C	C	C	1	
Ditemnus bidentatus Say			1											
Cyphon variabilis Thunb											1			1
Bruchus obsoletus Say							1			1	2	1		
Colaspis brunnea Fab	A	A	A	C		1		2	1	1				
Doryphora 10-lineata Say			1											
Chrysomela suturalis Fab											2			
Diabrotica 12-punctata Oliv					2			1	1	2	2	2	1	
Diabrotica vittata Fab											1			
Diabrotica longicornis Say				C	C	A	A	A	'A	A	A	A	C	2
Disonycha punctigera Lec.									C			2		
Longitarsus testaceus Lec.											2			
Phyllotreta vittata Fab.					2	1								
Systena frontalis Fab						1								
Systena blanda Mels.			1								1			
Crepidodera atriventris Mels.										1				
Chaetocnema confinis Cr		C	A	A		A	A	1	C		1	C	C	1
Mordella octopunctata Fab		1												
Epicauta vittata Fab.	A	C	A	C	C		1	2	1					
Epicauta lemniscata Fab.	A	A	A	C	2	1	2	1		1				
Epicauta cinerea Först.	3													
Epicauta pennsylvanica De G					1									
Centrinus picumnus Hort														2
Sphenophorus parvulus Gyll		1												
Sciara sp. ? (No. 31)				1	C	C	A	A	A	A	C	C	C	
Bibio sp. ? (No. 82)									2	2				
Anthrax sp. ?	A	C	1											
Sparnopolius sp. (No. 14).	1	C						2		C				
Stratiomyia sp. ? (No. 87).								1						
Oscinis sp. ? (No. 26).		1		3	2	C	C	C	3	C	C	C	C	
Oscinis sp. ? (No. 64).					C	C	A	C	C	C				
Chlorops sp. ? (No. 65).				C	A	A	A	A	A	A	A	A	A	C
Meromyza americana Fitch							1	C	C	1	2	C	1	1
Syritta pipiens Macq											C	C	2	
Oncomyia sp. ? (No. 89).										1				
Chelonus sericeus Say										1				
Aphis sp. ? (Root-form)							C	C	C	C	C			
Dactylopius n. sp. ?							C	C						
Jassus inimicus Say				C	C	C	C	C	C	C	1	C	3	2
Macropsis venatus Uhl				C	C	C	C	C	C	C	1	C		
Actualis calva Say (var.)											1			
Diedrocephala mollipes Say											1	1		
Euschistus servus Say										1			1	
Corizus lateralis Say				1			1				1	2	C	C
Blissus leucopterus Say							C	1						
Geocoris limbatus Stål	1			1	C	1								
Lygus pratensis Linn		C	A	C	A	A	A*	A*	A*+	*+A	A*+	A*+	A*+	A
Calocoris rapidus Say					2	C	C	C	C	C*	C*	C*	*1C	1
Plagiognathus obscurus Uhl		1	1	C	C	C		C	2	1	1			
Plagiognathus sp. ? (No. 24).		1	3		2		1	2	A	C			2	
Agalliastes sanvis Reuter.		1	1				C	3	C	C	C			
Triphleps insidiosus Say			A	A	A	A	A	A	A	A*	A*	A*+	C*+	2
Corius ferus Linn						2	C			1	2	C	C*	
Acholla multispinosa De G							1		2		C*			
Coleothrips 3-fasciata Fitch				C	C	C	C	A	A	A	C	3	1	
Oecanthus niveus.						1	3				2			
Orchelimum vulgare Harr						1	1		1		1			
Gryllus abbreviatus.	C	C	C	C	C	C	C	C	C	C	C	C	3	1
Melanoplus femur-rubrum Harr	A	A	A	A	A	A	A	C	C	C	C	C	C	C
Oedipoda carolina Linn							1	2	2	1			1	
Chrysopa externa ?							2	1	C		2		C	
Smynthurus sp. ?						3		C	A	A	A			

37 AG—'86

The Hymenoptera, as a rule, occurred most abundantly during the forenoon. Of the *Lepidoptera*, *Acontia* and *Eurycreon* were the most abundant. *Dichelia* was reared to the adult, but the *Geometrid* larva died, and it is very doubtful if this was really one of its food-plants.

The rarity of *Carabidæ* is quite suggestive as being in accordance with the lack of earth-inhabiting larvæ, and likewise the dearth of *Coccinellidæ* might be traced to the lack of *Aphididæ*. *Bruchus obsoletus* doubtless wandered from a plot of beans near by. *Colaspis brunnea* fed upon the buds. The lack of *Doryphora* was strongly indicative of disgust for the plant, as the adjoining plot was planted to potatoes, which they destroyed, and migrated to other localities, but studiously avoided the buckwheat. The same was true of *Epicauta*, excepting the *vittata* species, which fed upon the foliage quite freely. *Diabrotica longicornis* was one of the most abundant insects, and fed upon the blossoms. *Aphis* sp. ? and the *Dactylopius* were both found upon the roots. The spasmodic occurrence of *Blissus leucopterus* has the same signification as the single occurrence of *Doryphora*. *Lygus pratensis* was one of the most abundant species, and at the time of the last two observations it outnumbered all others ten to one. *Melanoplus femur-rubrum* seriously injured some of the young plants, but only along the margins. *Gryllus abbreviatus* cut off the plants and dragged them into its burrows, but only for about the first week after they came up. Larvæ of *Chrysopa* were quite numerous during August and September. Possibly these were of the same species as the adults. The *Anthrax* emerged from pupæ in the soil in considerable numbers during the early part of August.

Besides these, Dr. Riley (First Mo. Rep., p. 79) states that the larvæ of *Agrotis clandestina* and (Third Mo. Rep., p. 109) *Laphygma frugiperda* (*Prodenia autumnalis*) affect this plant, as also (Seventh Mo. Rep., p. 159) *Melanoplus spretus*. Dr. Cyrus Thomas (Sixth Ill. Rep., p. 171) thinks *Gastrophysa polygoni* might attack the plant, but we found nothing of the species in this case. In Riley's Seventh Mo. Rep., p. 43, a correspondent states that *Blissus leucopterus* did not affect his corn where buckwheat was sown among it. *Deiliphila lineata* (larva) is recorded as feeding upon this plant by Dr. Riley in Third Mo. Rep., p. 141.

INSECTS AFFECTING TIMOTHY.

THE GLASSY CUT-WORM.

(*Hadena devastatrix*, Brace.)

On June 29 of the present season Mr. J. G. Kingsbury, of the *Indiana Farmer*, called our attention to some rumors which had reached him relative to the depredations of some kind of worm in the timothy meadows about Richmond, Wayne County, Indiana, and we immediately wrote Mr. J. C. Ratliff, of Richmond, from whom, on the 12th of July, we received a reply fully corroborating the reports given us by Mr. Kingsbury.

On the 15th, in accordance with instructions from Mr. Howard, entomologist in charge, we visited the infested fields, three in number, situated to the northwest of the city, one on the grounds of the insane asylum, another about a half a mile north of this on the farm of Mr. Kreets, and the third on the farm of Mrs. Thompson, perhaps 2 miles farther to the northwest.

The field on the grounds of the asylum, of which about 15 acres were totally destroyed, had been plowed and planted with corn after the ravages had ceased, but the other two fields, of which about 15 and 20 acres, respectively, had been destroyed, remained intact. A critical examination of the affected portions of these two fields revealed the fact that even where every vestige of timothy had been destroyed red clover remained untouched, and a decided preference had been evinced for low, damp localities.

In the Thompson field chrysalids were found quite abundantly within a couple of inches of the surface; and with them, in almost equal numbers, were the larvæ of *Hadena devastatrix*, some of which were already in frail earthen cells, preparatory to pupating, all of these last being of a dingy-white color, with yellow heads. Interspersed among the *Hadena* larvæ were a very few of *Nephelodes violans*. In the Kreet field both chrysalids and larvæ were much less abundant, although the destruction had been equally complete. Here also the *Nephelodes* larvæ were found, but in a still smaller ratio as compared with those of the *Hadena*.

To settle any doubt which might arise as to which of the two species of larvæ were the authors of the destruction, we questioned the owners of the fields very closely, as well as the employés on the two farms, but all stated that the striped larvæ had never been numerous, and that it was the white ones with brown heads ("about half way between a worm and a grub," as they expressed it) which did the injury. In fact, an aged and intelligent gentleman, Mr. Vinnedge Russell, as soon as he learned of our arrival, went to the Thompson field and brought us therefrom a number of *Hadena* larvæ, remarking that the striped worms had occurred with them, but only in very limited numbers, and that those brought were the depredators.

From what we were able to learn, the effect of these worms was noticed for the first about the middle of May, and they continued to carry on their work for about three weeks, after which they appeared to do no injury, and the dried remains of the young grass seemed to attest to the statement, as in no case were any withered or dead clumps observed. The destruction appeared to lie solely in the amputation of the small roots, neither the bulb nor the blade having been ravaged, and we were informed that the worms were in no case observed feeding above ground, but invariably below the surface.

Although no such outbreak of these larvæ in meadows had been previously recorded, this habit of feeding below ground, and upon the roots of grasses was noticed long ago by Dr. Riley, who found that the larvæ would bury themselves in the earth, and feed in this manner from grass roots, although other food was provided them.*

That the *Hadena* larvæ, in both the Thompson and Kreet fields, originated in each case in excessive numbers throughout only a very limited area, and that they gradually extended their domains as the food-supply became exhausted, was very evident. In the Kreet field, which was very low, flat, and damp, the depredations began in the southwest corner, the worms gradually working eastward parallel with the highway, which was carefully avoided, and a margin of grass six to ten yards wide was left almost untouched, while they pushed farther and farther to the northward for a considerable distance, destroying every vestige of timothy, gradually seeming to exhaust themselves near the northern and eastern boundaries of the field.

In the Thompson field they originated in the northwestern portion, along a low, wide ravine, traveling eastward, following a narrow ravine near the northern boundary, a tributary of the former, nearly across the field, while elsewhere along the line of origin they did not extend their depredations more than about one-third as far, as that direction brought them upon the higher ground.

We were informed that while a few worms had been observed working upon the higher grounds in this field little damage had been done there, but as the tributary ravine reached high ground there had been a tendency to spread out at right angles, those on the south side being, as it were, thrown across the path of those worms proceeding east from the place of origin. As in the Kreet field, the boundary between the totally destroyed portion and the uninjured was irregular and poorly defined, a gradual fading of one into the other.

In this field larvæ and pupæ were found in considerable abundance, although many of the former did not appear in a healthy condition, and many of the latter had a blackened look, and some others had evidently been destroyed by some natural enemy. But in the Kreet field the case seemed different, for here it required considerable labor to obtain either larvæ or pupæ, even in limited numbers, and many of these were affected as in the Thompson field. Dead larvæ were found in the earth, stretched at nearly full length, rigid, and with a parasitic fungus, a species of *Isaria*, growing from between the thoracic segments, but more frequently from the neck, after the manner of *Torrubia* from the white grub, only that in this case they affect the upper as well as the under part. This was also observed to attack the larvæ of *Nephelodes violans*.

On July 17 a goodly number of larvæ and pupæ were secured from both fields and placed in earth in tin boxes. Returning home on the 19th, these boxes were at once opened, and found to be literally swarming with a species of *Pteromalus*. The larvæ and pupæ were placed in separate cages, the *Pteromalus* continuing to appear in that containing pupæ for several days afterward. Later there appeared from these pupæ a single individual of *Ichneumon jucundus*, a species of *Tachina*, and also a species of *Phora*. This last, however, was doubtless a scavenger and not a parasite.

The first moth appeared from the pupæ on the 22d, and the first appeared from the larvæ on August 11. All moths obtained were *Hadena devastatrix*, but not over 10 per cent. of the adolescent individuals developed to adults.

Had the appearance of the Glassy Cut-worms been more general, in such numbers as in the vicinity of Richmond, the loss would have been very serious; as it

---

*First Report Insects of Missouri, p. 83, 1868. Report Commissioner of Agriculture, 1884, p. 297.

was, Mr. Ratliff, who is a crop correspondent of this Department, estimated the damage to the three fields at about $1,600.

We have not been able to learn of any such depredations elsewhere, and Messrs. A. W. Butler, of Brookville; Stephen Gardner. of Cottage Grove; S. S. Merrifield, of Connersville; and D. E. Hoffman. of Winchester, all located in Wayne and adjacent counties, have written us disclaiming all knowledge of any similar ravages.

While we were on the ground too late in the season to observe the working of these worms or carefully study their movements. both the appearance of the affected fields at that time and the information obtained were strongly indicative of a slow, migratory habit.   Mr. Kreet stated that he had several times observed the worms collected in deep holes in the earth, from which they appeared to be endeavoring to escape.   All of this is very suggestive of preventing the progress of the worms by ditching, or even plowing a deep furrow across their course, and destroying them as they accumulate in the bottom, as with the Army Worm.

We again visited the locality on October 30.   The Kreet field had been plowed in the mean time, and was now covered with a luxuriant growth of wheat.   The Thompson field remained as we had left it in July, but neither there nor in other meadows could we find any young Cut-worms of this species, although a few of other species were observed.   We dug up the earth to a depth of several inches in places where it seemed most probable that they would occur, but found none.

We observed a considerable number of carnivorous larvæ in the Thompson field, and these, quite likely, aided in sustaining the check given the worms by the parasites of the spring brood.*

THE GRAIN SPHENOPHORUS.

(*Sphenophorus parvulus* Gyll.)

During the latter part of July of the present year the larvæ of this species were observed burrowing in the bulbs of timothy, their method of work not differing materially from what it was in wheat, as described in our last year's report, excepting that the bulb, being much larger than a straw, enabled the larva to attain to nearly or quite full growth before leaving it to pupate.   Several larvæ were often found infesting a single stool.   Pupæ were also found in the earth about these stools.

While examining the roots of timothy in meadows about Richmond, Wayne County, Indiana, on October 30, we found an adult of *Sphenophorus sculptilis* Uhl. in the midst of a mass of eaten bulbs, these last resembling in every particular those which had been destroyed by *S. parvulus*.

INSECTS AFFECTING WHITE CLOVER.

THE FLAVESCENT CLOVER WEEVIL.

(*Sitones flavescens* Allard.)

Early in the month of October, 1885, the foliage of White Clover (*Trifolium repens* L.) on the University grounds was found to be seriously injured by some insect depredator, and a plot of Alsike (*T. hybridum*) was likewise attacked, while Red Clover (*T. pratensis*) escaped with very little injury, even though growing up promiscuously among both of the former varieties.

This injury to the leaves of clover was of two patterns, one consisting of a circular disk extracted from the center and the other a more or less hemispherical portion taken from the margin. and, while there was never more than one circular space eaten from the same leaf, there might be several of the marginal pattern, or the two might be combined, thereby leaving only the leaf-stalk and bases of the mid-veins.

Careful search failed to reveal any insect about the injured plants in sufficient numbers to arouse suspicion, except a small, yellowish-brown curculio, *Sitones flavescens* Allard, an imported species, injurious to clover in Europe, but not previously known as such in America, although Dr. Riley had some years ago † directed atten-

---

* One of these species of larvæ was that of an Elater, probably *Drasterius dorsalis* Say.   The larvæ of this genus are known to be carnivorous, and we have observed this species destroying the larvæ of *Crambus zeellus* Fern., and also those of an undetermined species of *Macrops* which burrows in the roots of common plantain (*Plantago major* L.).—C. V. R.

† *American Naturalist,* Vol. XV, p. 751, and Report Commissioner Agriculture 1881, p. 177.

tion to its native habits, and Dr. Lintner had placed it in his list of possible enemies of the clover plant in New York.*

Dr. Le Conte† gives the species as inhabiting the Atlantic States in abundance, especially near the sea-shore, and states that the American race differs from the European by the color of the scales, being more rusty and less gray. We have for years found it plentifully here in the West, while Dr. E. R. Boardman reports both the beetles and their work in Stark County, Illinois, and Mr. Charles N. Ainslie, Rochester, Minn., makes a similar statement.

The beetles are rather timid, and, on being disturbed, drop to the ground and seek refuge among leaves and rubbish, and it was only after considerable patient watching that they were observed in the act of feeding upon the leaves. This they do by simply moving the head and thorax, the body remaining stationary, the circular disk being cut when the leaf is still folded, the two halves facing each other, the beetles eating through the back at the mid-vein. The half disk thus extracted from the two makes a full disk when the leaf is fully unfolded.

On October 17 a number of the beetles, confined alive in a small vial, deposited a number of eggs therein; and on the 25th of same month other adults, which had been placed in a breeding-cage with clover plants selected and transplanted from a locality where the leaves had not been injured, also oviposited, dropping their eggs about promiscuously, some being on the leaves, others scattered about on the surface of the soil, and one stuck to the side of the cage.

The eggs are nearly white, with a very slight tinge of yellow; slightly elongate, ovate, being a trifle less than 0.4^{mm} broad and a little more than 0.4^{mm} in length; not acuminated or depressed.

In a temperature of 65° F. these eggs hatched in about 48 hours after being deposited, the young larvæ at once disappearing. A few days later they could be found feeding upon the fresh lateral shoots, or even the softer parts of the main stem under the bases of the leaf stalks. The entire plant upon which the larvæ were confined withered and died within a few weeks, although it was kept well watered and under favorable conditions for growing.

A search in the fields about seriously injured plants revealed numerous small, white, footless larvæ in the earth, varying considerably in size, and for the most part much larger than those we had hatched indoors. None of the larvæ were observed in the act of feeding except one individual, a rather small one, which was engaged in devouring a seed. On being placed in glass tubes with stems of the plant they at once began to eat out the central portion, leaving only the epidermis. Similarly affected stems were quite common in the fields, but whether they were due to the work of this or another insect we find it still too much to say, although the former is the more probable, as there has been at no time anything to indicate that these larvæ attack the root, leaf, or leaf-stem portions of the plant, however near the latter might be to the surface of the ground.

Two larvæ found in the fields on the 1st of November being much larger than any previously observed, they were taken indoors and fed with stems of clover, upon the younger, tenderer portions of which they subsisted until the 2d of December, when one of them pupated, and twenty days later transformed to an adult, being at first nearly white, but assuming its normal color four days later. The second larva died before pupating.

The full-grown larva is 5^{mm} long; head small, testaceous, with brown mandibles; body white, wrinkled, first segment little larger than head, second and third larger, fourth to ninth nearly equal, gradually decreasing to thirteenth, which is very small and nearly pointed.

These larvæ when at rest in the earth lie in a hook-shaped position, the head and thoracic segments being kept at almost right angles to the fourth segment, where the rather abrupt curve begins. Prior to pupating they form a small earthen cell.

On December 9, the ground being frozen to the depth of from 2 to 2½ inches, affected plants, with the soil in which they were rooted, were dug up and brought indoors. After being thawed out this was carefully examined, and *Sitones* larvæ were found therein, varying in size from 1^{mm} in length to full grown, the major part being under 2.50^{mm} in length; but two fully grown were found, and these were in their cells preparatory to pupating. One larva, 1.50^{mm} long, began feeding as soon as thoroughly warmed. Two adults were also found, but no pupæ. One of these was kept in a breeding-cage, in a warm room, and was still alive on the 18th of the following February, when I left for an absence of a couple of months.

* The Insects of the Clover Plant, Report N. Y. Agricultural Society, Vol. XL, for 1880. Author's edition, p. 4.

† The Rhynchophora of America north of Mexico, Proc. Am. Phil. Society, Vol. XV, No. 96, p. 115.

Besides these, two adults were observed in the fields, in the act of pairing, on the 12th of November.

On account of absence from home no examination was made until the 13th of April of the present year, when larvæ were again found in the fields, in less numbers but in about the same stage of development as during the previous December. No pupæ were observed, but two adults were found, which died soon after, without having in the mean time deposited any eggs.

On May 25 both larvæ and pupæ were found, the former in still less numbers than they were during April, but now they were, for the most part, nearly or quite full grown. An adult, taken also on this date, died on the 30th inststant without ovipositing. June 14 several adults were observed, and from this time forward they appeared in increasing numbers until August, when they seemed to reach the upward limit.

The deposition of eggs may commence in July, but we obtained none until August 7, and then only after keeping adults confined in the breeding-cage for four days; nor could we at this date observe any larvæ in plants in the fields, although very small ones were common enough in and about the tender lateral shoots early in September, but in no case were they burrowing in the main stem except in the tenderer portions, under the base of leaf-stalks, as previously indicated.

In summing up the life-history of the species, they may be said to emerge as adults as late as July, and deposit their eggs from the last of that month until cold weather begins. The larvæ, hatching within two days after the eggs are deposited, feed upon the tender portion of the clover stems, probably burrowing into them sometimes, especially when they are from one-fourth to one-half grown, and, barely possibly, subsisting in part upon the roots when older. They pass the winter, for the most part, in this stage, but occasionally as adults. The larvæ pupate in spring, and after remaining about twenty days in this state emerge as adults.

The adults seem to wander about considerably early in the season, and we have observed them traveling about on fences, upon the heads of grain, and crawling up the trunks of trees, and also found them hiding away under rubbish.

THE CLOVER-STEM MAGGOT.

(*Oscinis* sp.)

Sufficient opportunity has not been offered to study more than a portion of the probable cycle of this insect, yet the very deceptive resemblance between the work of the larvæ and those of *Sitones* renders some account of it almost a necessity in order to prevent confusion.

The adult insect is a small, rather robust, black fly. The individual larva is 4^{mm} long, with a breadth across the thoracic segments of $.6^{mm}$, footless, slightly diminishing posteriorly, with the division of the segments after the first three very obscure. Color yellowish-white, with a tinge of green, becoming nearly white at extremities; oral parts quite large and jet black. Near the posterior extremity is an abrupt ventral restriction, and on the rounded anal segment are two short, robust, brown processes, each terminating in a corolla of small circular pustules.

The puparium is 2.4^{mm} long and $.8^{mm}$ broad, elongate, oval, slightly tapering posteriorly, and rather less obtusely pointed than at anterior extremity. The two posterior processes are here reproduced, and two others, shorter and more widely separated, are placed on the anterior extremity. Color at first yellowish-white, with tinge of green, but later turning to brown, and from this to nearly jet black.

The insect was first observed by us on August 6 of the present year in the pupal stage, and within a stem of white clover, which had evidently been destroyed by it while in the larval stage. During the four succeeding days other puparia were found, but only two larvæ. From the puparia one adult emerged on August 12, others following a few days later, thereby indicating that the brood of which they were a part was rapidly approaching maturity.

The exact time and place of oviposition it was, of course, impossible to determine, but the maggots are found singly in the stem, sometimes just under the epidermis and sometimes in the center, but in either case excavating parallel channels, working from the point where the stem originated. Hence we are led to infer that the eggs are deposited near the main roots, and the larva, as its pushes forward, is provided with a continual supply of fresh-grown food, the terminal or growing portion of the stem being in part sustained by lateral roots thrown out at equal intervals. It is also possible that the eggs are sometimes placed on the young lateral stems, through which the maggots burrow their way to the main stem.

As yet we have no trace of more than the one brood mentioned, although it is not at all improbable that there may be several in a season.

REPORT ON EXPERIMENTS IN APICULTURE.

By N. W. McLain, *Apicultural Agent.*

LETTER OF TRANSMITTAL.

UNITED STATES APICULTURAL STATION,
Aurora, Ill., December 31, 1886.

DEAR SIR: I have the honor to submit herewith my report of the work done under your instructions at this experiment station during the past year.

I desire to acknowledge my obligations to yourself for the valuable suggestions and assistance given me, manifesting the deep interest you have in advancing and developing the industry of bee-keeping.

I wish also to express my thanks to those engaged in the branch of husbandry in whose interest this experiment station was established for the very kind and unanimous expressions of appreciation and encouragement, some of whom have cheerfully aided me in my work; and especially to the publishers of the following apicultural and agricultural journals for the favor shown me in publishing my report and for files of their valuable papers, namely:

The American Bee Journal, Messrs. Thomas G. Newman & Son, Chicago, Ill.; *Gleanings in Bee Culture,* Mr. A. I. Root, Medina, Ohio; *The American Apiculturist,* Mr. Henry Alley, Wenham, Mass.; *The Bee-Keeper's Magazine,* Messrs. Aspinwall & Treadwell, Barrytown-on-Hudson, N. Y.; *The Bee-Keeper's Guide,* Mr. A. G. Hill, Kendaliville, Ind.; *The Canadian Bee Journal,* Messrs. Jones, Macpherson & Co., Beeton, Ontario, Canada; *Rays of Light,* North Manchester, Ind.; *The Southern Cultivator,* Atlanta, Ga.; and *The Cultivator and Country Gentleman,* Messrs. Luther Tucker & Son, Albany, N. Y.

Yours, very truly,

N. W. McLAIN,
Agent in Charge.

Dr. C. V. RILEY,
Entomologist.

THE "QUAKING DISEASE."

When bees are unable to obtain from ordinary sources a supply of saline and alkaline aliment, indispensable to their health and vigor and to the normal performance of their functions, they seek a supply from any available source. At such times they throng upon the Milkweed and Mullein, which exude a salty sap. At such times large numbers of dead bees may be found at the foot of the mullein stalks, and thousands perish in the fields, and thousands more which reach their hives, being low in vitality and unable to free themselves from the meshes of the silken fiber in which legs and wings are bound, die in the hive or crawl forth to perish. The actions of these starved and weakened bees when attempting to rise and fly or to rid themselves from the mesh of silky web causes a peculiar nervous motion, and this is one manifestation of that which is called the "quaking disease," or the "nameless disease." If examined with a microscope, many are found entangled with the filaments from the plants, and their stomachs are entirely empty.

The honey from hives containing colonies so affected has a peculiar and very disagreeable taste and odor, somewhat like that of fermented honey, indicating that some constituent essential in conserving it was lacking, and the cell-caps are dark, smooth, and greasy in appearance, and an offensive odor is emitted from the hive. An analysis of honey taken from such colonies, made by the Chemist of the Department, fails to reveal what element is lacking.

I have treated a number of apiaries so affected, using an application of strong brine, to which was added soda sufficient to make the alkaline taste faintly discernible. The hive should be opened, and each frame should be thoroughly dampened with spray from an atomizer, or the warm brine may be applied by using a sprinkler with very small holes in the rose, care being taken to use only enough to thoroughly dampen the bees and combs. The alighting-boards also should be thoroughly wet. The treatment should be applied morning and evening until the disorder disappears, which is usually in three or four days; a decided improvement being usually noticeable in twenty-four hours. The honey should be extracted and diluted by adding the brine, and, after being nearly heated to the boiling-point for ten minutes, may be safely fed to bees. The apiaries were last winter supplied with this food alone. Both wintered well. Vessels containing brine should always be kept in or near the apiary. Pieces of burnt bone or rotten wood should be kept in the vessels of brine, and these vessels should be protected from the rain.

Another form of the so-called "quaking disease" appears to result from hereditary causes; for, if the queen be removed from the colony in which the disorder prevails, and a young. vigorous queen be substituted, in due time the disorder disappears. In very rare instances bees also gather poisonous nectar from plants, such as Fox-glove or Digitalis, the eating of which, it is reported, results in paralysis; another manifestation of the so-called "nameless disease."

THE FOUL-BROOD DISEASE.

One of the most malignant diseases incident to bees is called the "foul-brood" disease. What pleuro-pneumonia and hog-cholera are to the dairyman and swine-breeder foul-brood is to the apiarist. This disease is so stealthy and so virulent and so widely distributed, no locality in the United States being assured of immunity, that much apprehension is felt, and some of the States have enacted laws having for their object its control and extirpation. In many States the ravages of this scourge have resulted in ruinous losses to bee-keepers, and many on this account have been deterred from engaging in this profitable branch of husbandry.

During the past year I have given much attention to the study of this disease and to experiments for its prevention and cure. In making my investigations and experiments concerning the origin and nature of this disease and the means for its prevention and cure, I have collected a great amount of information from my own experience and from the experience of many others. Concerning the origin of this disease and its means of communication the evidence obtained is somewhat conflicting.

That the disease is actively contagious appears certain. That it is always communicated through the commonly accredited agencies is uncertain. That the disease is persistent and usually reproduces itself whenever the germs find the proper conditions for development is verified by experience. That the germs of this disease may be carried upon the clothing of the apiarist and in and upon the bodies of bees from one apiary to another, and that they may be borne by the wind from one hive to another in the same apiary, and that the disease germs may be liberated from the decomposing bodies of other insects and scattered over other objects with which the bees come in contact. seem probable.

That the disease is destructive to bees as well as brood, that live pollen is the medium through which the contagion is most commonly and most rapidly spread, and that the disease yields readily to treatment which is simple, cheap, and easily applied, appear to be true, in support of which I submit the following detailed account of my experiments and observations:

On the 1st day of June an apiarist having over two hundred colonies in his apiary reported to me that he had discovered two cases of malignant foul-brood, and that unmistakable evidences of its presence were apparent in twenty-five other colonies. As I knew this man was not without experience with this disease, I could not hope that he was mistaken. I knew that he had had unenviable opportunities, having been a bee-keeper for many years where this disease had been prevalent, and two years ago he himself had consigned one hundred and forty-eight colonies to the flames as incurable. I at once gave him the following formula for a remedy:

To 3 pints of soft water add 1 pint of dairy salt. Use an earthern vessel. Raise the temperature to 90° F. Stir till the salt is thoroughly dissolved. Add 1 pint of soft water boiling hot, in which has been dissolved 4 tablespoonfuls bicarbonate of soda. Stir thoroughly while adding to the mixture sufficient honey or sirup to make it quite sweet. but not enough to perceptibly thicken. To ¼ of an ounce of pure salicylic acid (the crystal) add alcohol sufficient to thoroughly cut it (about 1 ounce), and add this to the mixture while still warm, and when thoroughly stirred leave standing for 2 or 3 hours, when it becomes settled and clear.

Treatment.—Shake the bees from the combs and extract the honey as clearly as possible. Then thoroughly atomize the combs, blowing a spray of the mixture over and into the cells, using a large atomizer throwing a copious spray; then return the combs to the bees. Combs having considerable quantities of pollen should be melted into wax and the refuse burned. If there is no honey to be obtained in the fields, feed sirup or the honey which has just been extracted. If sirup is used, add 1 ounce of the remedy to each quart of the sirup fed. If the honey is used, add 2½ ounces of the remedy to each quart of honey fed. The honey and sirup should be fed warm and the remedy thoroughly stirred in, and no more should be furnished than is consumed.

Give all the colonies in the apiary one copious application of the remedy, simply setting the frames apart so that they may be freely exposed to the spray. This treatment frequently reveals the presence of disease where it was not before possible to detect it. The quantity prescribed, applied by means of a large atomizer, is sufficient to treat one hundred and fifty colonies. Continue the treatment by thoroughly and copiously spraying the diseased colonies at intervals of three days, simply setting the frames apart so as to direct the spray entirely over the combs and bees. In order to keep the bees from bringing in fresh pollen, burn old dry bones to an ash and pulverize in a mortar and sift through a fine wire-cloth sieve, and make a mixture of rye flour and bone flour, using three parts of rye flour to one of bone flour, adding enough of the sirup or medicated honey to make a thick paste. Spread this paste over part of one side of a disinfected comb, pressing it into the cells with a stiff brush or a thin honey-knife, and hang this in the hive next to the brood. Continue this treatment until a cure is effected. Keep sweetened brine at all times accessible to the bees, and continue the use of the rye and bone flour paste while the colonies are recuperating.

As a preventive apply the remedy in the form of a spray over the tops of the frames once every week until the disease has disappeared from the apiary.

On June 20 the apiarist above referred to reported as follows:

"Number of colonies in the apiary June 1, 210. Number of colonies apparently diseased, 25. Treatment applied as directed to the whole apiary. Number of colonies actually diseased, 63. The disease present in all stages of progress; in some cases just appearing, in some well developed; in others the contents of the hives were a black mass, the brood combs nearly rotten, not an egg to be seen, and every cell of brood dead, and the stench from the hives nauseating. Have given the diseased colonies three applications, the first time extracting the honey. Effect of treatment instantaneous even upon apparently hopeless cases. Every colony save 5 is entirely free from any trace of disease, and these 5 are responding to treatment rapidly. I examined a colony to-day which two weeks ago had combs of brood almost rotten. No trace of the disease remains. I had 4,000 frames of extra comb. After hiving a few swarms, on some of them I found the disease present in every case. I then melted every one of these extra combs into wax, cleared and scalded and disinfected every hive, and hived the swarms on frames filled with comb-foundations. One of my neighbors, having an apiary of 60 colonies, had 38 cases of foul-brood, and before I was aware of it he had burned up a number of them. The remainder we treated as directed. His yard is now entirely free from disease. The cost of the remedy was just 10 cents. This prescription, if thoroughly applied according to your directions, will speedily and effectually cure the most hopeless and forlorn case of foul-brood."

It was afterwards found that the melting of the combs and scalding of the hives was not necessary.

After requesting this same apiarist to make some further tests, the nature of which will appear from what follows, August 1 he made the following report:

"In 5 of my best colonies, which had shown no symptoms of disease, I placed frames of brood from diseased colonies, treating them as I did the diseased colonies, and all evidences of disease speedily disappeared. To 1 colony from which the bees had swarmed out, leaving less than half a pint of bees between the black rotten combs and not an egg in the hive and every cell of uncapped brood dead and not more than one bee hatching to every square inch of brood, after thoroughly applying the remedy I introduced a queen just crawling from the cell. To-day I take pleasure in exhibiting this colony as one of the finest I own, lacking only a sufficient store of honey, and this without the addition to the original odorous hive and rotten combs of a single bee, cell, or brood, or anything whatever to assist, except the young queen.

"I extracted the honey from diseased colonies and treated the combs of such with the remedy as directed, and then exchanged hives and combs, giving the infested hives and combs to the healthy bees without cleansing or disinfecting a hive, and the diseased bees were given the hive and combs lately occupied by the healthy colonies. The contagion did not spread, and after two or three applications of the remedy all traces of it disappeared. I fed back the honey extracted from the diseased colonies for the bees to use in breeding, adding 2¼ ounces of the remedy to each quart; and I also fed the mixture of bone-ash, rye flour, and honey as a substitute for pollen by pressing the paste into the cells on one side of a comb, and this I placed next to the brood in each hive. I would not advise any one to feed this bone-flour and rye-flour paste unless they wish to raise a great many bees. I also fed the salt, alkali, and acid mixture outside in the apiary, so that all the colonies could help themselves. No; I do not fear that any of the mixture will be stored for winter or get into the surplus apartment, as the bees seem determined to use all they can get of it in brood-rearing. All my hives are running over with bees ready for the fall honey harvest.

"As requested, I placed frames of sealed honey from diseased colonies in healthy colonies, and the disease was not communicated; but the frames from which the honey had been extracted, such as contained pollen, uniformly carried with them the contagion. unless the combs were first thoroughly sprayed with the antidote, and colonies gathering no pollen, or but little pollen, recovered much sooner than those gathering pollen in considerable quantities—that is to say, the more pollen, the more treatment required.

"In reply to your question asking by what means and in what manner the disease was communicated to my apiary, I answer: I at first thought that it had originated spontaneously. but later and more careful inquiry leads me to believe that I introduced it into my apiary through my own carelessness. Both I and my neighbor (to whom reference was made in a former report) spent a day in some apiaries some distance from home in which the disease was raging. It would seem true that we brought the contagion home in our clothing. Other apiarists in our county who kept away from the contagion had no trouble. As to the progress of the disease in individual colonies, I would say that three or four weeks from the time the first cells of diseased brood are noticeable is sufficient to complete the ruin beyond redemption. I am surprised to hear that in some localities a colony may be affected for three or four months before ruin is complete. I have succeeded in raising some queens from one of these diseased colonies, treated with the remedy without removing the comb-frames, and I will give them every possible chance to reproduce and propagate the disease. I have no fears of a return of the disease where the treatment has been thorough."

2. Number of colonies in the apiary, 14. Every colony nearly ruined by the disease in most malignant form. This apiary is located on the same ground where 145 colonies perished last year from the same cause. The whole yard had been swept clean, everything had been burned up, and entirely new stock procured. Twelve colonies in this apiary were treated by copious and thorough applications of the remedy simply by setting the frames apart in the hive so that the spray could be directed over both sides. The frames containing brood were not removed from the hive, neither was the honey extracted. The treatment was applied every three or four days, and in three weeks the colonies were free from all appearance of disease. The other 2 colonies were treated with what is known as "the coffee cure," finely ground coffee being used as an antiseptic. The coffee failed to furnish any relief. Being dusted over and into the cells, it killed the little remaining unsealed brood. The salt, alkali, and acid remedy being applied, these 2 colonies also rallied, and "everything is all right now," was the last report.

3. Number of colonies, 100. Number apparently diseased, 48. A number of colonies had already been burned when the disease was reported. The remedy was thoroughly applied as directed, and in fifteen days the contagion had disappeared.

All the evidence so far obtained seems to prove that pollen is the medium through which the contagion is commonly introduced into the hive and by which it is communicated to both bees and brood.

The bacteria, "the disease germs," having been lately deposited on the pollen (from what source is not positively known, but probably from the decomposing bodies of other insects) before the organisms are washed from the blossoms by the rain or killed by the heat of the sun, as they lie exposed to his rays without any element essential to their culture and growth, are carried and stored with the pollen in the cell, or pass into the digestive system along with the live pollen taken by the bees for their own nourishment. By this means these agents of destruction are introduced into the organism of the bees, and through the same medium are they introduced into the cells of the uncapped larvæ. The bacteria, having found a lodgment in the organism of the bee, may or may not cause speedy death. If the bees are young and vigorous they may resist the ravages of the infection, yielding only after the organism is riddled with the bacteria, but if the bees are old and low in vitality the infection, if left to itself, brings speedy ruin. In the spring of the year I have dissected bees which had passed the winter in a colony in which this disease was present when the bees were put away in winter quarters the fall before. Their bodies had been completely honey-combed by the bacteria.

The fact that if a diseased colony is removed from the infested combs and hive and placed in an empty hive or in a hive with frames supplied with comb-foundation, even if the new hive be at once placed on the old location and the old hive and infested combs be burned and the bees at once liberated, the disease commonly disappears, seems also to furnish additional proof that the contagion is usually carried into the hive in the pollen, and, further, that the "disease germs" do not long retain their virility if exposed to the rain and rays of the sun; otherwise the bees would continue to carry in the infection. The bees being compelled to consume the contents of their honey-sacks in building new combs, none of the germs remain to be regurgitated in the new cells; but by this practice the bees are left to the tender mercies of the bacteria, unless they be treated with an antidote. For obvious reasons the queens in such colonies should in any event be superseded as soon as possible. This method of treatment also contemplates the destruction or renovation of all hives and frames, the destruction of all broods, and the melting of all combs; a large percentage of the capital in honey-producing.

Another reason for believing that, except in rare cases, the disease is introduced by means of pollen is found in the fact that the larvæ rarely ever exhibit any symptoms of disease until about the time when the process of weaning begins, at which time the character of the food is changed from the glandular secretion, the pap, to the partially digested and undigested food. Live pollen is then added to the larval food, and with it the bacteria in greater or less numbers; growth is arrested; death ensues; putrification follows, and the soft pulp, of a grayish-brown color, settles to the lower side of the cell. As the mass dries up it becomes glutinous and stringy and reddish-brown in color and emits an offensive odor. Some of the larvæ will be partially capped, some completely capped, and some left uncapped, the condition in which the brood is left depending, I believe, upon the virulence with which the disease attacks both bees and brood. The remedies prescribed appear to destroy the bacteria and cure the bees of the contagion and restore them to natural vigor. The worker bees then cleanse the hive of dead bees and brood and clean out and renovate the cells, and the colony resumes its normal condition.

That the contagion may sometimes be borne from hive to hive by the wind appears to be true, as it was observed in one of the apiaries which I treated for this disease during the past summer that of a large number of diseased colonies in the apiary, with the exception of two colonies, all were located to the northeast of the colony in which the disease first appeared. The prevailing wind had been from the southwest.

That the disease germs may be carried upon the clothing and hands appears probable, from the fact that in one neighborhood the disease appeared in only two apiaries, the owners of which had spent some time working among diseased colonies at some distance from home, while other apiarists in that locality who had kept away from the contagion had no trouble from foul-brood.

THE CONTROL OF REPRODUCTION.

The improvement which has been made in mechanical devices and methods of management by the scientific and practical apiarists of the United States during the past twenty-five years has resulted in establishing the claims of the industry of bee-keeping to a place among the various branches of rural husbandry which are the acknowledged sources of the nation's wealth. Improvements in the art of bee-keeping and in the devices by which the art is practiced are continually being made, and the degree of advancement made in the past is an earnest of the progress awaiting development in the future.

Improvements in devices and methods of management and importing races of bees reported to possess desirable qualities and characteristics have chiefly absorbed the attention of American bee-keepers. It is not strange that reliance has been placed upon these resources as the means by which the best results were to be realized, rather than upon a persistent and skillful application of the laws of heredity and descent and dependence upon the influence of intelligent selection and skillful crossing as a means for developing the highest attainable standard of excellence in *the bee*, the chief factor in permanent advancement.

The difficulties attending the control of the process of reproduction, of applying the laws of heredity and descent, and securing the influence of persistent, intelligent selection in breeding bees have appeared to be almost insurmountable. The very persistent efforts which have been made to improve the bees of the United States by yearly importations of the best races in their purity has also been attended with serious drawbacks and hindrances. These bees, bred for countless generations in a foreign habitat and under climatic conditions widely different from ours, are here submitted to conditions of domestication for which they are ill adapted. Any modification and adaptation of habits, instinct, and physiological structure which may have been secured by breeding a few succeeding generations under the altered conditions and requirements incident to domestication in the United States have been lost with each fresh importation of ancestral stock, and the work of securing the variability and adaptability of instinct, habit, physiological structure, and functional capacity essential to domestication here must be begun *ab initio*.

That some practical method might be discovered by which the process of reproduction could be controlled has long been the hope of all progressive apiculturists. With the control of fecundation assured, progress in scientific apiculture would be rapid and permanent.

In obedience to your instructions I have continued my experiments in striving to discover a practical method by which the fecundation of queen bees may be controlled. This I have endeavored to accomplish by two different methods, in both of which I have been in a degree successful. During the past summer, however, a drought set in in May, almost with the beginning of the breeding season, which was said to be the severest and most protracted known in this locality for twenty-five years. No rain fell during eleven weeks, and during the four weeks next succeeding the eleven weeks without rain we had but three light showers, scarcely sufficient to lay the dust, practically resulting in an unbroken, all-consuming drought fifteen weeks in duration. Under such conditions I found it impossible to bring many of my experimental tests to a successful issue.

Having discovered last year that it was possible to introduce the drone sperm into the spermatheca of the queen bee during the term of orgasm by artificial means, and that fecundation was practicable by such means, I attempted to perfect a method by which this could be done with ease and certainty. For the purpose of holding the queen bee in position for introducing the drone sperm I made what I call a queen-clamp, which consists of a block of wood 2 inches square and 4 inches long, in one end of which is an opening in size and shape like the upper two-thirds of a queen-cell, with the small end up. This block is sawed in two in the middle, leaving half the cell-shaped opening on either half. Grasping the queen by the wings or thorax I place her in one half of the cell-shaped opening and carefully close the other half over her. I then place a rubber band around the block and stand it on end. This leaves the queen in position, head downward, the lower half of her abdomen protruding, and confined in such a manner that she cannot receive any injury. For the purpose of appropriating and depositing the male sperm I used a hypodermic syringe. I removed the sharp injecting needle, and in its place substituted a nozzle having an opening of sufficient size to admit a knitting-needle of medium size. Over this nozzle I slipped a small, smooth tube, drawn to a point so small that the opening in the small end is not more than half as large as that in the nozzle. After selecting the drone I wish to use, I grasp the head and thorax between the thumb and finger, and by a continued pressure cause him to perform the expulsion act. I then remove the bean in which the spermatozoa are massed and squeeze the contents into a very small glass receiver, an eighth of an inch in depth and in diameter. I then add a drop of glycerine diluted with warm rain water, and take up the spermatozoa with the syringe, using the wide nozzle. I then slip the cap having a fine smooth point over the nozzle and inject the spermatozoa into the vulva of the queen. The queen, which has been held in position by the clamp while the preparations were being made, naturally bends the abdomen downward whenever so confined. The vulva is easily opened to admit the point of the fine nozzle-cap when the abdomen is lifted up straight. Of twenty-seven queens treated by this method the first week in May and the first week in June six proved to be successfully fertilized. After that time, although I was persistent in my efforts to succeed and made many and repeated trials, I met with success only occasionally.

Another method by which I succeeded in fertilizing a few queens in May, before the bees began killing the drones, was in the manner described in my report of last year. I took a number of young queens from nursery cages, clipped their wings, and introduced them to queenless nuclei. When they were seven days old, orgasm being well progressed, I placed them each in turn in a queen-clamp, and, holding them back downwards, I picked drones from a comb taken from a populous hive, and caused them to expel the generative organs, and selecting those in which the contents appeared of the color and consistency of albumen, I placed drops of the seminal fluid upon and in the vulva of the queen, which were eagerly received. After the introduction of the drone sperm these queens were treated by the bees as fertile queens, and in one or two days assumed the appearance of fertile laying queens, and in from three to six days began to lay fecundated eggs.

The fact that I did occasionally succeed in fecundating queen bees by these methods, which proved upon trial as prolific as any queens I had which had been naturally fertilized, queens which I had hatched in an incubator and in nursery cages, whose wings I had mercilessly clipped as soon as they had crawled from the cell, and which I knew had never been upon the wing, seemed to furnish reason to hope that I would be able to discover a method which would be uniformly successful. The hope of reaching this much-desired result made me persist in the face of discouragements incident to experimental work in breeding bees during the prevalence of a protracted drought. I am by no means discouraged by the partial success now realized. On the contrary, I am hopeful that under more favorable conditions better results may be obtained, and until other and untried resources fail I should not feel warranted in abandoning effort.

Observation and experiment lead me to believe that drone bees differ in degrees of procreativeness, and that the development and exercise of the procreative faculty are under the control of the worker bees.

First, there appeared to be drones of the impotent sort. If such be taken between the thumb and finger, no pressure short of crushing is sufficient to expel the sex organ. When forced to position external to the body, or if removed by a dissection, the organs are found to be nearly or quite empty, the few spermatozoa being massed in a hard lump, and but little mucus being present, and that little watery and clear and having no consistency.

Another sort of drones are those in which the mucus surrounding the spermatozoa is thick and curdy. With this sort I have not been able to fertilize a queen. The procreative principle is present in quantity, but the element in which it may be liberated and floated into the organs of the queen appears to be wanting.

A third sort of drones are those in which the sex organs are completely filled with spermatozoa and an abundant supply of albuminous fluid. It is only with this latter sort that I have been able to succeed in fecundating queens.

The facts observed seem to warrant the belief that it is the prerogative of the worker bees to determine the degree of development and dominate the function of the drones as they do the succeeding generations of workers and queens, the superior intelligence of the workers ordering the entire economy of the hive. During the first half of the severe and protracted drought of the past season I was able to rear a few drones by resorting to the usual methods employed for stimulating drone-rearing, but one-third of the entire number proved upon trial to be of the sort which I believe to be impotent, and nearly all of the remaining two-thirds were of the second class, not more than 5 or 10 per cent. of the entire number being furnished with the albuminous liquid necessary to enable the drone to voluntarily perform the expulsion act and complete the function of copulation, the filling of the spermatheca of the queen; for I am led to believe that the presence of this fluid, more than any odor or other influence from the presence of the queen during orgasm, excites in the naturally frigid drones the sexual desire and assists in the execution of the expulsion act and furnishes the element in which the spermatozoa are floated into the spermatheca, and also that the workers intelligently and purposely determine the sexual development and dominate the fitness, the desire, and capacity of the drone, as they do the physical development, the fitness, the desire, and capacity of worker and queen bees for the natural performance of their individual functions; that is to say, if drones are reared during a drought by artificially approximating the conditions under which the desire for drone-rearing normally arises, only a small percentage of the number will be sufficiently furnished with the food essential to complete sexual development, the counterpart of which is seen in a less degree in the rearing of worker larvæ; and, further, if there is a failure of honey or if for any reason the swarming impulse is absent and no emergency exists for the forming of a new colony, very few of the sexually mature drones are supplied with the food-elements essential in producing the secretion which excites sexual desire and supplies the agency by which the spermatozoa are freed and floated into the spermatheca, the counterpart of which is seen in the refusal of the worker bees to copiously supply the queen with the rich glandular secretion essential to oviproduction whenever their instinct warns them that ovipositing should cease and that further brood-rearing would only be a waste of energy, resulting in a generation of consumers and non-producers; for the queen is only a mother, and in no sense a majesty; only a machine, not a monarch. Other facts in my experience might be mentioned in support of this belief.

October 15, Mr. Otis N. Baldwin, of Clarksville, Mo., wrote me that he had met with success in practicing the method of fertilization described in my report of last year and that he had discovered that drones were of three kinds, namely: "Dwarfed, immature, and ripe." As directed by your letter of instructions of November 5, I went to Clarksville and interrogated Mr. Baldwin concerning his experience and observations, and I herewith give the substance of his statement made in reply to my questions. He said, "I first go to my nursery and take the queens and cage them. I then go to my hive of drones and pick out as many as I think I may need, and then proceed in the manner you describe in your report of 1885. I believe the whole secret of success lies in the drones, and I am not able to tell how old the drone must be, or how the right condition is brought about, or whether it was originally intended that only a very small percentage of drones should be capable of fertilizing a queen. I have, however, discovered that there are three kinds of drones. First, the drone which when squeezed bursts with apparently dry organs of generation. Second, drones which burst with an abundance of seminal fluid resembling a mixture made by adding bromides to a silver solution. Third, drones which bursting show a fluid resembling albumen. With the two former kinds I have succeeded in fertilizing a single queen. With the latter I have fertilized over two hundred queens the past season with but few failures after I found out the difference in drones. I carefully grasp the thorax of the queen between the thumb and finger of the left hand and with the right I pick up the drone which I have selected and press the thorax and abdomen of the drone until the generative organs are expelled, using as many as I need until I find one in which the color and consistency of the fluid suits me. Sometimes only a few of the right kind can be found in as many as one hundred. I place a few drops of the male fluid upon the vulva of the queen, which is eagerly received, using one, and only one, drone for each queen. I have fertilized queens by this method that were not a day old, and others more than fifteen days old, and after clipping their wings introduced them to their colonies, and they began laying in from six to eight days and were satisfactorily prolific. As nearly as I could tell, those fertilized early were more prolific than those treated after they were ten days old, but the right condition of the drone is very essential. It is very difficult to get drones ripe enough before the first half of May and after the first half of August, but during June and July this method may be operated with gratifying results. Queens fertilized by this method and directly introduced into a queenless colony are rarely ever molested by the bees. I clipped the wings of the first twenty or twenty-five queens I succeeded in fertilizing by this method, and finding the method worked to my satisfaction and with but few failures, I clipped no more wings."

The experience here detailed, as far as it relates to the procreativeness of drones, is in agreement with the facts within my own observation already set forth. The claim that a very large number of queens were successfully fertilized as set forth, and that, too, with but few failures in the whole number attempted, is lacking in the element of absolute certainty and completeness of detail which would entitle it to acceptance as of any scientific value. Mr. Baldwin assured me that "there could have been no mistake about it;" but in order to effectually guard against all possibility of the test being abortive, all the queens claimed to have been artificially fecundated should have had their wings thoroughly clipped before they were liberated. But the fact that the repeated successes were realized when the young queens were clipped upon being taken from the nursery cage, never having had opportunity to bear their weight upon their wings, is an encouraging step in advance towards the solution of the most difficult problem in practical bee-keeping. Another season, with the presence of favorable conditions, will determine the practicability and value of this method.

FERTILIZATION IN CONFINEMENT.

Realizing that natural methods nearly always possess advantages over artificial methods, I determined if possible to gain control of reproduction by the fertilization of queens in confinement. That some inexpensive and practicable method might be devised by which the natural mating of queens in confinement could be secured has very long been hoped for by all progressive apiarists. Very many attempts, in a variety of ways, some of which involved the outlay of considerable sums of money, have been made, but difficulties apparently insurmountable have been encountered.

I removed the queens from 6 colonies which I had had confined in the house for experimenting with bees and fruit, a house 10 feet by 16 feet, 8 feet high, partly covered on the sides with wire-cloth, a wire-covered sash in the gable, and large screen wire-covered doors in each end. These were strong colonies, which had been confined in this house for thirty days and had learned the location of their hives, and from these the bees flew daily in great numbers, returning frequently to their hives. Into these 6 colonies I introduced virgin queens hatched from cells which I had placed in wire cages. Into each colony the virgin queen was placed without being removed from the cage in which she was hatched. In due time they were accepted and liberated. The day these queens were five days old I liberated about ten drones near to the entrance of each of these hives. These drones were brought from hives in the apiary, and upon being liberated most of them persisted in flying against the wire-covered sides and windows in the gable, and few ever entered the hives. Here again there was frigidity or disability apparent among the drones. When the young queens flew from the hive seeking a mate they mingled among the drones, crawling over them and caressing them with their antennæ, meeting with no response. These queens, with one exception, seemed to have no difficulty in getting the location of their respective hives. The result of this trial was, one queen of the six was fertilized, and after she had laid eggs with regularity in two-thirds of the cells on both sides of one frame, after clipping the queen's wings, I removed this frame, with the queen and adhering bees, to a nucleus in the yard, and from the eggs laid in confinement worker bees hatched in due time, and the queen continued to lay as long as the nucleus was fed, there being nothing in the fields for the bees to gather. All the eggs laid by this queen were fecundated eggs. Being convinced that as far as the queens were concerned the difficulties in the way of success were not insurmountable, and that the main trouble was that the drones had not been furnished by the workers with the glandular secretion or the food suitable for producing the albumenlike secretion which I had been led to believe essential to produce sexual desire and to assist in the performance of the copulative act, from these same colonies I removed the remaining unmated queens, and to each 1 introduced another virgin queen as before.

I then went to a distant apiary, and secured an unusually strong colony which was under the swarming impulse. A few queen cells were being built and a moderate supply of drones was present. This was late in the season. This colony had not cast a swarm during the year, and was the only one I could find, after considerable search and inquiry far and near, having any drones, and probably owing to the excessive drought only an occasional one of the number examined had been prepared by the workers for the procreative function. I took this colony home and placed it in the wire-covered house at the end opposite that in which the virgin queens were located. I clipped the wings of the old queen so that she could not leave the hive, and upon being liberated the workers and drones of this hive made less effort to escape than those brought in from the apiary near by, and some seemed reconciled to their new surroundings. The workers soon learned their location and drones were soon to be found in nearly every hive in the house. The result of this trial was that three of the six queens were fertilized, and as soon as they had each laid five or six hundred eggs I clipped their wings and removed them, together with their colonies, to the yard and fed them, and all the eggs laid by these queens produced worker bees. I am much encouraged by the success so far realized under conditions so unfavorable.

With the return of spring I hope to follow out your suggestions and continue the test, using a large wire-covered inclosure for the purpose; with hives so arranged on the sides that the worker bees may have unobstructed flight, while the drones and queens, being restrained by means of queen-excluding zinc placed before the outside entrance to the hive, may fly and mate within the inclosure and readily return to the hives from whence they came. If practical control of reproduction can be secured by so simple and inexpensive a method—and the facts from my experience as given above seem to warrant the conclusion that this is true—then the Rubicon of scientific apiculture is passed.

EXPLANATION TO PLATES TO REPORT OF ENTOMOLOGIST.

Where figures are enlarged the natural sizes are indicated in hair-lines at side, unless already indicated in some other way on the plate.

EXPLANATION TO PLATE I.

THE COTTONY CUSHION-SCALE.

(Original.)

Fig. 1.—*a*, adult male—enlarged; *b*, hind tarsus of same; *c*, wing and poiser of same, showing hooks and pocket—still more enlarged.

Fig. 2.—*a*, newly hatched larva from below—enlarged; *b*, antenna of same; *c*, tarsus—still more enlarged.

Fig. 3.—Adult female, side view, showing the pale, greenish-gray form and with part of egg-covering torn away, showing the carmine eggs and egg-stain—enlarged.

Fig. 4.—Adult female, dorsal view, showing reddish-brown form—enlarged.

Fig. 5.—Male cocoon—enlarged.

Fig. 6.—Branch of orange tree with mass of insects *in situ* and as they appear soon after death—natural size.

EXPLANATION TO PLATE II.

THE COTTONY CUSHION-SCALE.

(Original.)

Fig. 1.—Outline of the egg—greatly enlarged.

Fig. 2.—Dorsal view of newly-hatched larva—greatly enlarged.

Fig. 3.—*a*, female larva, second stage, ventral view—greatly enlarged; *b*, antenna of same—still more enlarged.

Fig. 4.—Female larva, third stage, ventral view—greatly enlarged.

Fig. 5.—Adult female (fourth stage), dorsal view—greatly enlarged; *a*, antenna—still more enlarged.

Fig. 6.—Greatly magnified portion of lateral border of adult, showing bases of glassy filaments.

Fig. 7.—Male larva, second stage, ventral view—greatly enlarged.

Fig. 8.—Male pupa, ventral view—greatly enlarged.

EXPLANATION TO PLATE III.

ENEMIES OF THE COTTONY CUSHION-SCALE.

(Original.)

Fig. 1.—*Isodromus icerya*—greatly enlarged.

Fig. 2.—*Blapstinus brevicollis*—enlarged.

Fig. 3.—*Blastobasis iceryaella*—enlarged.

Fig. 4.—*Largus succinctus*—enlarged.

Fig. 5.—*Corizus hyalinus*—enlarged.

Fig. 6.—*Forficula* found preying on *Icerya*—enlarged.

EXPLANATION TO PLATE IV.

(Photo-engraved from a photograph.)

A lemon orchard at Los Angeles, infested by Cottony Cushion-scale.

EXPLANATION TO PLATE V.

(Photo-engraved from a photograph.)

Spraying outfit used in California in operation against the Cottony Cushion-scale.

EXPLANATION TO PLATE VI.

THE SOUTHERN BUFFALO-GNAT.

(Original.)

FIG. 1.—*Simulium pecuarum:* Larva—enlarged.
FIG. 2.—*a*, ventral view of head of larva; *b*, lateral; *c*, dorsal view of same—all greatly enlarged.
FIG. 3.—*a*, mentum of larva; *b*, labium, *c*, labrum of same—all greatly enlarged.
FIG. 4.—Pro-leg of larva—greatly enlarged.
FIG. 5.—*a*, antenna of larva; *b*, mandible of same—greatly enlarged; *c*, tip of mandible—still more enlarged.
FIG. 6.—Maxilla of larva—greatly enlarged.
FIG. 7.—Tip of abdomen of same, showing breathing organs—greatly enlarged.
FIG. 8.—Pupa—enlarged; *a, b, c*, spines of dorsal and ventral surface of abdomen of same—still more enlarged.

EXPLANATION TO PLATE VII.

THE SOUTHERN BUFFALO-GNAT AND THE TURKEY-GNAT.

(Original.)

FIG. 1.—*Simulium pecuarum:* Fan of larva—greatly enlarged.
FIG. 2.—*Simulium meridionale:* Larva—enlarged.
FIG. 3.—Same: *a*, antenna; *b*, mandible—greatly enlarged; *c*, tip of mandible—still more enlarged.
FIG. 4.—Same: Mentum—greatly enlarged.
FIG. 5.—Same: Breathing organs — greatly enlarged.
FIG. 6.—Same: *a*, empty pupa-case; *b*, case with pupa projecting from it—enlarged.

EXPLANATION TO PLATE VIII.

BUFFALO-GNATS.

FIG. 1.—*Simulium pecuarum:* Head of adult male—greatly enlarged. (Original.)
FIG. 2.—Same: Head of adult female—greatly enlarged. (Original.)
FIG. 3.—Same: Adult female from side—enlarged. (Original.)

FIG. 4.—*Simulium meridionale:* Adult male from side—enlarged. (Original.)
FIG. 5.—*S. pecuarum:* Dorsal view of adult female—enlarged. (Original.)
FIG. 6.—*S. meridionale:* Dorsal view of adult female—enlarged. (Original.)
FIG. 7.—*Simulium* sp.: *a*, portion of egg-mass from side; *b*, same, from top; *c, d*, individual eggs—enlarged. (After Barnard.)

EXPLANATION TO PLATE IX.

FIG. 1.—Larva of *Chironomus* sp.: *a*, dorsal view with pediform appendages retracted and jaws closed; *b*, lateral view with same parts extended; *c*, egg-mass—all enlarged; *d*, maxillary palpus; *e*, labial palpus; *f*, labium; *g*, mandible—still more enlarged. (After Riley.)
FIG. 2.—*Chironomus plumosus:* *a*, adult, dorsal view; *b*, pupa, ventral view—enlarged. (Original.)
FIG. 3.—*Hydropsyche* sp.: *a*, dorsal view of larva—enlarged; *b*, side view of anal hook of same—still more enlarged. (Original.)
FIG. 4.—Same: Side view of head and first thoracic segment of larva—enlarged. (Original.)
FIG. 5.—Same: Web of larva—enlarged. (Re-drawn from Clarke.)

EXPLANATION TO PLATE X.

THE FALL WEB-WORM.

(Original.)

FIG. 1.—*a*, dark larva from side; *b*, light larva from above; *c*, dark larva from above; *d*, pupa, ventral view; *e*, pupa from side; *f*, adult—all slightly enlarged.
FIG. 2.—*a-j*, wings of a series of adults, showing graduation from pure white form (*cunea*) to one profusely spotted with black and brown (*punctatissima*)—natural size.
FIG. 3.—*a*, moth ovipositing upon leaf—natural size; *b*, a few eggs *in situ*—enlarged.
FIG. 4.—*Meteorus hyphantriæ*. *a*, adult; *b*, cocoon—enlarged.

EXPLANATION TO PLATE XI.

(Photo-engraved from a photograph.)

View of a Washington street in late September, 1886, showing complete defoliation of the Poplars on the west side and almost complete exemption of the Maples on the east side.

www.ingramcontent.com/pod-product-compliance
Lightning Source LLC
Chambersburg PA
CBHW030609270326
41927CB00007B/1104